BUILDING COALITIONS

ANDREW M.
GREELEY

BUILDING COALITIONS

NEW VIEWPOINTS
A DIVISION OF
FRANKLIN WATTS, INC.
NEW YORK | 1974

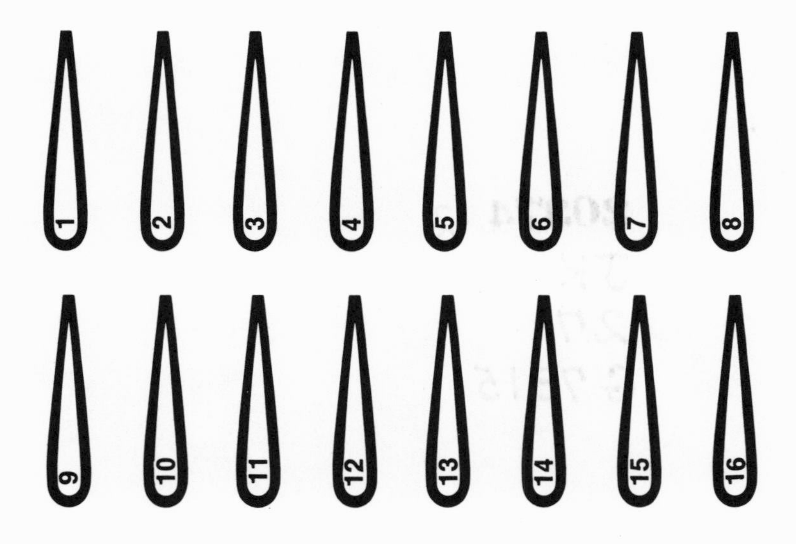

AMERICAN POLITICS IN THE 1970s

Library of Congress Cataloging in Publication Data

Greeley, Andrew M 1928–
Building coalitions.

1. United States–Politics and government—1945– 2. Political participation—United States. 3. Minorities—United States. I. Title.
JK271.G7315 320.9'73'0924 73-12797
ISBN 0-531-05354-7
ISBN 0-531-05561-2 (pbk.)

Printed in the United States of America
6 5 4 3 2 1

CONTENTS

FOR SENATOR EDWARD M. KENNEDY
In hope that once again the
multihued pennants of Camelot may
dance merrily in the brisk spring breezes.

BUILDING COALITIONS

SCENARIO FOR 1976

I began this final draft on January 20, 1973, the day Richard Nixon stood for the fifth time on the inaugural platform. As he began his second term as president of the United States, it was none too soon to begin to think about the 1976 election.

Richard Nixon was reelected in one of the strangest elections in the history of the United States. He shattered the liberal Democratic coalition that Franklin Roosevelt forged in the 1930s. Dwight Eisenhower defeated the coalition, but he was a military hero, a national symbol, and a man who resolutely stayed above the rough and tumble of party politics (or at least managed to convey the impression that he did). But Richard Nixon has never been popular and, indeed, was not even popular in his reelection; and while he utterly routed the Democratic coalition, his landslide victory was of no help to his party in congressional and state elections.

The country still has a Democratic majority and the chances of a Democratic comeback in 1976 are very great. No administration, not even a popular one, can govern the country for eight years and not stir up considerable popular antagonism. The Republicans do not seem to have an attractive candidate to succeed Mr. Nixon. The Democratic Congress can be counted on to hound the administration, to reveal its mistakes, and to uncover corruption, to which it already has proven itself prone. Since the Democrats are also likely to win something of a victory in the 1974 off-year election, one can expect even more congressional pressure on the Republicans as the 1976 contest draws near. It might make sense, therefore, simply to forget about the 1976 election and let the ordinary, "natural" political processes of the country do their work. While the Democrats do not have any clearly effective campaigner waiting in the wings for 1976, it would appear to be inconceivable that the choice three years hence could be as bad as it was during 1972. In any event, the country may be so fed up with Disneyland presidential courtiers by 1976 that almost any Democrat should be able to win.

And yet since 1967 the Democratic party has demonstrated a remarkable ability to overcome the advantage it has as the country's permanent majority party. The Vietnamese war—all by itself—cost Lyndon Johnson what would have been a certain reelection in 1968. Hubert Humphrey's inability to detach himself from his association with Johnson sent him down to a thin defeat. The 1972 presidential election ought to have been—given the political and social processes of the country—a tossup, with the incumbent minority president winning by a few percentage points because of his highly popular rapprochement with China and Russia and because by election day peace in Vietnam seemed "at hand" (though the hand turned out to be somewhat more distant than the public was led to believe). Instead of a narrow defeat in a closely contested election (or possibly a narrow victory), the Democrats managed to go down in one of the most spectacular defeats of political history. On the basis then of its performance in the late 1960s and the early 1970s, it would be a grave mistake to count on the Democratic party's ability to take advantage of the "natural" political forces at work in the country. On the contrary, a much more realistic appraisal would be to expect the Democratic party to continue to destroy its own best opportunities.

The Democratic coalition on the presidential level was shattered in the summer of 1972. I am concerned in this book with the reconstruction of that coalition. I am not prepared to take it for granted that such a reconstruction will take place automatically. It is not my intention to provide a detailed analysis of the 1972 debacle, for post mortems are already to be found in almost every journal one cares to read. The analysis of Seymour Martin Lipset in the January 1972 issue of *Commentary* seems to be plausible enough, though I have reservations about the second half of Lipset's assertion that while there was no political backlash in 1972, there was a cultural backlash. I am prepared to believe that the American voter does not particularly like gay liberationists, hippies, hard-eyed women liberationists, noisy militants, and loud-mouthed anti-Americans; but I am also convinced that these dislikes are not particularly salient politically. If you ask the middle American whether he likes "hippies" or "radicals," he is likely to say that he does not, but there is very little evidence that this dislike is high on his agenda of political concerns, or that under normal circumstances it has much influence on how he votes. His voting decisions, I would contend, are based on rather different sorts of concerns. To the extent that the Democratic presidential candidate and the men around him permitted the 1972 campaign to be identified with radicals, militants, protesters, hippies, and other disliked groups, they were guilty of political ineptitude of the most monumental proportions. For what they succeeded in doing was to make cultural backlash an election issue when there was no reason to have done so. Even more precisely, they made politically salient concerns that need not have been, and by so doing they persuaded the American public that George McGovern was not a man to trust and in whom confidence could not be placed. Professor Lipset is right, of course, about the existence of some cultural backlash in the society, but the cultural backlash did not lose George McGovern the election. His own ineptitude and that of his supporters was quite enough to lose it for him (or at least was enough to keep the election from being much closer).

But the bungling of the Democratic campaign in 1972 is only indirectly the concern of the present book. Although it would be the easiest thing in the world to produce quotations from John Kenneth Galbraith, Arthur Schlesinger, Jr., James McGregor Burns, Tom Wicker, Anthony Lewis, and Frederick Dutton to show how profoundly mistaken all these McGovern enthusiasts were in June and July of 1972, there is scarcely any point in such activity. The drubbing they took was punishment enough for their supremely self-confident foolishness. Nor do I wish to engage in a vendetta with Democratic liberals, for I am one myself. My concern is not to dwell on the mistakes of the past but to find ways to rebuild the Democratic coalition and to look for opportunities for the future of the party. My thesis in this book is that political victory for the liberal coalition in the years ahead will depend on the capacity of the leadership of that coalition to understand better than those who led it in 1972 how American society operates politically. I am more concerned with the underlying "pictures" or "images" of America that are in the heads of the coalition leadership. The mistakes made in 1972, I would argue, were caused by fundamentally distorted and misleading "pictures" of American political life. In this book I shall present my own set of pictures which, I shall argue, are more accurate and more politically useful than the set carried around in the heads of the McGovern New Politics enthusiasts of 1972. One reads men like Schlesinger, Burns, Dutton, and Galbraith not so much to ridicule them for the woeful inaccuracy of their predictions as to understand what the underlying assumptions were that made such intelligent and well-meaning men so wrong about how their fellow citizens would behave. It is my contention that for a variety of reasons the liberal left and the New Politics wing of the Democratic party internalized pictures about American politics that were profoundly mistaken, and that is why they lost the election, not because of stands on specific issues or mistakes in campaign strategy.

Everyone carries around in his head a set of intellectual images with which he organizes and explains the vast variety of phenomena that impinge on his consciousness every day. We cannot dispense with these pictures, and the problem with them is that they frequently become both undiscussed and undiscussable. As David Matza puts it:

> *Since assumptions are usually implicit, they tend to remain beyond the reach of such intellectual correctives as argument, criticism, and scrutiny. Thus, to render assumptions explicit is not only to propose a thesis; more fundamentally it is to widen and deepen the area requiring exploration. Assumptions implicit in conceptions are rarely inconsequential. Left unattended, they return to haunt us by shaping or bending theories that purport to explain major social phenomena. Assumptions may prompt us to notice or to ignore discrepancies or patterns that may be observed in the empirical world. Conceptions structure our inquiry.*[1]

[1] David Matza, *Delinquency and Drift* (New York: Wiley, 1964), p. 3.

So the powerful images and pictures with which we organize our experience are deeply embedded in our personalities. Even when something goes wrong in our expectations, it rarely occurs to us to question our basic assumptions. We blame our failures and our losses either on others or on mistakes in tactics and strategy instead of questioning our own fundamental meaning system or interpretive scheme on which both our strategies and our expectations of others had been based. It is clear that Senator McGovern and his staff have not seriously considered the possibility that their fundamental assumptions might have been wrong. The senator tells us that he feels sorry not for himself but for the American public—a public that apparently was not capable of rising to the level of moral excellence to which he called it. Gary Wills tells us that Nixon won because the American people were vindictive. Tom Wicker and Anthony Lewis suggest that the real but hidden issue in the election was racism (though none of these fallible journalists cite evidence for their assertions). Frank Mankiewicz, when asked why the election was lost, replied, "Hubert Humphrey, Arthur Bremer, and Thomas Eagleton." It never occurred to Mr. Mankiewicz that a more appropriate answer would have been "Frank Mankiewicz, Frank Mankiewicz, Frank Mankiewicz."

Many liberal news commentators broadly hint that it was the Wallace vote that caused the McGovern disaster, ignoring the obvious political arithmatic that if Governor Wallace's 12 percent of the national vote in 1968 had broken three-quarters for Nixon and one-quarter for McGovern in 1972, Mr. Nixon still would have won the election by fifteen percentage points. Furthermore, with the possible exception of Rhode Island, there was not a single northern state in which a Wallace candidacy would have tipped the electoral plurality for Senator McGovern. Or to put the matter somewhat differently, if every person who voted for a Democratic congressional or gubernatorial candidate in the North had also voted for Mr. McGovern, he would have had a fighting chance to win the election. Unless the liberal Democratic leadership stops blaming Senators Eagleton and Humphrey or the American people and asks what went wrong in its own basic assumptions, there is no reason to think that 1976 will be all that different.

This book will be about my own pictures of American political life. I shall argue with the pictures of the New Politicians only when it is absolutely necessary. But since there would be no reason to write this book unless the pictures of the New Politics dominated the 1972 Democratic party campaign, I must begin by outlining (without caricature, I hope) what the basic assumptions (as opposed to strategy and tactics) of the McGovern liberal left campaign of 1972 seem to have been.

The vision was, to begin with, profoundly religious. American society was "sick," "corrupt," "guilty," "diseased," "evil." The American people were "materialistic," "racist," "selfish," "thoughtless," "unconcerned about poverty, suffering and misery." Because of the sickness of the society and the corruption of its people, great new problems had emerged, particularly the war in Asia and racial strife and injustice at home. The American public was unconcerned about its war crimes in Asia and inattentive to its domestic problems. It was also unconcerned about the increasing environmental crisis. There were, of course, certain hopeful forces at work in society, particularly the "movements"—

black, Spanish-speaking, women, and youth. The leaders of these movements were the duly authorized representatives of the "disadvantaged" members of society. In combination with the more enlightened members of the professorate, the knowledge industry, and the more progressive political forces in the Democratic party, the movements would constitute a "new coalition." This coalition had going for it the powerful pressures of demography and social class, for there were higher proportions of young people and better-educated people in the United States in 1972 than in any previous election year. Indeed, there were twenty-five million new voters (or "great legions" of young voters, as they were frequently called). The new coalition could easily compensate for its losses by a powerful appeal to the young, the disadvantaged, the oppressed, and the well-educated.

Furthermore, there were deep spiritual resources within the American population that could be mobilized. Despite their fall from grace, the American people were still capable of repentance; they could be exhorted to "come home" to the best of their own authentic moral and political traditions. The country was going through a political and social realignment. There was an historical inevitability about such a realignment, and a call to penitence, reform, generosity, self-discipline, and self-sacrifice could accelerate the process.

If the New Politics had one legacy from the Kennedy years, it was a knowledge of how to build grass-roots political organizations. Hence it no longer needed the corrupt bosses of the old politics. The legions of the young, the well-educated, the socially committed would go out among "the people" and in rational political discussion persuade Americans that it was time to come home again, that George McGovern stood for the best in the American political tradition. If the American public was willing to do penance, willing to return to morality, willing to respond to a call for confession, reform, and renewal, then Richard Nixon with his corrupt, middlebrow entourage could be swept out of Washington.

There was a decided ambivalence about the American public in such a vision. It was corrupt and sinful yet capable of salvation; it had to do penance, indeed, harsh and severe penance, but it was expected to yield to moral excellence in gracious acceptance. It had been profoundly unconcerned about the "really important" political issues like abortion, marijuana, and amnesty, yet it was supposed to respond positively and favorably to appeals based on these issues even when they were made by those very groups for whom the American people had shown a notable lack of enthusiasm. But the power of the appeal to political morality was confidently expected to be so effective that their objections to militants, protesters, and radicals were expected to be overcome. For the whole country should rejoice, the public was told by the high priests of the New Politics, that those who were at one time excluded from the political life were now permitted to participate in it. The public was asked in effect, "Is it not better to have the young radicals inside the convention, as they were in 1972, than outside on the streets, as in 1968?" The public was supposed to say yes.[2]

[2] The historical inevitability argument—particularly as advanced by Frederick Dutton—had widespread appeal. There is nothing

I hope I do not exaggerate the religious and political vision of the New Politics. As I sat on an eroding Lake Michigan dune watching the Democratic party destroy itself in July of 1972, I kept asking myself what picture these people had of the American public. Do they really know what it does to the American voter to be told that Bella Abzug, Shirley MacLaine, Jesse Jackson, Bill Singer, Walter Fauntleroy, Robert Drinan, Abbie Hoffman, Jerry Rubin, and the Minnesota and New York representatives of gay liberation belonged on the floor of the Democratic convention while Richard Daley did not? As Professor Lipset was later to point out, the important thing about the Daley exclusion for the rank and file Democrat was not who was excluded but the arbitrary and vindictive way in which that exclusion was accomplished. Curiously enough, in that interminable session in which his delegation lost, the mayor probably represented more Americans than at any other time in his political career, because when he was expelled from the convention, millions of other Democrats were also excluded from the party—or at least felt that they were, which in an election is what counts.

In any event, the political vision I have described in the previous paragraphs seems to have been what was in the minds of the "reform" leaders who seized control of the Democratic party and nomi-

more exhilarating (or, as it turns out, more self-deceiving) than to feel that one is riding on the crest of the wave of history. Indeed, even some very sophisticated political scientists of my acquaintance argued in August that while McGovern was going to lose the election, he would play the role for the Democratic candidate in 1976 that Alfred Smith played for Franklin Roosevelt. I must confess that I have not heard that argument recently.

nated George McGovern. I would suggest that it is this picture, composed essentially of symbols like "corruption," "morality," "issue," "new," "young," and "future," that underpinned the strategy and tactics of the Democratic party in 1972 and that led to its disastrous defeat. I am prepared to concede for the sake of the argument that such a political and religious vision is a lofty and noble one. My argument is not against its moral superiority; it is that such a vision simply had nothing to do with how politics works and particularly with how American politics works. When men and women with that sort of vision won control of the Democratic party they would certainly lose the presidential election. Unless a new vision of the political process can be achieved by 1976, the chances of repeating the 1972 failure are very great indeed. (The Republican party cannot, after all, be counted on to nominate a trained chimpanzee.)

Let me note, as I turn to my own "counterpictures," that while I am an academic of a sort, a journalist of a sort, and even a religious professional of a sort, I write about American politics from a different perspective from that of most academics and journalists and clergymen who pontificate about political affairs. The academics and journalists (at least the nationally famous journalists) have seriously persuaded themselves that their role in society is an adversary role. Indeed, they seem prepared to argue that they have Constitutional guarantees to protect their exercise of this role. The academic and the journalist (and the latter frequently thinks of himself as a slightly different kind of "intellectual" than the academic) are fundamentally concerned with criticizing, not to say destroying or tearing apart,

American society. As "the best and the brightest," [3] these self-anointed critics assume that they have the right to stand against the rest of society, preaching its weaknesses and demanding that the society modify itself in response to their brilliant criticism. I take it that the role of the academic and the journalist is much more modest. Understanding, interpretation, explanation, reporting—these are appropriate functions for scholars and writers. I would prefer to leave messianic and apocalyptic visions to others, although I will confess that my preference now seems to mark me as a member of the minority. Nor am I an advocate of the "politics of love," which is pursued with so much charismatic vigor by some of my fellows in the Catholic priesthood. I believe in politics and I believe in love, but political strategy, tactics, or social policy cannot be derived from love. I certainly do not agree with Philip Berrigan that you cannot be an American and a Christian. Parenthetically, I wonder in what country could one combine citizenship and Christianity?

It seems appropriate for the cleric to urge his people to a maximum of generosity and enthusiasm and moral concern. But as I understand the political process, the politician has another role: he settles not for the maximum of morality but for the minimum of generosity he can get from the voter without losing the vote. In an imperfect world filled with imperfect humans, I do not see how politicians in a democratic political system can operate any differently. So I suppose my approach to the political process,

[3] Mr. Halberstam, who used this phrase to describe the intellectuals who got us into Vietnam, might well have applied the term to those intellectuals who led the Democratic party to defeat in 1972.

my collection of images about voting, the political culture, the compromise-coalition political leadership are very much a worm's eye view—the view, if you will, of a precinct captain who asks what it will take to get enough votes to carry his precinct. When someone tells me that all a particular politician wants to do is to win, I have to reply that it seems to me that that is what politicians are for. The politician who loses is no good to anybody. One does not, of course, want to win at any cost, but there are unquestionably costs in winning, and he who thinks that political purity comes free may be an admirable person but he'll never get elected. It is axiomatic that winners, not losers, shape the direction the country takes. If this book has a thesis that can be stated in a simple sentence it is that moral concern is an extremely useful and important political tool so long as it is combined with a shrewd understanding of the dynamics of politics, which is to say, of how to get people to vote for you.

By professional training I am a survey researcher, but I shall do my best to minimize the survey material in this book. The survey data were available to those who conceived the 1972 Democratic campaign. The problem was, I suspect, not that they did not read the surveys, but that their underlying images and pictures led them to misunderstand and misperceive the survey data. Hence it is to structures and processes that I shall devote most of my attention in this book, leaving more precise analyses of voting patterns in 1972 to such qualified authorities as Scammon and Wattenberg and the University of Michigan survey team. In some of the later chapters, I shall make moderately extensive use of research evidence, because the evidence is so contrary to the "pictures" of the liberal Democratic leadership that it is essential that at least some of it be made available immediately to those who read this volume. The misperception of this leadership about American attitudes toward race and the Vietnam war were so monumental that evidence against their pictures on these subjects is essential to the argument I am trying to make.

The reader might well ask by what authority I claim to know more about politics than, let us say, Frank Mankiewicz or James Reston or John Kenneth Galbraith. Do I think I am smarter than these men, or more sophisticated, or have had more experience in the cosmopolitan world? I am afraid I am unable to answer such questions. Obviously, I am not as sophisticated or as experienced or as knowledgeable as the theorists and practitioners of the New Politics, but I insist that I know more about politics than they do. More than that, what I know about politics seems to me to be almost self-evident, and I cannot understand how such brilliant men could have so badly missed the point. Perhaps at the very high levels of national society in which they move, some things do not seem nearly so obvious as they do from the worm's eye view of the precinct and the neighborhood. Or maybe it has something to do with being Irish.

In any case, while I shall buttress my argument with sources made available by political science, political theory, history, and sociology, I must be honest in the beginning and say that my pictures of the political process are primordial and antedate the social analytic arguments that I use to articulate and explicate them.

I trust I will be excused for not being explicitly outraged at the injustices in American society. I am outraged at injustice wherever I encounter it, but it seems to me that it has been demonstrably ineffective as a political style. I also trust that I will be excused from detailing programs on how injustice in America can be eliminated. I do not think there are any detailed programs that will solve any of our social problems quickly and easily, though I believe we could do many more things than we are now doing. I am a liberal Democrat and have been all my life, but I do not think that should necessitate my support of busing, quotas, or even affirmative action, particularly when I think such tactics are counterproductive and will not work, and that there are other and better ways of accomplishing the goals for which such programs have been designed. This is not a book about how American society might be made better; it is rather about some of the aspects of American political life that ought to be a matter of explicit knowledge for those leaders who are committed to changing American society.

The late Richard Hofstadter is alleged to have said that the 1960s were an age of rubbish. It was certainly a decade of exaggerated and romantic political rhetoric in which the rhetoricians began to take their own exaggerations seriously. The "establishment," "generation gap," "backlash," "youth culture," "police state," for example, may have been highly useful rhetorical symbols but they were also taken seriously as precise social analysis and the basis for social action. Anyone who insisted that radical rhetoric was inaccurate and that the crisis, while serious, was not necessarily the beginning of the end was accused of acquiescing in racism and war crimes.

Yet there ought to be at least the possibility of a middle position. In newspaper headlines and on the evening news there are no crises that are not prelude to disaster. The real world is far more fuzzy and complex. Life has a way of bumbling on even after Armageddon. Problems can be very serious yet not fatal. Men and women rarely follow their prejudices and fears to the most logical conclusions. Trends have a way of collapsing or generating countertrends. Some problems seem to solve themselves despite all that we do.

In other words, it ought to be possible to be gravely concerned about the future of America without having to give up hope. It ought to be possible to recognize the serious injustices in American society and still see both certain strengths and the possibility of change. It ought to be possible to say that we have a long way to go before we become a just society and still not deny the very real progress of the past. It ought to be possible to be outraged over war, racism, and dishonesty in high places without writing off American democracy as a complete failure. It ought to be possible to work for sweeping social change within the political system and without yielding to the inadequacies of that system. We ought to be able to acknowledge the obstacles to social change without being forced to deny the existence of resources that make change possible. We ought to be able to describe the complexities of American politics in a relatively dispassionate manner without being charged with lack of social concern and immoral complacency. It ought to be possible to say that radical rhetoric and, even more, radical action are frequently counterproductive and still share a commitment to the building of a better society with the radicals.

Whether such a middle stance may be espoused

in the part of American culture where most of the books are written and read is problematic. But the fundamental assumption of this book is that effective political action is still possible with many other segments of American society. Politics, this volume will argue, is the art of coalition building, and effective coalitions can still be built. There is some polarization and even something of a generation gap, but perhaps four-fifths of the American republic is not yet polarized. The majority of the young and the poor and the blacks still want in, not out. It is not too late for a reformist coalition—not even almost too late.

Some apocalyptic rhetoric is motivated by the conviction that without it there will be no sense of urgency. People must be frightened if they are to accept social change. Some fear is indeed useful for social change, but panic is counterproductive and can be expected to lead not to reform but to reaction. The most effective position from which to work for social change is one in which the reformer is able to balance outrage and a passionate moral commitment with an understanding of the complex nature of social and political reality and the skills of coalition formation.

There is still time for the United States, and to say that does not justify complacency. We need skilled visionary political leadership. We need theorists who are sensitive to the geographic, racial, religious, economic, social, and ethnic complexities of America; and we need innovators who can improve our organization performances without depriving us of freedom.

There are four groups of people who I hope may find this book useful.

1. The young. Serious research has demonstrated

that the young are not really very different from their parents—perhaps a little more likely to have supported Eugene McCarthy in 1968 if they were in college and a little more likely to have supported George Wallace if they did not go to college. The "young" about whom the media pontificate represents a small and volatile segment of their age cohort. This segment is not unimportant for setting cultural patterns but it ought not to be identified with the rest of the youthful population, a majority of which supported President Nixon in 1972.

Neither should the temper tantrums of the late 1960s about the "system's" never listening be taken seriously. The "system" was given its chance when Gene McCarthy was nominated; it could have listened after the war protest moratoriums or the Cambodia invasion protest demonstrations were mobilized. Since the "system" didn't respond by immediately acknowledging the superiority of the "young" in both morality and wisdom, they were then absolved of all further political responsibility. Politics, it would seem, is to be taken seriously if you win the first time you try. If the system doesn't concede you victory the first time around, then it has had its last chance.

So from awe over the "enthusiasm" of the "young," we have moved to disappointment over their "apathy." But both the awe and the disappointment have less to do with reality than with the descriptive rhetoric we use to talk about reality. This rhetoric is shaped for us by men who have very little understanding of what social reality is; and the "youth" question is an excellent example. Most of what is written about the "enthusiasm" and the "apathy" of the young is based on the changing fads and fashions of a minority of students at elite colleges. These changes are fascinating, make splendid media copy, and provide editorial writers and columnists with lots of material to view with alarm or to take comfort from; but politically such fads mean very little.

The reality is that young people are rather like the rest of us, only perhaps more so. Most of them are neither enthusiastic nor apathetic but somewhere in-between. Like the rest of us they move periodically along the continuum from enthusiasm to apathy and back. Because they are young their progress back and forth is likely to be more rapid and occasionally more dramatic, but there is no reason to think that they are as a group more likely to save society than any of their predecessors.

And yet, there is a new consciousness among the young that may represent (it is still too early to say) an important cultural change. This consciousness is not to be found among Professor Charles Reich's young friends at Yale, who are drifting off into a world of communes and drugs waiting for the arrival of the Eschaton; it is an assumption of political and social responsibility as a long-term commitment that is to be found in a rather small but critically important segment of the youthful population. This sense of commitment may be strong only in a very few and may not exist at all save in a minority. But it is there. Some of these young people who are determined to devote their lives to political and social action are beginning to ask whether the models of political strategy provided by the "New Politics" have much value. It is for them that this book is written.

2. This book is also for those American adults who are confused by but interested in politics. Although there is considerable variation in the trends of political participation, the work of my colleague, Norman

Nie, has demonstrated quite clearly that Americans have become much more "political" in the last decade and a half. Such "politicization" is not automatically a good thing. The arrival of the amateurs on the scene may well guarantee defeat rather than victory. It was, as Professor Nie observes, the amateur Republicans who created the Goldwater disaster in 1964. But, on balance, increased participation is, potentially at least, a good thing for democracy; and the desire of young and old, men and women, black and ethnic, rich and poor, to have a greater "say" in what happens to their society is more healthy than not. However, the amateur who thinks that the political process is simple and that all that is required to reform the political and social order is sincerity, good will, and honesty may well be a menace to society and is almost certainly going down the same path that the sincere, honest, and enthusiastic supporters of Barry Goldwater and George McGovern did.

3. This book is also for politicians. The mayor of Chicago is alleged to say frequently, "Those experts, they don't know anything." And yet as government grows more complicated, political leaders have no choice but to rely on the advice of men who are trained to think on a more general and abstract level than most politicians can or ought to do. There is nothing wrong with such a procedure so long as the advice is good and taken with a grain of salt. Unfortunately, sometimes that advice is very bad and is taken seriously. It was, after all, intellectuals more than anyone else who involved us in the war in Vietnam.

When one watches how a candidate defines the political issues and shapes the rhetoric with which he discusses the issues, one is increasingly suspicious that behind the scene there is lurking an "expert" who is assuring the politician that the speeches he (the expert) has written embody the best possible political strategy. The "experts" are so articulate and so confident that the politician may go along with the strategy even against his own better judgment (especially since his favorite newspaper columnist is saying the same thing). It probably does no great harm in the long run, since defeated political candidates can find well-paying jobs elsewhere in American society.

The mayor of Chicago is indeed right about those "experts" who ignore the need to rebuild the coalition: they don't know anything. My message to the politician who reads this book is that if the bright young Ph.D's on your staff are not talking about rebuilding the coalition (though they might not use the word), fire them. Better they be unemployed than you.

4. Finally, this book is for my colleagues in the social sciences. Many of them have helped form my ideas on the political process, and I owe it to them to set down my perhaps unorthodox views so that they can criticize them. Maybe they can learn something from me now in return for all they have taught me.

There are a number of different sources from which I have composed this book. I have relied heavily on the work of such scholars as James Q. Wilson, Robert Dahl, Nathan Glazer, V. O. Key, Seymour Martin Lipset, Peter Rossi, Daniel Moynihan, and my colleagues Sidney Verba and Norman Nie.

The purpose of this book is to facilitate social change. I yield nothing to the radicals in my concern about the serious problems that face American society. My disagreement, rather, is on the question of what strategies are appropriate for bringing about social change—and perhaps on the question of how easy and successful the change is going to be.

I take it that long-range social change cannot be accomplished in the United States as we now know it without building a coalition that will win elections and provide support for policies between elections. Winning isn't everything perhaps, but, as Charlie Brown has observed, losing isn't anything. The radicals don't mind losing because it reinforces their feelings of moral superiority and because they are convinced that a revolution is going to occur which will impose their programs for reform. There may be a revolution—though I doubt it—but if there is, it won't bring the radicals to power, only to concentration camps. However, since revolutions of either the Right or the Left are unlikely, there is no other course available to those interested in creating change than to use the creaky, imperfect, frustrating democratic process of coalition formation—unless one wishes to devote oneself to the satisfying but useless practice of performing liturgical gestures.

Deep concern about social evil, outrage over injustice, a profound sense of the importance of morality in public affairs—these qualities are a critical if not absolutely indispensable prelude to effective social reform. But in this volume the presumption is that the reader already has such moral commitments. The pertinent question is how does the morally concerned person operate within the political system and what are the tools available for his use? If a reader is convinced that American society is so corrupt that change is impossible, or that the political system is so immoral that it ought to be destroyed by violence or be permitted to topple of its own dead weight, then the ideas in this book will be of no use to him.

But most Americans have not yet come to such drastic conclusions. Even most young Americans believe that the system can be made to work—if not with the total morality of an ideal society, at least with a good deal more morality than is to be presently observed. It is for those who believe in the workability and the improvability of the system that I am writing. It is not too late.

Since this book was written the Watergate scandal has broken wide open. At this time (June 1973) three comments seem appropriate:

1. Massive electorial "mandates" do not dispense an American political leader from seeking consensus and building coalitions. A 60 percent presidential victory or a 52 percent victory represents very little difference in real presidential power—particularly when there is little change in the Congressional distribution of power. A landslide president has to deal with the same social and political structure in the nation, the same Congressional committee power elites, the same governmental bureaucracies, the same informal alliances between the bureaucracies and the Congressional committees, the same veto groups and power alliances in the larger society, the same recalcitrant social problems, and the same hostile media. He may have additional prestige for a time, but it deteriorates very rapidly and does not impress such key "check and balance" figures like Wilbur Mills one bit.

Yet each mandate president seems to think that in his case Mr. Madison's system is no longer required.

After 1936, Roosevelt tried to govern without the Supreme Court; after 1956, Eisenhower tried not to govern at all; after 1964, Johnson tried to make war without the consent of Congress or the people; and after 1972, Nixon tried to govern the country not only without the cooperation of the courts and Congress but also without the cooperation of the bureaucracy, the cabinet, and the Republican party. In each case the result was predictable to the politicians who had not been hypnotized by the majesty of the presidential office, the size of the presidential majority, or the ruthlessness of the presidential advisers. Watergate merely brought disaster to Mr. Nixon sooner and quicker than it came to other mandate presidents. Our political system is designed for 55–45 percent majorities (at the most). Any president with a larger majority is ill-advised to take his mandate seriously.

2. The checks and balances system of Mr. Madison still works. The courts (in the persons of Judges John Sirica and Matt Byrne), the Congress (in the person of Senator Sam Ervin), and the media (in the form of the *Washington Post*) tumbled the southern California house of cards rather quickly. Nor do I think this victory for Madison's scheme was merely accidental or lucky. The system did exactly what it was designed to do: it prevented tyranny. Of course, the cost of such a jolt to the country is very high indeed. A parliamentary system, which would sweep the Nixon administration out of office, would have been much more efficient *in this instance.* The question remains whether that system would be more desirable than the present strong presidential system for a society as large and as complex and as unstable in its pluralism as ours. My own hunch is that there are costs in both the parliamentary and presidential systems, and that the

United States at the present has the one best suited to it. And while Americans probably still believe in the strong president system, at this point they are perhaps willing to admit that there must be some new mechanisms to inhibit the isolation of the president from political realities.

3. Watergate gives the Democratic coalition the greatest political trump card since the Great Depression. There is no reason to think, however, that the conflicts that defeated the party in 1968 and 1972 will not again cause the Democrats to misplay—particularly if the ideological liberal left component of the coalition continues to make the same mistake it did in 1972. Mr. Nixon made it, too, after his reelection: In American politics no political faction can assume that it has either the right or the capacity to govern unless it wins the cooperation and consent of other factions. And this holds true for factions in the governmental structure as well as for the larger society.

I am forced to let out of my hands the final galleys of this book the day after the Special Prosecutor in the Watergate Case, Archibald Cox, has been fired and the Attorney General, Elliot Richardson, has resigned. Many observers are calling this moment one of the great constitutional crises in American history and are speculating on any number of Republicans as possible presidential candidates in 1976. At this juncture all predictions seem foolish. The American presidency is in its most serious crisis since Andrew Jackson. One has the impression that the president and his advisers are digging themselves into a deeper crisis. No more can safely be guessed on this last day of June.

Yet for all its dramatic and traumatic impact on American political life, Watergate does not lessen the importance of building coalitions. On the contrary, the failure of political kills in the leadership of both parties is responsible for the present crisis. One party was presided over by the "best and the brightest" (even more true of Senator McGovern's entourage than President Kennedy's) and the other by the "worst and the dumbest." Neither, it turns out, had much in the way of politicians. Self righteousness and bugging are no substitute for coalition building.

MR. MADISON'S EXPERIMENT

Stewart Alsop, in a bitter denunciation written to Anthony Lewis, had some extraordinarily harsh words to say about currently fashionable liberalism:

> *Consider the results of your kind of liberalism. The old liberalism identified itself with the interests of ordinary people, people who work for a living, enjoy "I Love Lucy," and wear American flags in their buttonholes. Your kind of liberalism excludes such people as rigidly as old Joe Pew's "real Republicanism" excluded them.*
>
> *One result was last November's liberal disaster, which saw an unloved president, burdened with a snowy scandal, score a historic landslide. The reason was not that your kind of liberalism was against Mr. Nixon, hardly anybody likes him very much, or against the war, which nobody likes at all.*
>
> *The reason was that a great many ordinary Americans perceived your kind of liberalism as against* them *and worse, against the United States.*

Leaving aside Mr. Alsop's rhetoric, there can be little doubt that he has put his finger on the critical dilemma of contemporary American liberalism. It does not have the votes to win an election by itself, and it does not have the patience, taste, or sympathy to work very hard at winning allies among those people whose sympathies used to be an important part of the old liberal coalition.

There was considerable talk after the 1972 Democratic convention about broadening the base of the McGovern coalition, but there was some ambivalence about such an enterprise. Some liberals thought it was unnecessary because the young people would compensate for the loss of those who "enjoy 'I Love Lucy' and wear American flags in their buttonholes." Others thought, as did Frank Mankiewicz when he forced Senator McGovern to dump Larry O'Brien as chairman of the National Committee, that such behavior was a rejection of "compromise with the old politics." But even those who were convinced that it was necessary to win the support of "ordinary people who work for a living" seemed to think that the way to do it was to preach at them, to exhort them to virtue, and to urge them to "come home" to generosity, sacrifice, and morality. Any other technique at coalition building, it was apparently felt, would be demeaning and inappropriate for the New Politics.

One can sympathize with the problem of the New Politics liberals. Men and women of superior intelligence, morality, and commitment, they were being asked to enter into a political alliance as more or less equal with vast hordes of people who did not read the *Village Voice* or the *New York Review* or even the *New York Times* and the *Washington Post.* To build a coalition in which such people were treated as equals would have required time, patience, compromise, concession, and even a consideration of the possibility that such people might have something useful to say about American politics. Professional politicians, whose livings depend on it, find coalition building a wearisome and difficult task, but the New Politicians—most of whom clearly do not depend on success in coalition building for their livelihoods—found it ultimately an affront to their integrity. In 1972, they attempted to substitute morality for the degrading task of making political "deals" with their inferiors. In 1976, one suspects from the preliminary signs, they will attempt to substitute charisma. Morality did not work in 1972, and if the New Politicians think that charisma will work in 1976, they are wrong again. As a union leader said to a meeting of the New York American Civil Liberties Union (quoted by Lucian Truscott IV in the *Village Voice*), "I have the sense that the people sitting around this table know more about and care more about the average peasant in North Vietnam than they do about the kind of people who make up my union." Care and concern about peasants all over the world is admirable, and there should be more of it; but lack of knowledge about those whose votes you need to win an election is political folly.

Why must the "best and the brightest" of American liberals be constrained to deal politically with the kind of people who watch "I Love Lucy?" Is it not an unjust political system that requires this kind of condescension? Ought not coalition politics be abolished? Indeed, who thought up coalition politics in the first place? It sounds like a plot dreamed up by Richard J. Daley.

No one would deny that the mayor of Chicago is a master at coalition politics. But he didn't originate it. If we want to find a single person who is responsible for imposing coalition politics on American life, we will discover the offending party to be a gentlemen far more elegant and more reflective in his prose style than the mayor of Chicago. He was a young man named James Madison.

There is a new "school" of historical literature emerging on the beginnings of the American nation.[1]

[1] Bernard Baylin, *The Ideological Origins of the American Revolution* (Cambridge, Mass.: Harvard University Press, 1967); Gordon S. Wood. *The Creation of the American Republic 1776–1787* (Greensboro, N.C.: University of North Carolina Press, 1969); and Michael Kammen, *People of Paradox* (New York: Alfred Knopf, 1972).

This literature ought to be required reading for all New Politics liberals as well as for those hardy souls who are going to try to put the American liberal coalition back together again in the next four years. They should also, incidentally, probably read the *Federalist Papers,* particularly the tenth and the fifty-first. One may not like Mr. Madison's political experiment (though I happen to think it is the most noble work of polity that human ingenuity has ever devised), but whether one likes it or not is ultimately irrelevant if one has decided to engage in politics in American society, because it is the political structure with which we happen to be stuck.

Michael Kammen argues persuasively in his *People of Paradox* that there were two fundamental political problems in colonial America. The first was the quest for legitimacy. The confusion of charters, royal grants, dubious legal interpretations, and provisional governments with uncertain powers created a situation in which it was very difficult for the citizen to know from whence came legitimate political power:

> *At a time when new groups were seeking access to the political process, and at a time when new social assumptions were taking shape, countervailing legitimacy could not be located in the continuity of traditional integrative institutions. For some years prior to 1689, repeated deterioration in governmental effectiveness had made the stability of legitimate systems precarious at best. In the years immediately following the rebellions, the most effective (albeit illegitimate) regimes proved to be even less stable than their predecessors.*[2]

[2] Kammen, *People of Paradox,* pp. 37–38.

To compound the legitimacy problem and make it even worse was the fantastic pluralism of late seventeenth- and early eighteenth-century American society. One might have expected, Kammen says, that the governmental and cultural impulses of American society ought to have been in the direction of uniformity and away from multiplicity. Nonetheless, such factors as the labor shortage, military requirements, recruitment patterns for colonization, and, of course, the geographic immensity of the continent all contributed to pluralism. And other factors were at work that made the pluralism not only extensive but also unstable.

> *So many of the immigrants to the colonies came for anti-authoritarian reasons, came with hostilities against restraint already well formed. Moreover, plural societies gain in stability where major political parties cut across ethnic lines. Such has been the case in nineteenth- and twentieth-century America, where the history of party is remarkable for continuity and longevity. But such was not the case in colonial America, where there were Quaker parties, German parties, Presbyterian parties—where each group might have its own faction, each sect its own school, each dogmatist his own ideology.*[3]

Thus pluralism in American society did not come into being when the Irish and the Italians and the Poles began to flood our shores. Pluralism in the society—economic, geographic, religious, and cultural—existed long before the new republic was born. The Constitution emerged not as a means of guaranteeing pluralism for the future but rather as a

[3] Kammen, *People of Paradox,* pp. 60–61.

means of legitimizing and coping with a well-established phenomenon.

As Kammen says:

> *The concept of balanced government which emerged so vitally in 1787–8 embodies institutional means whereby a viable political system could be maintained in a diffuse society. And so it was that American colonial history, which had begun with a quest for purity and homogeneity, ended with a sophisticated rationale for pluralism and heterogeneity. What had happened was not really so paradoxical as it may seem, for the so-called melting pot had been a boiling cauldron all along, from Jamestown to James Madison. There is a very real sense in which the American nation emerged, not in response to new-found national unity, but rather in response to provincial disunity, in response to a historical problem of long duration: how best to control unstable pluralism, how best to balance the areas of compulsion and freedom in American life.*[4]

Gordon Wood's *The Creation of the American Republic* is a study of the evolution of political thought among the leaders of the republic between the time of the Declaration of Independence and the Constitution. It makes extraordinarily fascinating reading because it is a chronicle of fantastic change in political beliefs. The Americans began their struggle for independence as essentially radical Whigs. They believed that they were not so much replacing the British constitution (the vesting of power in king, Lords, and Commons) as that they were attempting to return to the freedoms and integrity the British consti-

[4] Ibid., pp. 73–74.

tution guaranteed and which were being rapidly corrupted in Britain itself. They were firmly convinced that once tyranny was eliminated a republic of virtue would come into being. The separation of powers in the British constitution was perceived as a check on the abuse of power by government, not as a check against the abuse of power by one faction of the society against another faction of the society. The Americans were convinced that self-sacrifice, self-discipline, and virtue were required in a republican society and that all members of the republic would be willing and eager to make whatever personal sacrifices were required for the common good. What impeded such virtue, they argued, was the fact that governmental power had deteriorated into tyranny. When a proper balance was established once again within government, when the old British constitution was revitalized in an American context, republican virtue, indeed the greatest republican virtue in human history, would emerge.

So, British rule was overthrown, state constitutions were established, and the Articles of Confederation were written. Much to the horror of the Americans, virtue did not emerge at all. The people turned out not to be particularly virtuous, and unwilling to sacrifice for the common good. Various factions within the population fought bitterly among themselves. Nor did the governments set up by the state constitutions prove either intelligent or virtuous. On the contrary, state governments seemed to alternate between incompetence and oppression. The splendid republican dream crumbled into dust before the horrified eyes of Americans like Alexander Hamilton, John Jay, James Wilson, and James Madison. Something had to be done, and quickly.

Two ideas emerged around which the Constitution

was built. The first was the notion of "limited sovereignty," an idea that was both new and absolutely unintelligible to the critics of the Constitution. All political thought until the time of Madison was convinced that absolute sovereignty rested in the government. As Patrick Henry exclaimed in bafflement, "How could sovereignty that was not absolute be sovereignty at all?" In the British constitution, according to the pre-Federalist theorists, the check on the abuse of government powers came from a division of the government into three separate parts. Madison and the Federalists were convinced that this would no longer work in the United States, and the check on the power of government had to be built into both the theory and structure of government. The people, they argued, would come together (and at the Constitutional Convention the representatives did just that) to delegate certain specified powers to the government. Within those limitations of power, once the leaders of government were elected, they had great discretion as to how they exercised their powers. But they were strongly forbidden to go beyond those powers that the people had delegated to them. Limitation of government abuse of power, then, came not so much from internal division of governmental authority (though that, of course, was to occur too) as from the fact that government had only certain specified powers, a limited sovereignty, while the rest of the power of the state remained with the people.

It is interesting to note in Wood's book how the Federalists developed their theory to explain what they were doing not before but at the same time and, indeed, to a considerable extent, after they had designed their political structure. James Wilson, in particular, in arguing in his native state of Pennsylvania in favor of the Constitution, explicated most clearly and in a sense for the first time the notion of limited sovereignty that is at the very root of American constitutionalism.

But more important for our purposes in this book was the Madisonian conclusion that freedom and justice in a society would be guaranteed not by eliminating diversity and interests but in fact by playing off various interests one against another. Gordon Wood summarizes his six hundred pages of research on the creation of the American republic with two brilliant paragraphs that tell the entire tale of the evolution of thought of the founding fathers (most of whom, incidentally, were too young to have children much beyond infancy).

> *The Americans had reversed in a revolutionary way the traditional conception of politics: the stability of government no longer relied, as it had for centuries, upon its embodiment of the basic social forces of the state. Indeed, it now depended upon the prevention of the various social interests from incorporating themselves too firmly in the government. Institutional or governmental politics was thus abstracted in a curious way from its former associations with the society. But at the same time a more modern and more realistic sense of political behavior in the society itself, among the people, could now be appreciated. This revolution marked an end of the classical conception of politics and the beginning of what might be called a romantic view of politics. The eighteenth century had sought to understand politics, as it had all of life, by capturing in an integrated, ordered, changeless ideal the totality and complexity of the world—an ideal that the con-*

cept of the mixed constitution and the proportioned social hierarchy on which it rested perfectly expressed. In such an ideal there could be only potential energy, no kinetic energy, only a static equilibrium among synthetic orders, and no motion among the particular, miscellaneous parts that made up the society. By destroying this ideal Americans placed a new emphasis on the piecemeal and the concrete in politics at the expense of order and completeness. The Constitution represented both the climax and the finale of the American Enlightenment, both the fulfillment and the end of the belief that the endless variety and perplexity of society could be reduced to a simple and harmonious system. By attempting to formulate a theory of politics that would represent reality as it was, the Americans of 1787 shattered the classical Whig world of 1776.

Americans had begun the Revolution assuming that the people were a homogeneous entity in society set against the rulers. But such an assumption belied American experience, and it took only a few years of independence to convince the best American minds that distinctions in the society were "various and unavoidable," so much so that they could not be embodied in the government. Once the people were thought to be composed of various interests in opposition to one another, all sense of a graduated organic chain in the social hierarchy became irrelevant, symbolized by the increasing emphasis on the image of a social contract. The people were not an order organically tied together by their unity of interest but rather an agglomeration of hostile individuals coming together for their mutual benefit to construct a society. The Americans transformed the people in the same way that Englishmen a century earlier had transformed the rulers: they broke the connectedness of interest among them and put them at war with one another, just as seventeenth-century Englishmen had separated the interests of rulers and people and put them in opposition to each other.[5]

In the tenth *Federalist Paper* we see how far the idealistic James Madison had come from his 1775 belief in a republic of virtue. Realistically, almost cynically, he defines "faction": "a number of citizens, whether amounting to a majority or a minority of the whole, who are united and actuated by some common impulse of passion, or of interest, adverse to the rights of other citizens, or to the permanent and aggregate interests of the community." [6] Madison then points out two ways of eliminating the "mischiefs of faction": one either removes the causes or controls the effects.[7] He quickly concludes that the causes cannot be removed—at least without eliminating liberty. It therefore becomes necessary to control the effects. And how are they to be controlled? Basically by preventing the faction from getting sufficient amounts of power to impose its own "passion" on the rest of society.

One of the stronger arguments that Madison and the other Federalists used for the new Constitution was that the very size and diversity of the country being established would prevent any faction from obtaining the power of political oppression. In a state,

[5] Wood, *Creation of the American Republic,* pp. 606–7.
[6] James Madison, "The Federalist No. 10," in *The Federalist,* ed. Jacob E. Cooke (Middletown, Conn.: Wesleyan University Press, 1961), p. 57.
[7] Ibid., p. 58.

he argues, where the population is small and rather homogeneous, it may be possible for factions to obtain such power (as they had in fact during the era of the Articles of Confederation); but in a national government the built-in diversity of the various groups constituting national society will make it most improbable that factional oppression can occur.

Madison returns to this theme in the fifty-first *Federalist Paper.* After pointing out that the divisions of powers in the government and the division between state and federal government provides a limitation and a check on the power of governmental oppression, he turns to the question of guarding "one part of the society against the injustice of the other part." [8] There are, Madison says, two ways that one might effectively prevent such oppression:

> *The one by creating a will in the community independent of the majority, that is, of the society itself; the other by comprehending in the society so many separate descriptions of citizens, as will render an unjust combination of a majority of the whole, very improbable, if not impracticable. The first method prevails in all governments possessing an hereditary or self appointed authority. This at best is but a precarious security; because a power independent of the society may as well espouse the unjust views of the major, as the rightful interests, of the minor party, and may possibly be turned against both parties. The second method will be exemplified in the federal republic of the United States. Whilst all authority in it will be derived from and dependent on the society, the society itself will be broken into so many parts, in-*

[8] James Madison, "The Federalist No. 51," in Ibid., p. 351.

terests and classes of citizens, that the rights of individuals or of the minority, will be in little danger from interested combinations of the majority. In a free government, the security for civil rights must be the same as for religious rights. It consists in the one case in the multiplicity of interests, and in the other, in the multiplicity of sects. The degree of security in both cases will depend on the number of interests and sects; and this may be presumed to depend on the extent of country and number of people comprehended under the same government.[9]

It is fascinating to note in passing that Madison uses religious pluralism as a model of the structure required for political pluralism. While I have not been able to find any detailed historical research on this subject, I am inclined to suspect from certain passages like the one I have just quoted, that the denominational pluralism of the colonies before the emergence of the American republic was the most important model that the Americans had in their minds when they were trying to create a politically pluralistic society. Denominational pluralism preceded and to some extent caused political pluralism.

Madison then goes on to repeat his argument of the tenth *Federalist Paper* that a large society is likely to have more freedom than a small one precisely because there is likely to be greater diversity within the large society. Rhode Island left by itself could become a tyranny; Rhode Island in a federal republic would be part of a variegated whole in which majority oppression would be extremely unlikely.

[9] James Madison, "The Federalist No. 51," in Ibid., pp. 351–52.

So in the former state, will the more powerful factions or parties be gradually induced by a like motive, to wish for a government which will protect all parties, the weaker as well as the more powerful. It can be little doubted, that if the state of Rhode Island was separated from the confederacy, and left to itself, the insecurity of rights under the popular form of government within such narrow limits, would be displayed by such reiterated oppressions of factious majorities, that some power altogether independent of the people would soon be called for by the voice of the very factions whose misrule had proved the necessity of it. In the extended republic of the United States, and among the great variety of interests, parties and sects which it embraces, a coalition of a majority of the whole society could seldom take place on any other principles than those of justice and the general good.[10]

Madison, of course, may have been unduly naïve. There have unquestionably been times when majority coalitions have taken place which have not operated on principles of justice and general good. Nonetheless, the need to put together a majority coalition to accomplish one's purpose, a need, in other words, to make "deals" and to win allies, has been and continues to be a serious problem for factions, particularly for moralistic factions, who are convinced that their own goodness and virtue precludes negotiation, concession, and compromise.

Madison was interested in restraining oppression. He was less concerned about how coalitions could be put together that would make effective government, but it is clear from the paragraph quoted

[10] Ibid., pp. 352–53.

above that he and his colleagues deliberately and consciously set forth to establish a political system in which power could only be put together by establishing coalitions. Indeed, no one who reads the fifty-first *Federalist Paper* carefully could possibly deceive himself into thinking that coalition building was not at the core of politics in the American constitutional structure. One may ultimately decide in terms of one's own philosophical principles that coalition building must go (though even to do that, one would have to build a coalition that would accept such a change or, alternatively, impose one's will by raw power). But one should have no illusions: to eliminate coalition building from American politics would mean to terminate Mr. Madison's experiment.

Gordon Wood notes at the end of his book that the Federalists were extraordinarily proud of their effort. They were persuaded that they had put together a constitution that would make republicanism possible. They had conceived a "constitutional antidote 'wholly popular' and 'strictly republican' for the ancient diseases of a republican polity—an antidote that did not destroy republican vices but rather accepted, indeed endorsed and relied upon them." [11]

Federalists may have been partisan aristocrats. They may have believed that their own intelligence and training made them fit to rule while those who were governing under the Articles of Confederation were not fit to rule. The system they developed has never worked perfectly, and there are obviously too many deficiencies in their thoughts; but as Wood remarks: ". . . the Federalists' intellectual

[11] Wood, *Creation of the American Republic,* pp. 614–15.

achievement really transcended their particular political and social intentions and became more important and more influential than they themselves anticipated."[12] Their creation could be changed, modified, expanded, developed by others with different interests and different aims even to the extent of destroying the aristocratic world of tide-water plantations, which had given rise to Federalist thought. The system, then, even in its beginnings, had its weaknesses and failings, yet it was a remarkable system, and, as Wood puts it in his closing paragraph:

> *So piecemeal was the Americans' formulation of this system, so diverse and scattered in authorship, and so much a simple response to the pressures of democratic politics was their creation, that the originality and the theoretical consistency and completeness of their constitutional thinking have been obscured. It was a political theory that was diffusive and open-ended; it was not delineated in a single book; it was peculiarly the product of a democratic society, without a precise beginning or an ending. It was not political theory in the grand manner, but it was political theory worthy of a prominent place in the history of Western thought.*[13]

On balance, how has Mr. Madison's experiment worked? It has produced a political structure and a political culture that has demonstrated extraordinary flexibility for absorbing new groups and for undergoing rapid social change without collapsing under the strain. In a reasonably stable nation with

[12] Ibid., p. 615.
[13] Ibid.

one culture and long political and legal traditions behind it, there might be other and more effective ways to govern than the complex pluralistic system devised by Madison and his colleagues. However, if anyone has discovered a better way of governing a large, variegated, and new society, this alternative is not clearly visible. Precisely because the United States had a political structure and political culture that took coalition building for granted, it was able to integrate the vast diversity of immigrant groups that descended upon its shores after 1800. The native Americans may not have wanted these immigrants to come into American society, and they may have been grimly suspicious of sharing political power with them. Yet the principles of the American republic demanded that they be admitted, and the styles and protocols of American political bargaining and coalition formation permitted these new groups rapidly to acquire enough of a base of their own so that they too became partners in coalition construction.

The principal failure of Madisonian federalism was, of course, race. The nonwhite groups were not duly certified and licensed coalition bargainers until very recently. The Civil War was fought—from one point of view—both as a result of a failure in coalition politics to cope with the slavery question and an attempt to permit the black population to become a licensed coalition party. Tragically, this attempt of the northern "faction" to impose its will on the southern "faction" was not very successful, and while one can be more hopeful today that there is a majority coalition in favor of eliminating the residual effects of slavery and admitting nonwhites as partners in the political coalition, one is still uneasy about the possibilities of permanently resolving this traditional "American dilemma."

Two things should be said in defense of the Madisonian experiment: (1) The experiment did not create the racial problem in the United States. Slavery existed before the Constitution, and by outlawing the slave trade after 1808, the Constitution at least made clear the Federalist ambivalence about slavery. (2) More important for our purposes is the fact that America's failures to cope with its racial dilemma come from being false to its own Constitutional principles. It is not that the principles have failed; it is that on racial matters the principles have been imperfectly and belatedly applied. The principles of the Madisonian experiment (not practised by Madison and his colleagues either, for that matter) make it perfectly clear that blacks, too, should be admitted as full participants in the coalition-formation enterprise. One can only conclude that the American constitutional framework cannot solve the racial problem at such a time when even though blacks have become partners in the coalition, they are still unable to obtain freedom and justice in American society. The society has failed to resolve its racial problems, and to say that does not imply that the constitutional principles have failed or even have impeded a solution. To paraphrase what G. K. Chesterton said about Christianity: as far as blacks are concerned, coalition formation has not been tried and found wanting, but found hard and not tried.

So Madison and his colleagues began by believing in the possibility of a republic of virtue and ended up believing that they had created a republic in which, broadly speaking, virtue was irrelevant. In their view, the American Constitution guaranteed a certain minimum of justice and freedom regardless of how virtuous its people were. It guaranteed that minimum precisely because it imposed on any group within the society that sought to achieve its own aims the unconditional need to win allies. By so doing, the Federalists not only legitimated the pluralism that already existed in the society, they opened the door for a dramatic increase of pluralism, the like of which may well have horrified them. The political and cultural structure they created not only makes pluralism possible, it almost makes it necessary. The Federalists created not merely a society where bargaining, compromise, and coalition formation was a political option; they created a society in which such behavior became a political necessity. If a person wanted to have political influence, he had best find himself a "faction" (union, trade organization, national association, ethnic group, political party, etc.) with which he might affiliate. Indeed, the wise man found several different "factions" to join.

It is a messy, disorganized, inept, frequently bungling way of operating. Are we reconciled to it yet? As Michael Kammen observes:

> *. . . stable pluralism in a democracy also requires a strong and lasting inventory of psychological legitimacy: understanding, acceptance, and pervasive confidence in the composite system necessary to make it run smoothly rather than by fits and starts. Americans continue to celebrate pluralism in the past, but are reluctant to honor it in the present. Have we fully accepted the legitimacy of pluralism? How highly do we value cultural, moral, and regional autonomy, absolute toleration, community control over education, the*

continued integrity of divergent groups? Partially: some of us, some of these, in some places, at some times. Our ambiguity about the implications of our own system—"the huge, unrecorded hum of implication"—ought to prompt us to look more closely than we have at the historical background of our ambivalence.[14]

One has the impression that ambiguity about the structure and history of American politics is today very powerful indeed among the nation's intellectual and cultural elites. Lip service is given to coalition formation, of course, but in fact the New Politics seems really to want to form coalitions only with those who already agree with it. Trade-offs, compromises, development of programs that large numbers of people can "live with" (if not enthusiastically endorse)—all of these things seem to the New Politics liberal as somehow or other corrupt and immoral. It is so much simpler to appeal to the moral imperative, to call for virtue, to attempt to stir up guilt, to find a leader with "charisma." That the collective bargaining negotiations between management and labor might be merely a specification of a general American political style is an extraordinarily offensive idea to many of the elite leaders of the liberal New Politics. It is all right for management and labor to compromise with each other, but how can a New Politics liberal compromise with someone who will not admit the totality of his moral superiority and confirm his claim to leadership and guidance?

Mind you, throughout the history of the United States since the beginning of Mr. Madison's experiment, there has been no lack of appeal to morality in politics. Indeed, the rhetoric of morality is perva-

[14] Kammen, *People of Paradox,* p. 85.

sive in political dialogue. No effective American political leader eschews the use of moralistic rhetoric or doubts the effectiveness of an appeal to moral impulse. But the smart politician is well aware that morality is not nearly enough, and he never counts on it to help him win an election or to effect a social change unless he has devised a program that includes "something for everyone." Walter Lippmann pointed out long ago that major social change will occur successfully in America only when the program establishing such change has benefits for a very broad spectrum of the population. It will probably be an extraordinary affront to many New Politics liberals to read what I am about to write: We will have effective racial integration and racial justice in the United States when the techniques and the policies designed to achieve such admirable social goals will bring clear benefit and profit not merely to blacks but to much of the rest of American society. If there is a profit to be made in integration, then integration will work. A newspaper columnist's suggestion that everyone with a nonwhite neighbor should be granted a thousand dollar income tax deduction may have been intended as a joke and it may be impractical as a social policy recommendation, but it does display an approach to the solution of social problems that ought to be taken seriously. I am sorry if this suggestion is offensive to some readers, but as one who believes in racial integration, I am convinced that making it economically profitable is the most effective way to accomplish it. As a believer in Mr. Madison's experiment, I think such an approach is perfectly consistent with the political ideas that gave birth to our republic and that have sustained it in existence despite its heterogeneity and the centrifugal forces constantly at work within it.

No reconstructor of the liberal coalition is going to be successful (unless the conservative coalition commits political suicide, which it very well may) unless he can devise broad social programs that have something in them for all those partners of the coalition on whose support he will rely and unless the cost of such programs are distributed with some sort of equity through the whole of society. Those costs should not be imposed on the members of the lower middle and working class who happen to live in closest proximity with the expanding black ghettos. The most obvious sort of issue on which there is broad consensus among all potential members of a reconstructed liberal coalition is crime. Despite the stubborn and dogmatic refusal of the liberal elites to face the fact (secure behind their barred windows and apartment building guards) that crime is not a right-wing issue—save to the extent that liberals have conceded it to the right—black and brown Americans are at least as concerned about crime as are white Americans. It is quite proper for them to be so concerned, because they are much more likely to be its victims. The liberal cant responds that crime will only stop when one eliminates social problems, but such an assertion is small consolation to someone who has been mugged. Social policies for improving opportunities for health, education, and employment are going to have to be accompanied by other social policies that will effectively make the streets of the cities safe again. How George McGovern and his *Wunderkinder* could have failed to make more of the crime issue simply escapes me. A man, I think, could be elected president of the United States at this point in time solely on the basis of an intelligent, clearly thought out and comprehensive program for reducing crime in the large American cities. There is no more compelling evidence of the woeful political ineptitude of American left liberals than their inability to take the crime issue away from reactionary demagogues. In a political system that originates from Mr. Madison's experiment, such ineptitude is simply intolerable.

One can be very troubled when one goes through the *Federalist Papers* in 1973. Madison and his colleagues would have been horrified at the immense powers of government bureaucracies and the arbitrary and raw exercise of force by governmental agencies—particularly by the president and the Supreme Court. They would, I think, be very much afraid that the tyranny they opposed was returning. They would also be dismayed, I think, by the apparent collapse of Congress's ability to administer its own affairs effectively. If, on the other hand, they were told that there were strong though inarticulate demands in the rank and file members of the American public for reforms that would make the governmental bureaucracy both responsive and responsible, they would take heart, I think. It would not be difficult to persuade those sophisticated men of the world that in a large and complex society like ours there is no way to escape the need for big government. Their fear would be that there were no opposing forces in society to check and restrain the power of big government and to prevent it from becoming itself a faction to oppress the rest of society. As long as the ordinary citizen could expect government agencies to be efficient, responsible, and responsive, the Federalists' experiment might be deemed to be working relatively well.

But the New Politics liberals of 1972 did not seize that issue either, leaving it Mr. Nixon's meat-axe approach of "Don't ask what Washington can do for you." The critical question in American society, as far as big government goes, is not whether there should be more or less of it, but how it can be made humane, responsive, responsible. One of the big advantages of urban organization politics is that the citizen had something the precinct captain wanted—a vote. When you dealt with a precinct captain he had to be careful not to offend you, because you had something he needed. If he was officious, insensitive, or unhelpful, you could always go to the ward committeeman. But in dealing with a contemporary government bureaucrat, you have nothing he wants, and he can clobber you over the head with his books of rules and regulations. It is always possible, of course, to appeal to the courts or to Washington (or to the state or city governments), but they are a long way away and not nearly so likely to be interested in you as the ward committeeman was. When my precinct captain offends me, I can get the committeeman on the phone the same day and seek redress. When a federal bureaucrat oppresses me it will take months and years and money to bring the case before proper authority.

I am not suggesting that federal bureaucrats are inept or tyrannical men and women. On the contrary, they are in most cases serious and dedicated individuals working under extraordinary demands and pressures. The problem is not malice or stupidity among bureaucrats; it is the bureaucratic *system* that is not designed to facilitate meaningful interaction between citizens and the government, which in the Federalist view of things belongs to him, not the bureaucracy.

This book, as I said in the first chapter, is about building coalition politics. I shall not attempt to detail here the sorts of reforms that might be appropriate to make large governmental bureaucracies operate more effectively and more humanely. I am not seriously suggesting a return to the precinct captain style of government, though I think some ways must be found to reintroduce the precinct captain function into the governmental process. My point is that crime and governmental responsiveness are two obvious political issues for someone who wishes to recreate the liberal coalition. They are of tremendous importance to the society, and they are problems that affect virtually all the population groups within the society. To provide solutions to these problems will require ingenuity, imagination, and creativity, which liberals have a lot of if they can divert themselves from moral denunciation. As Lucian Truscott said in the January 18, 1973 issue of the *Village Voice* about the crime issue:

> *Liberals have traditionally reacted quickly to challenges, ideological and otherwise, from the Left. But this time, the challenge is coming from the Right, and so far, liberal reaction has been either woefully misbegotten (as in "Protect our community and to hell with the rest of them.") or completely non-existent. Still liberals have two things to offer . . . however belatedly, with respect to the problem of crime. We have our minds, our ideas, our voices. And we have our political leadership. We know that when these have come from the Right, they have been woefully bereft of substance, compassion, and justice. And more to the point, they have simply done nothing about crime. Nothing. So we better damn well get some new*

thought, some new leadership from the Left. But will we?

A fair question. At this stage of the game only a fool would assay an answer. What, after all, is a liberal elite for if it can't think up new and ingenious and creative and broadly acceptable solutions to the problems of crime and big government? I shall return to this question and the "new issue" of responsiveness and responsibility in a subsequent chapter.

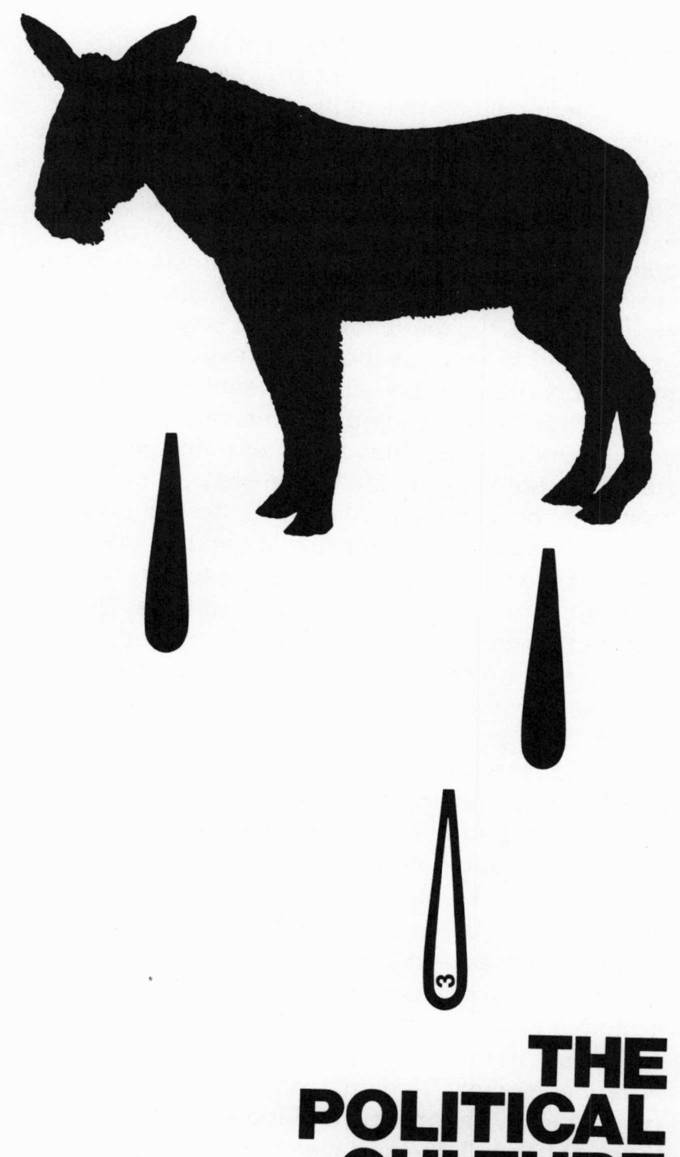

THE POLITICAL CULTURE

Negativism about American politics is so widespread that it is difficult to attempt an objective and an unemotional analysis of the American political culture. The forest is seen as inhabited by monsters called Establishment, Power Elite, and Military-Industrial Complex. The average citizen is thought of as apathetic or indifferent or, worse, the victim of a conspiracy to deprive him of the satisfactions of exercising political power. The mass media are described as part of the technique the power elite has established to serve as the modern equivalent of bread and circuses to keep the disenfranchised masses happy. Depending on which apocalyptic is your favorite, the people are either politically frustrated, do not know it, and hence are beyond redemption, or they are politically frustrated, do know it, and hence are ready for revolution. In addition, we are assured that ours is a violent society with little respect for the civic and legal traditions, the rights of dissent, and the viewpoints of others. Force and repression have been characteristic of American life from the beginning and are even worse now. Why?

One sober writer, Seymour Martin Lipset, compared the respect for the legal tradition in the United States and in Canada and showed that legal institutions are far more respected in Canada. According to Lipset, that is because the American nation came into being as a revolt against the political order and because many of the more conservative and traditional components of American society migrated to Canada after the revolution.

Other writers have emphasized the diversity of American society. Regional, economic, social, religious, racial, nationality, and ideological differences lurk just beneath the surface of this large, complex society that was patched together from variegated components over a brief period of time. The Civil War was but an exaggeration of the conflict characteristic of American society from the beginning.

If one combines a rather low level of respect for legal institutions with great social diversity and a tradition of settling difficulties and conflicts by direct action, one is forced to marvel that we have a society at all and that we have fought only one civil war.

Obviously some of the charges in the preceding indictment of the American political culture are contradictory. How can a society be simultaneously apathetic and violence prone? How can the individual citizen be politically indifferent and still ready to do his enemies in? That there is both apathy and a proclivity for illegal and violent means in the United States surely cannot be denied by anyone who knows anything about American history. However, we might well ask *relative to what?* Is the American political culture deficient by the abstract standards of political excellence we learned in our high school civic books? Or is it deficient compared to other nations in the world? Is there more violence in the American political tradition, for example, than there is in Ireland, France, Spain, Italy, or Germany? Or is there more apathy among the American public than one would find in similar countries? The comparisons always seem to be made with Sweden, New Zealand, Great Britain, and Canada. The people who are fond of making such comparisons were considerably embarrassed recently when it turned out that the supposedly civilized and libertarian Canadian society had far less protection for dissent than did corrupt, repressed America.

The work of Sidney Verba and his associates on

the "civic culture" provides a considerable amount of both theory and data in response to these questions, theory and data that is, I might add, decidedly nonapocalyptic.[1] Gabriel A. Almond and Verba distinguish three kinds of political culture: the "parochial," the "subject," and the "participant." In the parochial culture, characteristic of tribal societies, there is little in the way of specialized political roles, investment in the larger political system, expectation of service from the system, or even concern about what the political system does. The parochialist is detached and indifferent on the subject of politics.

In the subject political system, there is an awareness of governmental authority, a feeling about it, either positive or negative, and an acceptance, willing or grudging, of its existence. However, the subject relates to his political and governmental system as a passive recipient. The political system, good or bad, is characterized by a downward flow of activity. The subject is conscious of the "output" of the government but does not see himself as engaged in significant "input."

But in the participant culture the citizen takes an active part in both output and input. He is not just a passive recipient of government activity; he views himself as a self-conscious agent in shaping governmental policy. He not only is governed, he governs.

In the modern industrial world, the pure form of any of these three styles does not exist. The pertinent question is, what combination of the three characterize a given society? Democracy, Almond and Verba note, is not a purely participant society; if

[1] In this chapter I rely heavily on Gabriel A. Almond and Sidney Verba, *The Civic Culture* (Princeton, N.J.: Princeton University Press, 1963), subsequent papers by Professor Verba, and repeated conversations with that worthy gentleman.

men are not willing to combine the roles of participant and subject, they will be unwilling to accept governmental decisions with which they disagree. It works the other way, too; if a subject is unable to combine his acceptance of governmental decisions with some sense that he shares in the making of such decisions, he will feel alienated from the political process. Finally, if there is not a touch of parochialism in the society, then the level of constant political agitation makes the society extremely volatile and unstable.

According to Almond and Verba, the political culture of the United States and Great Britain—they call it the "civic culture"—is a "fragile, intricate, and subtle" combination of all three styles, a combination that emerged gradually in the course of the history of the Anglo-Saxon world.

> *Independent aristocrats with secure local power in the countryside, courageous nonconformists, rich and self-confident merchants—these were the forces that transformed the tradition of the feudal estates into the parliamentary tradition and enabled Britain to pass through the era of absolutism without destroying her pluralism. Britain thus entered the industrial revolution with a political culture among its elites which made it possible to assimilate the gross and rapid changes in social structure in the eighteenth and nineteenth centuries without sharp discontinuities. The aristocratic Whigs found it possible to enter a coalition with nonconformist merchants and industrialists, to establish securely the principles of parliamentary supremacy and representation. The traditional aristocratic and monarchic forces assimilated enough of this civic culture to compete with the*

secularist tendencies for popular support and, indeed, to mitigate their rationalism and impart to them a love and respect for the sacredness of the nation and its ancient institutions.

What emerged was a third culture, neither traditional nor modern but partaking of both; a pluralistic culture based on communication and persuasion, a culture of consensus and diversity, a culture that permitted change but moderated it. This was the civic culture. With this civic culture already consolidated, the working classes could enter into politics and, in a process of trial and error, find the language in which to couch their demands and the means to make them effective. It was in this culture of diversity and consensualism, rationalism and traditionalism, that the structure of British democracy could develop: parliamentarism and representation, the aggregative political party and the responsible and neutral bureaucracy, the associational and bargaining interest groups, and the autonomous and neutral media of communication. English parliamentarism included the traditional and modern forces; the party system aggregated and combined them; the bureaucracy became responsible to the new political forces; and the political parties, interest groups, and neutral media of communication meshed continuously with the diffuse interest groupings of the community and with its primary communications networks.[2]

In countries like Great Britain, Canada, Scandinavia, and the United States, the political issues focus rather on policy differences than on fundamental differences towards the political structure. Both the Left

[2] Almond and Verba, *The Civic Culture*, pp. 7–8.

and the Right (save for the extremes of each side) "accept the existing political structure and differ only on the substance of policy and political personnel." [3] Almond and Verba insist that the civic culture is not the culture one finds in high school civics textbooks. There, the citizen is expected to be active in politics, to be guided by reason rather than emotion, to be well-informed when he makes his decisions, and to make those decisions on the basis of careful calculation and detailed consideration of principles and interests. Such a model is that of a "rationality-activist" political culture, and while there is an element of it in the civic culture, there is much more.

For instance, while the citizen accepts the political structure and participates in it, he does not do so out of rational considerations alone. There are also present the styles of a subject and a parochialist. These styles of passivity and traditionality moderate the passions and emotions that can be stirred up by total political involvement. Fundamental loyalty also plays a part. So, in a country whose political style is the civic culture, politics is not a life or death matter. It is not that the citizens are not interested or do not like politics; their stake in political affairs is just not so deep that they withdraw their consent from the government or society should a decision go against them.

There are two questions that can be asked of this theory. Is it an accurate description of what goes on in American politics? If it is, is it good?

The second question obviously depends on one's philosophical values. If one is a radical or an anarchist, the civic culture is an abomination; its ability

[3] Ibid., p. 29.

to combine stability with a sense of political competency is either the result of a deliberate trick of the ruling class or a manifestation of the perverse political effects of capitalism. If, on the other hand, one is a liberal reformist, one delights in the civic culture, because it enables society to combine peace and stability with social progress—though it does not guarantee either.

To the question of whether the political style of the United States is indeed that of the civic culture, one can say that to some extent it surely is. One need only observe what goes on in American life to see that there is some congruence between the model of Almond and Verba and reality. Most Americans enjoy the political game, but few seem to have high emotional stakes in it. Fortunately, however, we do not need to rely on just these impressions, because Professors Almond and Verba have collected data on the political attitudes of Americans as well as attitudes of citizens in England, Germany, Italy, and Mexico. This enables us to test the model of the civic culture as it manifests itself in the United States with the political styles to be found in those other countries.

The first thing that emerges upon inspection of the Almond and Verba data is that Americans tend to be more involved in politics than the citizens of the other four countries (Table 3.1). Americans are more likely to think that the national government has a great effect on their lives (41 percent), and they are considerably more likely to report that they pay much attention to political campaigns (43 percent).

Almost two-thirds of the American population is able to name four or more party leaders, a percentage comparable only to that found in Germany. A mere 7 percent of the American population feels

TABLE 3.1
Attitudes Toward Government in Five Countries [1]

Attitude	United States	United Kingdom	Germany	Italy	Mexico
Percent agreeing that national government has a great effect on life	41	33	38	23	7
Percent who pay much attention to political campaigns	43	25	34	17	15
Percent who can name four or more principal political leaders	65	42	69	36	5
Percent alienated both locally and nationally	7	14	13	38	35
Percent proud of governmental institutions	85	46	7	3	30
Percent expecting serious consideration for their point of view from bureaucracy	48	59	53	35	14
Percent who talk about politics with others	76	70	60	32	38

[1] Adapted from Gabriel Almond and Sidney Verba, *The Civic Culture* (Princeton, N.J.: Princeton University Press, 1963).

alienated from both the local and national political governments as opposed to 14 percent in the United Kingdom, 13 percent in Germany, 38 percent in Italy, and 35 percent in Mexico. Furthermore, Americans are overwhelmingly proud of their governmental institutions; 85 percent in the U. S. as opposed to 46 percent in the United Kingdom, 7 percent in Germany, 3 percent in Italy, and 30 percent in Mexico.

This phenomenon of intense pride in governmental institutions is something anybody who is concerned about serious reform in American society must bear in mind.[4] The social reformer is not likely to talk most Americans out of this vigorous pride in their polity. The style of social reform, then, which concentrates on denouncing the failures of the American political system and insisting that the existing system must be replaced, is going to fall on deaf ears if not hostile ones. Perhaps this fundamental allegiance to the American political system explains why Professor Philip Converse of the University of Michigan discovered that three-quarters of those who were Vietnam doves approved the way the Chicago police handled the convention disturbances.

Radical protesters are perceived as attacking a political system that has the support of more than four-fifths of the population. Their strategy is inevitably self-defeating. You cannot win with four-fifths of the population against you; they will turn you off without listening. Those who wish to change American society need not limit themselves to a rhetoric that calls for the destruction of American political institutions. Surely there is enough in the political

[4] The data on which the Almond-Verba book was based were collected in 1962. However, Professor Verba tells me that more recent data indicate no change in this pride in governmental institutions.

ideology and tradition of the United States to justify both peace and social progress in the name of American democracy and patriotism. Opposition to the war could have been just as well based, I think, without any hypocrisy, on loyalty to the flag rather than on flag-burning. Support for racial justice could easily have been rooted to the traditions of American political government and not as a call for overthrow of that government. Granted that large numbers of people in the peace movements were patriotic, loyal Americans, they nonetheless managed to yield to their extreme colleagues control of the rhetoric of protest, thus precluding any possibility of effectively communicating with four-fifths of the population.

I take it as axiomatic that if you wish to change American society, you will do so not by denouncing political institutions but by showing how change is not only consistent with the genius of those institutions but also actually required by that genius.

Interestingly enough, the American public has less confidence that the governmental bureaucracy will give serious consideration to their own point of view than do the publics of either the United Kingdom or Germany (48 percent as opposed to 59 percent and 53 percent respectively). The balance in American society, in other words, is somewhat more on the participant style than on the subject style. Americans are more confident in the participant role; perhaps for Professor Lipset's reason that America was born in revolution and lost many of its more subject-oriented citizens to Canada at that time. If one compares the fifth and sixth items in Table 3.1 one can see the roots of American populism. We are as a nation very proud of our governmental institutions, much more so than any other of the countries studied. We are also skeptical of the governmental bureaucratic structures. Here, I think, there is an important hint for those engaged in political and social reform movements: One does not attack the fundamental governmental institutions of American society, but one can be extremely critical of the governmental bureaucracy, preferably in the name of the more fundamental political convictions. Finally, Americans are more likely than citizens of any of the four countries (76 percent) to discuss politics with others.

Involvement in politics, the feeling of governmental impact on their lives, a familiarity with political leaders, pride in governmental institutions while critical of its bureaucracy, discussion of politics with others—on each of these items the response of the American population is more definite and more vigorous than that of the populations in any of the four countries studied. Whatever the absolute failings of the American political culture are, the culture looks rather good when compared with the political cultures of the other four countries. This is a phenomenon that political and social reformers—or coalition conveners—can ill afford to forget.

Not only are Americans relatively satisfied with their political system, they also are more likely than the citizens of the other four countries to enjoy the political game (Table 3.2). Almost three-quarters of them get a sense of satisfaction from voting; two-thirds enjoy political campaigning. On the other hand, only 3 percent would be upset if one of their offspring married a member of the opposite party, as opposed to 15 percent in Great Britain, 20 percent in Germany, 57 percent in Italy, and 22 percent in Mexico. Also, more than half of the Americans find campaigns silly or ridiculous (as opposed to 37

TABLE 3.2
Attitudes Toward Partisanship in Five Countries[1]

Attitude	United States	United Kingdom	Germany	Italy	Mexico
Percent who feel satisfaction when going to the polls	71	43	35	30	34
Percent who enjoy election campaigns	66	52	28	18	34
Percent who sometimes find campaigns silly or ridiculous	58	37	46	15	32
Percent who sometimes get angry during campaigns	57	41	46	20	26
Percent who would be displeased at child marrying someone from other party	3	15	20	57	22
Percent open partisans	82	61	44	14	42
Percent intense partisans	10	14	25	20	25

[1] Adapted from Gabriel Almond and Sidney Verba, *The Civic Culture* (Princeton, N.J.: Princeton University Press, 1963).

percent in the United Kingdom, 46 percent in Germany, 15 percent in Italy, and 32 percent in Mexico). Americans are involved in politics, they enjoy it, are capable of getting angry in the course of the political debate, and enjoy casting their votes; but they do not take politics so seriously that they are unable to laugh at it or condone marriage across party lines.

Almond and Verba draw a political type they call "the open partisan." "This is the respondent who expresses indifference toward interparty marriage yet describes himself as emotionally involved in election campaigns." [5] Eighty-two percent of the American population falls into this category as do 61 percent of the British, 44 percent of the Germans, 14 percent of the Italians, and 42 percent of the Mexicans. On the other hand is the "intense partisan" who is "both sharply divided from his party opponents and emotionally involved in electoral contests." [6] He is represented by only 10 percent of the American voters, 14 percent of United Kingdom voters, 25 percent of the Germans, 20 percent of the Italians, and 25 percent of the Mexicans.

One may not like the American "open partisan" whose involvement is real but limited. One may feel that the "intense partisan" is a more logical and admirable sort of person. One had better face the fact, however, that the open partisan is the typical American political animal, and without his consent no coalition will be effective and no social change will occur.

Almond and Verba summarize their findings about the different feelings about politics and partisanship in the five countries.

[5] Almond and Verba, *The Civic Culture,* p. 154.
[6] Ibid., p. 155.

In the United States and Britain there is a widespread sense of freedom and safety in political communication; partisan feelings are relatively cool, and feelings of all kinds flow relatively freely into the political system. In Germany people seem to feel more restricted in these communications, partisanship appears to be more intense, and anger and contempt seem to be the emotions most frequently expressed in election campaigns. In Italy the proportion of the population that feels free to communicate about politics and admits to having feelings about elections is extremely small. At the same time, the intensity of partisanship is extremely high. In Mexico political communication is restricted, but not to the same extent as in Italy. The expression of feelings about elections is also low, but not as low as in Italy, and the level of partisanship is high, but again not so high as in Italy.[7]

The controlled emotionality of American and British political life may be objectionable both to ideologues and to the authors of civics textbooks. Both would like to see much higher levels of political involvement, and the former would like to see more intense emotion and more emphasis on the importance of doctrinal differences. But whether they like the "cool" of the culture or not, it is nonetheless the specific culture they are stuck with, which in all likelihood they will find impossible to change.

Americans are also more likely to think that the ordinary man should be active in his community and to be persuaded that they enjoy political competence and have exercised it (Table 3.3). Thus 51 percent of the American population think the ordinary

[7] Ibid., pp. 153–54.

TABLE 3.3
"Political Competence" in Five Countries [1]

Political Competence	United States	United Kingdom	Germany	Italy	Mexico
Percent agreeing that ordinary man should be active in his community	51	39	22	16	26
Percent feeling they can do something about unjust national regulation	75	62	38	28	38
Percent who have attempted to influence government	33	18	21	13	9
Percent feeling they are "politically competent"	65	63	45	40	38

[1] Adapted from Gabriel Almond and Sidney Verba, *The Civic Culture* (Princeton, N.J.: Princeton University Press, 1963).

man should be active in his community as opposed to 39 percent in the United Kingdom, 22 percent in Germany, 16 percent in Italy, and 26 percent in Mexico. Three-quarters of the American population think that they are capable of doing something in response to unjust regulations of the national government as opposed to approximately three-fifths of the English population, approximately two-fifths of the German and Mexican populations, and a little more than one-quarter of the Italian population. Furthermore, 33 percent of the Americans assert that they have in fact attempted to influence governmental decisions as opposed to 18 percent of the British, 21 percent of the Germans, 13 percent of the Italians, and 9 percent of the Mexicans. The critics of American society who lament that only one-third of the American population has ever tried to influence a decision of the national government would do well to ponder that this is a far higher proportion than can be found in the countries Almond and Verba studied. Critics also say that there is something seriously wrong with a society when one-quarter of the population does not think it can do anything about an unjust national regulation. Perhaps they are right, yet almost two-fifths of the citizens of the United Kingdom think that they are powerless before an unjust national regulation; and even higher proportions of the other countries feel the same way. The critics can then retreat to their last barrier and say that those citizens who think they can influence the national government have simply been deceived by the treachery of the power elite or the military-industrial establishment. But then why have Americans been so easily deceived—more than the inhabitants of the other four countries? There is no way of getting around the data: Americans are more satisfied with their political system than are the British, Germans, Italians, and Mexicans.

Verba and Almond composed an index of subjective political competence, which measures whether one feels he has some control both locally and nationally over his political destiny. We can see in the last item of Table 3.3 that the Americans and British are about equally likely to feel politically competent (65 percent of the former and 63 percent of the latter), while less than half of the Germans, Italians, and Mexicans report a feeling of political competence (45 percent, 40 percent, and 38 percent respectively). Again, the critics can say that fully one-third of the American population feel excluded from the political process. One must concede that that is an important fact. The United States should do all in its power to increase the feeling of political competence among its citizens. Nonetheless, given the weaknesses of human nature and the human condition and given the size and composition of American society, the fact that Americans are slightly more likely to feel politically competent than Britons must be regarded as astonishing.

Almond and Verba conclude by demonstrating relationships that exist among the variables represented in Table 3.3.

> *In many ways, then, the belief in one's competence is a key political attitude. The self-confident citizen appears to be the democratic citizen. Not only does he think he can participate, he thinks that others ought to participate as well. Furthermore, he does not merely think he can take a part in politics: he is likely to* be *more active. And, perhaps most significant of all, the*

self-confident citizen is also likely to be the more satisfied and loyal citizen.[8]

The persistent critics will say that Americans ought not to be satisfied and loyal. Perhaps they are right, but in fact Americans are likely to be satisfied and loyal; this is a reality, however distasteful to the political reformist.

One is immediately faced with the question of how all this can be. How does a political system that obviously has so many things wrong with it function as well as it apparently does? Part of the answer can be found in the fact that Americans—and their British cousins—are more likely to believe that others can be trusted, and they are more likely to belong to voluntary organizations (Table 3.4). Thus more than half of the Americans and 49 percent of the Britons believe that most people can be trusted, while only 19 percent of the Germans, 7 percent of the Italians, and 30 percent of the Mexicans would agree. Furthermore, 57 percent of the Americans, 47 percent of the Britons, 44 percent of the Germans, 29 percent of the Italians, and 25 percent of the Mexicans belong to voluntary organizations. By a set of complicated mathematical cross-tabulations, which we will not duplicate in this volume, the two authors demonstrate that there is a powerful connection between belief that others can be trusted and membership in voluntary organizations on the one hand and satisfaction with the political system on the other. The American and British social systems, in other words, seem to maximize both trust and voluntary associations and thus provide the social matrix in which the two styles of politics are able to operate.

[8] Almond and Verba, *The Civic Culture,* p. 257.

TABLE 3.4
Environment for Political Culture in Five Countries [1]

Environment	United States	United Kingdom	Germany	Italy	Mexico
Percent agreeing that people can be trusted	55	49	19	7	30
Percent who are members of voluntary organizations	57	47	44	29	25
Percent who had some influence in family decisions as children	73	69	54	48	57
Percent who had freedom to discuss decisions during education	45	35	34	29	40
Percent who had freedom to protest job decisions	82	89	75	55	70

[1] Adapted from Gabriel Almond and Sidney Verba, *The Civic Culture* (Princeton, N.J.: Princeton University Press, 1963).

Politics do not tear the countries apart because the social structure, for all its diversity and potential for fragmentation, is held together by rather strong bonds. In situations of political stress or threat, an American or Briton can mobilize his own "personal and community network," or, as the two authors suggest, "The right of revolution has now been institutionalized in a widespread capability to act outside the organized infrastructure of democracy . . ." [9] They suggest that the combination of group activity and interpersonal trust provides a "reserve power" for the citizen who wants some sort of independent access to political influence.

Men can cooperate with one another in political activities precisely because whatever their political differences "they are tied to their fellow citizens by a set of interpersonal values, and these values overarch the political and nonpolitical aspects of the system." [10] Hence, however important the issue or however deeply involved in the issues a citizen may be, the potential for fragmentation is "impeded by the force of shared social values and attitudes, which permeate all aspects of society." [11]

Critics will angrily insist that many Americans (and Britons, too, one supposes) are excluded from this overarching value consensus. And they are perfectly right, though it is worth noting that the consensus is much broader in the United States than it is in the other countries being studied. But the point is that the style of American political culture is shaped by this overarching consensus; he who wishes to broaden it must understand both its origins, its power, and its popularity. Furthermore, he

[9] Almond and Verba, *The Civic Culture,* p. 299.
[10] Ibid.
[11] Ibid.

should realize that a strategy that demands the right of those who are excluded to be admitted to the consensus is likely to be much more effective politically than one who denies the consensus exists or is bent on destroying it.

It would also appear that there is some relationship between family, school, and occupational patterns and the emergence of a civic culture. Americans and Britons are more likely than the citizens of the other three countries to see themselves as having influence on family, educational, and occupational decisions—with the Americans ahead of the Britons on family and educational decisions and somewhat less likely (82 percent to 89 percent) to claim that they enjoy freedom to protest job decisions. While the pattern of relationships between personal competence in other areas of life and political competence is complex and involved—and beyond the scope of this volume—there is still no doubt that after reading the careful analysis of Almond and Verba, one can see that a general tendency for competence in other areas of life correlates highly with political competence. The American and the Briton is more likely than the Italian, the German, or the Mexican to experience competence in all areas of his life, including the political. He may be deceiving himself; he may be the victim of the manipulations of a shadowy establishment or clever military-industrial complex, but I suspect no one could persuade him of it.

It is difficult to come away from the work of Almond and Verba without concluding that American political culture is a rather remarkable phenomenon. It ought not to work as well as it has. Black, white, Protestant, Catholic, Polish, Irish, Southerner, Northerner, seem all to share a good deal of satisfaction with, enjoyment of, and competence in the American political process. The political culture apparently reflects a more general social system in which trust, personal competence, and voluntary organization characterize a society in which men feel they have considerable control over their own destinies.

The purpose of this summary of the Almond-Verba research is not to "defend" the American political system, much less to deny its faults and imperfections. It is frequently sluggish and unresponsive and cannot quickly mobilize the resources necessary to deal with critical problems. It frequently is satisfied with the lowest common denominator of public consensus. Some groups have relatively little access to it. A number of extremely important social problems have been ignored for unconscionably long periods of time. Dishonesty, corruption, incompetence, venality are widespread. Yet for all its faults, the system lumbers along and works moderately well, at least part of the time, and does command the loyalty of the overwhelming majority of its participants. There are two principal conclusions that seem to follow: (1) He who wishes to reform the American political and social system is going to have to cope with the phenomenon that most Americans fundamentally accept the political system, and (2) it, therefore, behooves the reformer to understand why they accept it and how the system works.

In the next chapter I will suggest that most Americans consider politics to be a game. The data of Professors Almond and Verba suggest that it is a game that Americans find more delightful than their British counterparts and more meaningful than their Italian, German, and Mexican counterparts. The reason may well be that those who shaped the American political process knew implicitly that it had to be a game if it was not to tear the society apart; so they set about making it a game that anyone and everyone could play. More than that, it was a game in which no one could ever be certain of winning or losing permanently.

A good deal happened to the United States of America between the time James Madison wrote his contributions to the *Federalist Papers* and Gabriel Almond and Sidney Verba wrote *The Civic Culture.* One wonders what James Madison would think if he were to read the Almond and Verba book. Presumably he would have mixed emotions. He would probably wish that the level of intelligence and informed participation in American society were higher, though he would not, one suspects, be all that surprised. Doubtless he would be pleased that in most respects the American political culture seemed more satisfactory than that of the other countries the two twentieth-century authors had studied. What would truly have astonished Madison, however, is the fact that there is as much continuity between the *Federalist Papers* and the *Civic Culture,* given the fact that in the ensuing century-and-three-quarters fifty million immigrants had come to the shores of the United States and the nation had expanded across an entire continent in the midst of an incredible technological revolution. Madison might well be proud of the work he and his colleagues had done.

But what does all of this mean for those whose responsibility it is to rebuild the liberal Democratic political coalition? It would seem to me that these rebuilders might at least conclude that there is in the American political culture immense residual sources of strength. Compared to its own ideals and to absolute norms of goodness, the American political culture is clearly deficient. But compared to other countries, it does not look all that bad. While there has been in the last decade an increase of polarization, America is not a polarized society. And while large numbers of Americans are not deeply involved politically, neither are they politically apathetic or indifferent. The political culture is not a guarantee of national survival, but it does create a relatively benign context in which such survival is more secure and in which the democratic process, as conceived by Madison and the other Federalists, can improve and flourish. Minimally, the rebuilders of the coalition can take comfort from the thought that the political culture need not inhibit and may even facilitate their work. It is not a political culture, in other words, that should move one to despair.[12]

[12] Although the Almond-Verba data are more than a decade old, research done in 1967 by Verba and Norman Nie, as well as a study of political participation in the United States over the last two decades by Verba, Nie, and the present writer, would indicate that the American political culture has not changed drastically since the Almond-Verba book. If anything, political activity and participation in the United States increased rather than decreased during the 1960s. See Sidney Verba and Norman Nie, *Citizen Participation in American Political Life* (New York: Harper and Row, 1972).

THE VOTER

Was it really a clear choice in 1972? Everyone seemed to think so. The candidates, their campaign managers, and the pundits like Eric Sevareid and David Brinkley and James Reston and Mr. T. R. B. not only asserted that it was so, they did so in a tone of relief, virtue, and satisfaction, indicating that they thought it was a "good thing." They seemed to say that whatever else may be wrong with McGovern's selection, at least we can be satisfied that the choice was clear.

Well, maybe. But perhaps one who was fishing on Lake Michigan on election day may be permitted to dissent. As the sports editor of the old *Chicago Herald-American* remarked of the disastrously comic 1945 World Series between the Cubs and the Tigers, "I don't see how either team could possibly win." I would submit that those who think it was both a clear and good choice were deceived by the social road maps they carry around in their heads, road maps which, if they are taken too literally, are not only false but dangerous. There is a clear choice in Ulster just now between the Vanguard and the Irish Republican Army (IRA), and that is not a notably happy province. Choices that are too clear can be disastrous for a society.

Unlike our fellow animals, humankind is given to interpreting. The incredible variety of phenomena that impinge on our consciousness must be organized, categorized, explained. Hence we are given to building taxonomies, mental pigeonholes in which we can sort the information and events we experience. The categorization of reality is almost as natural to man as breathing. Humans almost automatically make the primordial categorizations of "we" and "they," male and female, raw and cooked, sacred and profane, and then begin to elaborate more sophisticated categories, such as Greek and barbarian, Hebrew and Gentile, Christian and pagan, believer and infidel, Harvards and Yales. These categories become "pictures" that we carry around in our heads to help us organize, interpret, and shape our experience.

Such pictures are frequently expressed as generalizations: "Jews are well-to-do," "Poles are blue-collar workers," "blacks are poor," "the Irish drink too much." If we are pushed, we admit that there are exceptions and qualifications to such generalizations. Some Jews are poor, some blacks are well-to-do, some Poles are not blue-collar workers, some Irishmen do not drink at all. But our generalizations are not intended to be precise descriptions of reality. They are, rather, broad interpretive rubrics in which the qualifications and nuances are implicit. Generalizations stop short of being stereotypes precisely because of the implicit qualification. But because the qualification is implicit, the generalization cannot but on occasion become dangerously close to a stereotype.

Political ideas must also be categorized, and to the North Atlantic world in the last two centuries there have been two sets of binary divisions—"conservative" and "liberal" and "right" and "left," the former set having its origin in the French Revolution and the latter in the conflict between Marxism and the bourgeois society. Such political categories are extremely useful and perhaps necessary shorthand devices for organizing political reality, but, like all other binary categories, they are not able to cope with much of the richness, complexity, ambiguity, and confusion of the real world. When the category stops being a crude map of reality and becomes a rigid model that reality must be reordered to fit, then it becomes deceptive and potentially dangerous.

There is no great risk when journalists use binary categories like "young" and "old," "rich" and "poor," "reformer" and "boss," "black" and "ethnic." If in their haste to meet deadlines they do not themselves make the implicit qualifications, most viewers and readers will. But when a serious political strategist like Mr. Frederick Dutton allows his mental image of the upper-middle-class college youth to obscure the fact that the majority of young people do not even go to college and that large numbers of the noncollege young may not be liberals at all, he and those who listen to him are in deep trouble.

If liberalism is seen as an ideological position held by a minority or a strain or a tendency of thought that influences a larger minority, then it is a useful intellectual tool. But when liberalism becomes an elaborate clearly defined program that the electorate is given the choice of accepting or rejecting in toto, reality is being shaped to fit the model, not the model to fit reality. Is there an essential and inevitable connection linking liberal stands on peace, inflation, poverty, abortion, marijuana, amnesty, busing, military spending, and racial quotas? Surely for some people all these positions are linked in a coherent political fate, but for many other Americans there is no such connection. If a clear choice means they must buy the whole package or buy exactly the opposite package, then they are put in an awkward position and begin to believe that they have no choice at all.

An Irish lawyer is against the war and against abortion, for a family assistance program and against the legalization—or even against the decriminalization—of marijuana. He thinks his positions are consistent: war and abortion are murder, family assistance and drug control are both necessary for an orderly society. Is he a "conservative" or a "liberal"?

A Detroit housewife, who is vigorously opposed to busing even though her son is in an integrated high school and she strongly supports integrated schools, thinks of herself as consistent, because, in her judgment, both stands come from a concern over quality education. Is she a "conservative" or a "liberal"?

The black man who dislikes the militant leaders (and slightly more blacks dislike the militants than like them), is opposed to busing (as are about 45 percent of the blacks in the country), and is bitterly opposed to the legalization of marijuana (as are about 66 percent of the blacks in the country); but, nevertheless, he enthusiastically supported George McGovern as a friend of the black people. Is he inconsistent? Is he a "liberal" or a "conservative"?

The Polish physician who is against the war but also against the decrease in military spending on the grounds that both weaken America's international position—is he inconsistent? Is he a "liberal" or a "conservative"? There was a time when the position opposite to his would have been called "isolationism."

And the Italian steelworker who argues that the war was started by college professors, and that the hippies, the radicals, the women liberationists, and the television commentators are all part of the rich establishment that is out to exploit him—is he a "liberal" or a "conservative"? He was against the war, deeply concerned about the economy, views crime on the streets as a very serious problem (as do 65 percent of the blacks in the country), and has voted Democratic all his life. His suspicions about the rich establishment would have done credit to a Marxist not so long ago, but now the only leader in public life who he finds vigorously attacking the "rich kids and their Wall Street supporters" is Spiro Agnew.

We lump such men and women into the political "center," but our propensity for special categorization may deceive us about the richness and the ambiguity of social reality. The word "center" implies a group that stands somewhere in between the official "conservatives" and the official "liberals," holding a "moderate" position on the same issues on which the liberals and the conservatives hold more vigorous positions.

Such a one-dimensional approach to political life ignores the fact that those who are consistently neither liberal nor conservative may hold vigorous positions that are not at all moderate in either substance or tone. They may be passionately with the "liberals" on one issue and on another on the side of the "conservatives," with equal passion. What is more, even though both the liberals and the conservatives may think of such citizens as inconsistent, those who are consigned to the "center" think that *they* are the only ones truly consistent.

But if by their own standards they are consistent, surely they must be described as uninformed. How can a well-informed person be for stiff regulation of polluters and against decriminalization of marijuana? How can a well-informed person be against the war and for continued high levels of military spending? How could he be for welfare reform and against abortion reform? How can anyone who reads the newspapers and listens to the wise television commentators miss the inevitable connection between improving the lot of minority groups and the establishment of some kind of quota system? A clear choice in an election would surely be a good thing if people were well-informed, and a clear choice campaign ought to contribute greatly to the amount of information available to the average citizen.

Let us leave aside the questions of what it takes to be well-informed and of who determines how much one has to know to be termed "well-informed." It is surely true that the ordinary man is interested only marginally and intermittently in political issues. He is caught up most of the time in the ordinary cares of his ordinary life—home, family, job, neighborhood, mortgage payments, health, the weekend holiday. He does not know nearly as much about political issues as does the person who is passionately involved in and concerned about the crises of the day. Even if one concedes that Ordinary Man may be protected from the peculiar narrowness that passionate commitment sometimes creates and also that he is isolated from the fads that periodically sweep the intellectual elites, it still must be admitted that he is likely to be woefully uninformed.

On the subject of marijuana he simply may not have the facts, and indeed he may be dead wrong—though his worry about the drug problem is hardly invalid, and his memory of the time not so long ago when most of the elites were saying that there was no physical danger in LSD is accurate. Nevertheless, if he were well-informed, he would probably understand that his concern about the drug problem should lead him to support a decriminalization of marijuana instead of opposing it. His lack of information, then, impedes a politically sophisticated decision. If he knew more he might be more consistently a liberal or a conservative. But the question is an academic one. In no imaginable future of American society will we ever have an electorate that will be as well-informed as that segment of the population that reads the *New York Times* and the *Washington Post* every day. Virtually all the research evidence indicates that there are rather low correlations in the general population between the liberal stand on one political issue and a liberal stand on other political issues. Inconsistent and uninformed Ordinary Man may be, but there is little likelihood that he will change or that even a "clear choice" election will change his inconsistency and lack of information.

In one vision of republicanism such lack of information would disqualify Ordinary Man from influencing political discourse and decision-making; in another vision of republicanism an act of faith is made in the presumption that over the long haul the instincts of the average man can be counted on sufficiently to permit him to participate in the political process even if he is uninformed on many specific issues. The former vision is that of Plato; the latter is the republicanism of Mr. Madison. The well-informed activists of the Right and the Left may frequently lament it, but we are stuck with Mr. Madison's republic, and the well-informed elites—no matter how vigorously and persuasively they may lead—still have to wait for the average man to catch up.

The assumption of Madisonian republicanism is that the ordinary citizen can be led by men who can sympathize with his problems, understand his fears, and appeal to his best instincts. He will not, however, be led by those who attempt to impose on him in the name of "liberalism" the obligation to support causes and persons who stand for much that he does not like.

Let us put the matter differently. If it had not been for Chappaquiddick, Edward Kennedy would likely have been the Democratic presidential nominee. Can one imagine a Kennedy convention from which labor, the Catholic ethnics, and the professional politicians were excluded? His stands on most issues would have been little different from those of Mr. McGovern—though perhaps they would have been qualified and nuanced earlier. The "new" political forces would have been at the convention (perhaps a little less exuberantly), and the "old" forces would have been there, too. Most of the campaign would not have to have been devoted to "binding wounds" since there wouldn't have been any in the first place. Whether such a convention would have been "new" politics or "old" politics would have been a moot question. It certainly would have been "smart" politics. But then there wouldn't have been a clear choice in the election.

Some people may think that driving at least one-third of the Democrats in the country into Mr. Nixon's camp was a high price—unnecessarily high—for a clear choice. "Smart" politics assumes that people ought to be drawn together, not torn apart. The smart politician abhors binary categories, because he fears that forcing clear choices on voters usually means losing elections; clear choices destroy coalitions instead of creating them. The "good" politician feels that it is his role to operate in the area where coalition, consensus, and compromise are possible. But in politics, it would seem, compromises are evil. Everyone rejoices when Russia and the United States compromise or when labor and management, parent and child, husband and wife, Namath and Rozelle do the same. A compromise solution to the war was welcomed by practically everyone. But the politician who is willing and even eager to work out a compromise—alas, he has no integrity, and, of course, he precludes clear choices. Without binary categories—and a presumed binary reality—you can't have those clear choices.

The large majority of the American electorate is neither "liberal" nor "conservative." A majority of Americans were against the war, worried about the economy, in favor of racial integration, supportive of strict pollution laws, in favor of welfare reform, and for maximum effort to eliminate poverty. On the other hand, a majority is deeply concerned about crime and drugs, against amnesty, quotas, and busing, and deeply suspicious of "radicals," "militants," and "hippies." Ignorant and inconsistent they may be, but they are still the ones who decide elections.

On most of the major substantive political issues, however—peace, race, poverty, pollution—some three-fifths of the American population was willing to support general liberal postures. If the liberals were not able to convert that support into electoral majorities, the reason may well be that they seemed to be imposing on Ordinary Man a clear choice of buying the whole liberal package or none of it. The *New Democrat* told us that amnesty, abortion, and marijuana were the criteria by which "liberalism" was to be judged today. Putting aside the question of whether these three issues are more important than peace, pollution, poverty, and race, one can only say that if such be the hallmark of liberalism or of the "new" liberalism, then it will have to wait a long time before it wins another election.

Was it necessary to impose such a clear choice on political reality? Does the conservative-liberal dichotomy merely deprive reality of its complexity and ambiguity? May it not also be a dichotomy that points in a misleading direction, especially for an American political reality where the conflict between the revolution and the old regime, between socialist and bourgeois, are hardly important dimensions of political life? Social class may be an important aspect of American politics (though if there ever was a haute bourgeois convention, it was the Democratic gathering in Miami Beach); but also in the United States there is conflict, competition, collaboration, and compromise among the various religious, racial, ethnic, and geographic groups that constitute an extraordinary variegated nation. To impose the essentially European intellectual notion of "liberal" and "conservative" on such a different kind of political reality may blind those who are enamoured of such a dichotomy to what is most important in American political life. American intellectuals have yet to devise a scheme or a model that does justice to what is different about American political reality. The elites, then, may well be imprisoned in a categorization that is not only inadequate, as are all characterizations, but that is fundamentally wrong.

A clear choice between liberal and conservative may be meaningful to French, German, Swedish, or even English politics; it may also be meaningful to one dimension of American political life. But a vast and complicated nation like ours does not have a one-dimensional (for instance, social class) politics but a multidimensional politics. What looks like a clear choice on one dimension may not be so clear and may even be politically irrelevant on other dimensions. A clear choice between war and peace? The American electorate would surely vote for peace. A clear choice between busing and not busing? The American electorate would surely vote against busing. In a one-dimensional view of politics such inconsistency may seem incredible. But if busing is seen not as a liberal-conservative issue but as an effort by one social group to impose on another social group something that is alleged to be for the advantage of a third social group (even though it is not altogether clear that the third group really wants it), then the inconsistency vanishes. It is not surprising that a substantial segment of the population was disturbed when it was told that when it wished to support the candidate who was more likely to bring peace it must also support the candidate who was more likely to bring busing. What is surprising, rather, is that political elites would think that such a dilemma did indeed represent a clear choice.

Is fear about crime in the streets a conservative stand? If so, then two-thirds of the blacks in the country must be conservative. Is support of the police a conservative position? Then 90 percent of the citizens of the republic must be conservative—and, again, two-thirds of the blacks. But would it not be more fruitful to see differences over crime to be largely a function of how close one lives and works to high crime areas, and not an ideological problem at all?

Is disagreement over abortion best understood as a liberal versus conservative controversy, or does it make more sense to see it as a religious difference over the meaning of human life that need not correlate with stands on other issues?

Are public housing controversies (like Forest Hills, N.Y.) adequately described by calling one side liberal and the other conservative? Are not such painful and complex problems better seen as part of the ethnic succession process in a large city?

Is the conflict between "hippie" and "square"—of which the pot question is one manifestation—really political or is it rather cultural? Do not both cultures have long traditions and advantages and disadvantages? Is it not a disservice to both the counterculture and to politics to permit such a conflict to become an election issue?

And what does "liberal" really mean on the parochial school question? Would it not be more satisfactory to see it for what it is—a battle between Catholics and native Americans that has gone on for more than a century and that is totally unrelated to any other major political question?

There was even a time when a rapprochement with Red China was a liberal, not to say radical, position.

Finally, who is more liberal or more "black" of two black participants in the 1972 convention Chicago delegation fight—Cecil Partee or Jesse Jackson? The former has the highest position of any black in a state legislature in the country and was elected by a large number of black people. The latter never won an election and frequently does not find the time to vote. To say that the two men are engaged in an old fashioned intraethnic power struggle describes the situation quite precisely (and such power struggles are surely legitimate), but to call one man a "liberal" and the other a "conservative" says little if anything about the nature of that struggle.

There are, then, many political divisions in American life—though few of them fit elegant binary categories. Some, perhaps, can be accurately described as liberal or conservative divisions. Others have nothing to do with such labels; and to use them even as shorthand is to deceive oneself if no one else.

We cannot do without categories and taxonomies. Journalists must have them if they are to describe what goes on in the world in a one-minute news spot or a three-hundred word article. And social scientists must have them too if they are to write their obscure and elaborate papers. However, both journalists and social scientists are in trouble when they become so enthused with the neatness and the symmetry of their taxonomies that they forget the implicit qualifications. It is not merely the uneducated who permit the category to become stereotyped.

Stereotyped dichotomies of either the educated or the uneducated are relatively harmless until they become part of the climate of politics. A passionate precision for symmetry, elegance, and intellectual neatness is a dangerous trait for someone playing the political game. The temptation is to construct a neat, consistent set of responses to all critical questions and to expect that all of those who are on your side will accept the same responses. In such a symmetrical model humankind is divided into those who are with you and those who are against you; and those who are not with you on all issues must be assumed to be against you on all issues. Consistency will be forced upon them whether they want it or not; they will be offered a clear choice whether they want it or not. The binary division between "liberal" and "conservative" is not just a crude tool for interpreting reality; it is now reality itself.

Robert Coles has argued with painful care that the middle American is a complex mixture of conservative and liberal, rightist and leftist, bigot and altruist. The anger of much of the response to Coles's work indicates that there is a certain kind of American intellectual who has tremendous emotional interest in protecting his own symmetrical model of reality. I have often thought that the passionate ethical intensity of many brilliant scholars results from the blinding clarity with which their powerful intellects separate the good from the evil, a clarity which may not always do full justice to a gray-toned world. To such intense moralists, Coles's agonized defense of complexity must indeed seem heresy.

If men and women are the inconsistent, complex, ambiguous creatures that Coles claims they are, then he who forces a clear choice on them may simply be driving them into the enemy camp. There may be a good deal of intellectual neatness in cleaning all the conservatives (those who are against busing and the decriminalization of marijuana) out of the Democratic party. As the lady said at the convention, "It was a purifying experience."

One may think that the dichotomous categorization of people and issues, particularly in the United States, is all right for everyone but politicians, and for them it is a disastrous mistake. The difference between professional politicians and amateurs is that the former make that mistake much less frequently than the latter—mostly because they can't afford to lose too often. The professional politician must understand who the American voter really is. He cannot rely on the fictional accounts that appear on the "Op-ed" page of the *New York Times.*

The typical American voter is very much a citizen. Politics is a game [1] that he pursues with a fierce

[1] One sensitive and intelligent critic of an early draft of this chapter objected strenuously to the use of the word "game." He observed that "contest" would be a better word. The trick in politics, he said, is to work in such a way as to be able to cooperate on issues with those in the other camp. This isn't playful but rather a mature exercise of judgment, intelligence, and wiles. I thought seriously about accepting his suggestion, but, on balance, I don't think "contest" would be accurate, at least

partisanship frequently and with considerable enjoyment usually. If you watch the "typical" American voter in front of his television, enjoying the drama of a political convention, or on election night as the returns come pouring in or listening to two political antagonists sparring with each other, you cannot escape the conclusion that his approach is not too different from that with which he watches the world series, the superbowl, or the world's heavyweight championship fight. He dearly loves the slugfest; and a runaway victory for either side is somehow disappointing and frustrating. He doesn't like to lose and is sometimes quite furious at his fellow citizens for being so stupid as to vote for the other side. On the other hand, like the pro football partisan, he won't desert the losing team. He glares at the other side and says, "Wait till next time!" Furthermore, he expects the contestants to be good sports. Just as he would be horrified to see his pro football favorite fighting after the final gun has sounded, so he expects the losers of the election to send the telegrams of congratulations and the winners to acknowledge them graciously.

The typical American voter is not an activist. He is not likely to canvass for a candidate, to make a political contribution, to hold a formal membership card in a party, or to try to persuade someone he doesn't know to vote his way. He knows that he has

not to describe the average American's political activity. Leaving aside for the moment the question of whether there really is a contradiction between "play" and "mature exercise," it still seems to me that the average American does view politics as a game more than a contest, as my critic defined it. However, and here I think his point is well taken, for the political elites and for those who are deeply concerned about politics, "contest" is a better word.

the right to be an activist and would jealously defend that right. He may argue with others about parties and candidates, but argument, observation, and voting are the usual extent of his political behavior —although in the last decade the amount of formal political activity has increased notably in American society.

The American voter considers himself interested in the American political game but not fanatically committed to it; he has other interests in life besides politics. He refuses to let political activity take precedence over his other interests. He does not equate politics with society nor political behavior with citizenship; he casts his vote, he pays his taxes, he keeps the law (at least most of the time), and is content to criticize the frailties and failings of politicians. He suspects the inherent corruption of the political process yet enjoys the battle between political candidates.

He is most likely to belong to the party his parents belong to largely for reasons that many deem irrational. The region of the country he lives in, his religion, his ethnic background, the size of his pay, the political history of his family—all of these seem to have at least as much influence on his political affiliation as do the more "rational" claims of class and party ideologies.

His political affiliation is likely to be something that he is born with, much as he is born with his religion; and though he is more likely to change his political affiliation as his economic fortunes change, there is still a strong tendency for that affiliation to continue. He may be a "strong" party member or a "weak" party member, or he may consider himself to be "independent," yet even as an independent he is likely to lean more toward one party than the other. The principal difference between the "weak" Democrat and the "independent" who leans in the Democratic direction is that the latter is slightly more likely to vote for a Republican.

There are, of course, economic and social interests that correlate with political affiliation and behavior. A doctor is more likely to be a Republican than the manual worker, who is more likely to be a Democrat. There are other factors at work, which from the point of view of class politics would suggest that being a Republican or a Democrat for many people is about the same thing as being a Yankee or a Mets fan in New York and a Cubs or White Sox fan in Chicago. On the other hand, it will not do to tell the "typical" American voter that his political affiliation is irrational; he doesn't think it is at all. In an extreme case, for example, both the Democratic doctor and the Republican manual worker will thank you to leave it to him to decide what rational political behavior is and what it is not.

The American voter does not like the other party. He may assert, perhaps with some reason, that the Republicans are the party of recession or the Democrats are the party of war. To some extent, his objections to the other party may be based on an accurate notion of its policy orientations; but more, his suspicions are based on the fact that it is the "other side," and he is out to beat them. To want to beat the other side doesn't mean that he is afraid of them. A Democrat may fiercely contend that if the Republicans win, the working man will suffer, but he doesn't really think that he will be thrown out of his job, or that his children will be expelled from school, or that he runs the risk of being interned in a concentration camp. Similarly, for a Republican (except for the very extreme wing), a Democratic victory does not mean that practicing Bolsheviks are going to take over the administration of the nation. One cheerfully predicts all sorts of dire results should the other side win, but one does not take the predictions any more seriously than the campaign rhetoric of many of the candidates.

Similarly, your political positions may very well be unpredictable. On foreign policy you may be a liberal, on domestic policy, a conservative. You may be for more government aid to schools and at the same time a hawk on Vietnam. You may not like Spiro Agnew and still be concerned about the crime problem. You may be for federal health insurance and against increased taxes. You may sympathize with modifications in the welfare program and be against revenue sharing.

From the point of view of the ideologue, this is woefully inconsistent; everybody should be either a consistent liberal or a consistent conservative. Nevertheless, every study that has been done on the correlations of political attitudes among Americans indicates that ideological consistency is rather rare, in part because there are so many different components that enter the political decision-making process of each individual.[2] Thus a Polish Catholic doc-

[2] In a technical monograph being prepared by Sidney Verba, Norman Nie, and the present writer, it will be noted that between 1956 and 1968 there was an increase in ideological "consistency" among American voters. Most of the increase happened between 1960 and 1964. The phenomenon is an interesting one and has considerable importance for practical politics. However, despite the increase, there is still a very low level of political consistency among American voters. Only about a fifth of the variation on one scale that measured liberalism can be explained by variation on another liberal measure. In other words, while consistency did increase in the early 1960s, there is still much more inconsistency than not.

tor who lives in Chicago in a neighborhood close to the ghetto and whose son is about to be drafted, is obviously caught in many cross-pressures urging him to diverse political decisions. His profession would incline him to be Republican but his religion and nationality to be a Democrat. His nationality would also orient him toward taking a militant stand against communism, but his personal interest in protecting his son's life would incline him against the Vietnam war. His educational background might make him more enlightened on the race question, but the proximity to the ghetto and the threat he perceives to his neighborhood might make him extremely conservative, if not reactionary, on the subject of race. As a Catholic he is likely to be more prointegration than is a Protestant, but his geographical location might make him more likely to be antiintegration. As a doctor he is likely to be against health insurance but strongly in favor of aid to medical schools and hospitals. As a Pole, he probably is in favor of liberalized immigration laws. As the son of a truck driver, he is sympathetic to labor unions. He is a close friend of the Democratic precinct captain down the street and thinks Mayor Daley is doing a good job. He likes Spiro Agnew's forthrightness but voted for Adlai Stevenson III in part because the senator's father was "a great man."

My Polish doctor friend would be the absolute despair of the ideological liberal or conservative. Why can't he make up his mind and attach himself to one ideological allegiance or another? But it will not do any good to rail; he doesn't think he is irrational or inconsistent at all, and by his own standards he is not. Furthermore, he was positively delighted at the prospect of one of his own kind (the senator from Maine) running as his party's presidential nominee.

It is also important to note that the doctor is likely to have a relatively different agenda than have those who are angry with him for his inconsistency. He may have only a marginal concern about the Ugandan revolution. He may not care much about the conflict between India and Pakistan over Kashmir. He may not even know that Singapore is an independent country. He may be willing to take a stand on Eastern Europe, but it may be more ritualistic than anything else. He is not moved by denunciations of South Africa even though he does believe that black and white can get along with one another. He doesn't understand the biological or economic complexities of the pollution issue, though he figures the government damn well better save Lake Michigan. If you ask him what he thinks about college professors, he is probably wary of them, but he supports higher education.

He is very much concerned about inflation, taxes, getting his children into college, keeping them out of the war, having his streets shovelled after snowstorms, protecting his home and family from crime, efficient garbage removal, and uninterrupted city services in an atmosphere free from labor strife.

In other words, from the point of view of the ideologue, my Polish doctor has a badly mixed-up scheme of priorities. But he will resent anybody's telling him that his priorities are either wrong or mixed-up, especially if such criticism is couched in the language of intellectual or moral superiority.

You may not care for my Polish doctor. You may think he is ignorant, uninformed, bigoted, irrational, racist, and unable to confess his guilt feelings. But whether you like him or not, you will have to deal with him, because it is he and people like him who constitute the American citizenry and the American electorate. And without his consent and cooperation you will not change a thing. Nor are you likely to win him over to your side by denouncing him as a racist or a bigot or a hardhat or a war criminal. He does not feel that he is any of those things or any other pejorative adjective you or anyone else may fling at him. He may be open to persuasion but not by appeals to guilt feelings.

How is this confused and inconsistent Polish doctor likely to have voted? If he were of voting age in the 1930s, he certainly would have been for Roosevelt. He would have rejected Tom Dewey in 1948 and cheerfully voted for Eisenhower in 1952 and 1956 (despite his conviction that Stevenson was a great man—but "ahead of his time"). In 1964 he wouldn't have hesitated much about supporting Lyndon Johnson, but in 1968 he would have had a very hard time making a last-minute choice between Humphrey and Nixon. In 1972 he would have voted unenthusiastically for Richard Nixon because he "didn't trust McGovern." He would have consistently supported Paul Douglas for the United States Senate and just as consistently voted for Everett McKinley Dirksen. Of course his vote is safely in Richard Daley's camp in the mayoral election, and just as safely there for his alderman in the City Council. His representative to the United States Congress is more likely to be on the liberal column in most domestic issues, perhaps somewhat less so on foreign policy issues.

Before my Polish medical friend is written off completely, I would like to say a few words on his behalf. First, he stands accused of not being nearly as interested in politics as he ought to be. The ideologue is convinced that political sophistication and participation are a necessary moral obligation and a required means of personal development in modern society. The doctor's position would be that what is really important is that one be able to participate in politics to the extent that one wishes to, but one should not be constrained to do so. The exercise of the franchise, in other words, is a privilege, not an obligation. Freedom of choice in American society includes a determination of what kinds of behavior are important and what kinds are less so for oneself.

Secondly, my friend stands accused of being irrational and inconsistent. But is it so irrational to be loyal to the Democratic party because it has facilitated, however inadequately, the acculturation of the Polish immigrant group in American society? There must be enough uncertainty, ambiguity, and complexity in the political process to make possible more than one pattern of consistency, and it must be possible to forge alliances between people who agree on some matters and disagree on others. Because we can articulate a highly sophisticated rationale for our own political consistencies does not mean that those who are less skilled in articulation do not have a perfectly plausible case for coherence in their positions. Or to put the matter somewhat differently, because those who shape the rhetoric of the national media decide that concern about crime is a conservative political emphasis does not mean that anyone who takes a position defined as liberal on other issues is automatically inconsistent if he persists in thinking that crime is a very important problem in American society. The inconsistency of many American voters may be more apparent than real. It may result from a narrow and *a priori* definitions of what constitutes consistency.

Thirdly, my Slavic surgeon seems to think of politics as a game instead of a serious business. He roots for the Democrats much as he would root for the Chicago White Sox or even, in the old days, for the Chicago Cardinals. And yet is it that unhealthy or irrational to approach politics as a game? Is it not possible that one can be very serious about one's games and that they can have profound influence on one's life and society? Can it be that the game approach to politics makes possible both social stability and the elaboration of coalitions that can facilitate social progress? If politics is seen as a game, one is not false to "the true faith" if he collaborates on given issues with people with whom he disagrees on other issues. But if politics is a deadly serious matter, how can one cooperate with those who do not share one's entire faith save under pain of heresy, infidelity, and immorality? A society is not likely to be stable if political coalitions for change are difficult to convene. Is it not possible that the cool and controlled approach to political emotion, which Almond and Verba documented in the book cited in Chapter 3, may produce an electorate that is both more sophisticated and more flexible than the approach that sees politics as an all-consuming passion demanding the totality of one's selfhood? My Polish doctor is open to persuasion precisely because he views politics as a game. I can sell him on part of my platform for reasons not unlike those I use to persuade him that my wide receiver is better than his. It is better, in other words, to argue about wide receivers than to argue about God.

The typical American voter, I would argue, is also immune to demagoguery, at least in the long run, although he has been a pushover for war heroes. He tends to be suspicious of politicians, wondering why any honest and moral man would ever get into such an easily corrupted profession. He is ambivalent about his political leaders. He expects big results from them and scapegoats them when things go wrong. He has little tolerance for mistakes and while he may give a leader a second chance, he is not likely to give him a third. He can be periodically swept off his feet by men like Joseph McCarthy—but not for very long. The rise and fall of the militant style of Spiro Agnew would suggest that today the short run is likely to be very short indeed.

The American voter is skeptical about campaign promises and, as we shall see in a later chapter, quite unhappy about campaign rhetoric. He does not like taxes, he opposes the busing of school children, he is restless with the selective service system, he does not like communism, and he is very ambivalent about what is happening in American education. He strongly dislikes protests, riots, violence, and those whom he considers to be self-righteous loudmouths. He is vigorously against drugs, he is afraid of crime, and is looking for someone who will draw American society together. He is committed in theory to the open society, but in practice he is skeptical and suspicious of other groups, particularly of those members of other groups who seem to be self-appointed spokesmen. If he is white, he has become increasingly sympathetic to integration (as we shall document in a later chapter), but he will not be won over by threats, exhortations to guilt, or warnings that he should be afraid. He is not fooled by television; candidates have, with one or two exceptions, not succeeded in fooling him by clever public relations packaging or advertising merchandizing. (Despite Joe McGinness's clever book, *The Selling of the President,* the president was not "sold" in 1968. Quite the contrary, the 1968 election could be summarized by saying that the previous president managed to "unsell" himself long before the 1968 campaign and that his vice-president got "unsold" in the process.)

The typical American voter is extremely suspicious of the moralistic, self-righteous reformer who thinks he knows all the answers—particularly if this reformer is young or a clergyman, and most especially if he is both. Nevertheless, despite his suspicions about reform and reformers, he has been part of liberal majorities for the last forty years. My Slavic surgical friend did not like Abbie Hoffman or Eldridge Cleaver, yet with rare exceptions his vote has gone to liberal candidates who have stood for social change. He did not support Joseph McCarthy for very long; he did not vote for George Wallace; Spiro Agnew didn't talk him out of supporting Adlai Stevenson III; and he was attracted by both Robert Kennedy and Eugene McCarthy in 1968. Furthermore, my Polish doctor has stayed in the liberal coalition for forty years, and all the protest, agitation, confusion, and polarization of the 1960s did not drive him away. It took the concerted efforts of his own party's "liberal" elite to do that.

If the view of the American voter I have presented here is at all accurate, it follows that the swings to the right or left that the national columnists talk about really do not mean very much. These political swings probably represent no more than 5 or 6 percent shifts in attitudes or behavior and are short-range shifts under the pressures of transient circumstances. My Polish doctor may have voted for Eisenhower in 1952 and 1956, perhaps for Nixon in 1968, and certainly for him in 1972; but the long run political strain in his life is predictably and consistently Democratic. When he votes another way, he is likely to have been influenced by grave dissatisfaction with the course of government or because an issue of particular interest to him has for some reason come to center stage in the political drama. Thus if aid to parochial schools was important in his list of political priorities and two candidates for the state legislature chose to fight it out on this issue, my friend may shift from one party to another, but only as a temporary phenomenon.

It will be perceived that the Polish doctor of this chapter is a relative of Scammon and Wattenberg's famous machinist's wife from Ohio, their "typical" voter. The two of them live in that center, which Scammon and Wattenberg rightly argue is where American politics takes place. And it is, as they say, a floating center. But there are a number of important differences between our Polish doctor and the machinist's wife.

1. He is a much more complicated person than she is, or, if you wish, much more inconsistent. He has "liberal" tendencies that she does not display. Neither are his "conservative" convictions nearly as simple as hers. He may frequently sound as though the "social issue" obsesses him, and on occasion it does. Nonetheless he voted for Adlai Stevenson III, whose position on the "social issue" was certainly very different from his own—at least as his own is expressed in his more irate moments. He did not trust George McGovern, but neither does he really trust Mr. Nixon.

2. Because he is more complicated, the Polish doctor is easier to deal with. He is not merely a frightened, recalcitrant character with his heels dug in against any more change. Skeptical and suspicious he may be, but he is also responsive to appeals from liberal leadership that is able to understand him and speak his language. He can be "won over"; he is, indeed, in some respects already won over, and is merely waiting for the kind of leader who "speaks his language."

3. Therefore, while the machinist's wife in Ohio may be properly considered something of a threat to

social progress, the Polish doctor could very well turn out to be an asset. He is worried about the state of the country and is not convinced that problems can be solved simply by repression. He is willing to be led by leadership in which he has confidence. One might go even further: he is desperately eager to be led by those in whom he has confidence.

4. Thus, the Polish doctor lives not merely in a floating center but in a *leadable* center. This is the principal addition that I wish to make to the model of Scammon and Wattenberg. The American center not only "floats," it can be *led.* Scammon and Wattenberg are perfectly correct when they say the American politician must, if he expects success, find out where the center is. But once he has found the center, he is not constrained to remain there. On the contrary, if he is not willing to lead the center in the direction in which it dimly and confusedly wants to be led, then he will find in a short while that where he is, the center is no longer. The center "floats" indeed, but not comfortably. Rather, it floats fretfully, bobbing about on the water, as it were, trying to find a strong current with which it can move.

The great men of American political history are those who have been able to lead the center. The men who feel constrained to stay within the limitations of where the center is when they find it are quickly forgotten. If one wishes to lead the center, it is not merely enough to have a splendid vision of how American society can be improved or to have a profound sense of moral outrage about what is wrong—though these two qualities are also probably essential. It is necessary to understand the people in the center with all their rich variety, inconsistency, and complexity. The American political leader is caught in a bind. He surely cannot ignore the limitations of his followers, but if he wishes to be successful and reelected, neither can he be content with these limitations.

The Polish doctor is looking for someone who will make sense out of the present confusion in American society and who will offer some promise of leading him out of it. But if he is looking for a leader, he is not looking for a Messiah or a man on horseback or a self-righteous prig. Like most Americans, the Polish doctor is profoundly suspicious of politicians. He is experienced at sniffing out a demagogue or a man who uses clever words or television charm as a substitute for intelligence and conviction. A leader who will interpret, explain, guide, encourage, reprove, warn, inspire, and direct—that is who he's looking for. He feels justifiably cheated because there don't seem to be any such leaders around these days.

So those who will assume the responsibility for rebuilding the coalition need not despair over the absence of potential coalition members. On the contrary, they are out there where they always were. But those who are engaged in reconstruction must not try to impose on their potential colleagues ideological consistencies that the rank and file members of the coalition could not understand and would not like if they could. No one will have any success in rebuilding the Democratic coalition unless he is willing to concede that human beings are complex and frequently inconsistent creatures. The wise politician will take this into account and not try to pretend it isn't there or, worse, try to eliminate it. If ideological purity is to be a prerequisite for membership in the reconstructed liberal Democratic coalition, then that coalition will never be bigger than the New Politics coalition of 1972.

CONFLICT, CONSENSUS, COALITION, AND COMPROMISE

At the conclusion of his book, *Patterns of Dominance,* the British anthropologist Philip Mason observes:

> *. . . in a free society the government can do only so much. It can stimulate and encourage something of which the germs exist—but the response it can elicit is limited by the consensus, the nature of the people to whom it appeals. . . . In a democracy the opinion-forming function rests in every part of society. There is no separate licensed caste of opinion formers. . . . The consensus cannot be ignored. It must be led, molded, analyzed, persuaded.*[1]

At first, Philip Mason's statement seems unexceptional until one realizes that he is speaking about race relations. An Englishman may be able to get away with such statements and still have his book favorably reviewed, but for an American to make such assertions at the present time would almost certainly lead to his being denounced as a white racist.

CONFLICT

The theoretical underpinning of the assumption that those seeking social changes need not be concerned about seeking allies consists of two assertions:

1. There is a group called the "establishment," or the "system," or the "power elite" that either through conscious conspiracy or unconscious community of interests controls American society.

[1] Philip Mason, *Patterns of Dominance* (New York: Oxford University Press, 1970), pp. 331 and 336.

2. All coalitions and the political consensus are simply the tools of this group.

Once these two facts have been exposed it becomes clear that one must engage in "militant" action. Such action will convert the controlling group from its erroneous ways either by an appeal to virtue or by the threat of dire consequences to follow if the control group does not convert. Persuasion, coalition formation, recruitment of allies, and (that ultimate immorality) compromise are a waste of time. One can and should short-circuit such processes by a direct attack on the sources of power.

There is an element of truth in such analysis. Foundation officers, government officials, intellectuals, and the idea men of the mass media can be moved, whether by virtue or by fear, when confronted with the politics of unnegotiable demands. In the short run, funds can be made available to some blacks and power to some students, but eventually one comes up against the harsh reality asserted by Philip Mason: The response to a minority group from the rest of society is limited by the consensus, and the consensus in a democracy rests in every part of society, not in a separate licensed caste of opinion-makers. All the romantic amateur Marxism in the world cannot change that basic fact. Social elites in the United States have only a very limited power over the political reactions of most of the population. The capacity of the elites to respond to the legitimate demands of the young and the blacks is severely limited by their ability to obtain consent from majority groups within the population.

When one argues this case with militants, the response frequently is that the appropriate strategy is to give the establishment a vigorous kick (which means, of course, to give *society* a vigorous kick).

Two critical points:

1. Kicking is not enough.

2. Kicking is a very subtle art. If one kicks at the wrong time or in the wrong way, one is likely to be kicked back—hard.

Appeals to morality or the exercise of political pressure are not techniques that are to be abandoned in any movement for social change, but they must be used judiciously if they are to be effective. Judicious use of them implies that other tactics be used as well. He who really wants to win does not content himself with making threats about what he will do to potential allies if they do not in fact become allies. Nor does he devote much of his time informing these potential allies that they are immoral, indeed, quite possibly worse than the Nazis. On the contrary, he builds his own political muscle (which means that he organizes those votes he can count on). He tries to persuade other groups with whom he thinks he has common interests; he tries to persuade groups with which he has no common bond to remain neutral or at least passively indifferent to his cause; he makes vigorous demands and develops a fine sense of when the time is appropriate to negotiate and make a deal. None of this is nearly as brave as demanding "freedom now!" Unfortunately, and the point cannot be repeated frequently enough, in a democratic society a minority group really has no other option—other than self-destruction.

One can understand why the black and the young were outraged during the 1960s at the immorality that is endemic in American society. Outrage by itself, however, is not a viable political strategy. Minority groups are not excused from politics simply on the grounds that they are the victims of injustice. In the final analysis there is no alternative to the recruitment of allies. Nothing else will work. Threats, nonviolent confrontation, even violence may have their places as short-run tactics, but they do not constitute a viable strategy for a minority group. The critical group in molding a consensus is the large segment of the society that is not strongly supportive of social change but is "able to live" with it. If one threatens them or frightens them too much and applies too much pressure to them, their willingness to live with social change will be converted into reactionary panic.

After the death of Martin Luther King, Jr., it became fashionable for a while among militants to say that nonviolence does not work. But violence works even less, because it reduces that essential component of potential consensus that can "live with" social change even though it will not actively support it.

Another truth from which both the young and the blacks were shielded is that however noble "equality now" is as an ideal, it is also an unachievable reality. Even if everyone wanted it and were willing to positively support it, it is dubious that society knows how to achieve it while retaining any semblance of freedom. We can be properly outraged that we are still so primitive in our ethics that we do not have an overwhelming consensus in favor of "equality now." We can also be outraged that we really do not know how to achieve it. But what comes after outrage?

The answer is "militancy." But it must be a politically effective militancy that pushes, shoves, argues, demands, and does not drive the other side to panic and to rage of its own. One must emphasize that most blacks and many young people have engaged in precisely this kind of politics—blacks with ever-increasing success. The elected black political leaders around the country have proven themselves masters at building coalitions, winning allies, and obtaining consensuses. But for some reason these political leaders, elected by the black people (as well as substantial numbers of white people), were frequently reduced to silence by the self-anointed militant spokesmen who speak for tiny minorities. I have been at several meetings where the militants go through their exhibitions of the rhetoric of rage, and after they leave to attend another meeting (where the same show will be performed), the black political leaders begin to speak and implicitly reject what has been said. What is especially interesting is that the militants are in almost all instances employed by or financed by white liberal organizations. Occasionally, in a very unguarded and off-the-record moment, a political leader will permit himself to wonder out loud why someone like himself, who depends on black support, can be called an Uncle Tom while a militant spokesman who depends on white support is not.

Perhaps as good a way as any to summarize the argument is to say that while it was great emotional fun to denounce another human being as a pig, it did not win allies and it does not change social reality.

The above applies equally to the student protest movement. A small handful of extremists were somehow equated, by themselves, by the mass media, and by the larger society, with youthful objection to the war and to the absurdities of contemporary higher education. This identification probably served to prolong the war. It has certainly served to postpone, if not permanently defeat, any meaningful higher education reform. The principal difference between the blacks and the students is that there are among the young no equivalent of the elected black political leaders. But the net result is the same: the intellectual elites have identified a whole social group with a handful of militant spokesmen. The rest of society has accepted this identification but put a very different interpretation on it.

Social change is inevitably and necessarily gradual, even when it is a change from a situation that appears to most to be immoral. I am sorry that this is the case. I wish that the human race were different, that it had the will and the knowledge to change rapidly and dramatically once its elite groups have determined that a given situation is immoral. But I do not see any escape from the wisdom of Philip Mason's observation about a democratic society. "The consensus cannot be ignored. It must be led, molded, analyzed, persuaded." It can even, I think, be kicked, but not too often.

And now both the student and the black protest movements seem to have deflated and fragmented, not to say collapsed and dissolved. They didn't win everything. In fact, as a young friend of mine said, "Our generation hasn't won anything. We lost on McCarthy, we lost on the war, we lost on educational reform. There doesn't seem much left for us." What does one say in response? By what right does this young man or any of his generation demand instant and easy victory? By what right do they think they can impose their viewpoints and their solutions on the rest of society without "leading, molding, analyzing, persuading"? Who do they think they are that they, unlike any generation before them, have the right to instant victory? Why do they think they are excused from a lifelong commitment to political involvement and to social change? And after they lost again with McGovern in 1972, will they learn anything about political reality? The blacks are learning, I think. As for the young (in the elite colleges, at any rate), I'm not so sure.

CONSENSUS

To say that politics is the art of shaping consensus is not to say that the existing consensus is one we can accept complacently. The logical and psychological line between recognizing the constraints of political realities and acquiescing in those constraints is a thin one. But those who are interested in politics, particularly the politics of social change, have no choice but to walk that line. If they stray too far to the right and acquiesce in the consensus the way it is, then the social problems around them will simply get worse. If they walk to the left and put more pressure on the consensus than it is presently prepared to bear, they will find that they have become ineffective and quite possibly counterproductive. The answer to the problem is not to abandon political militancy, for that would be acquiescence; nor is the answer to be found in militancy that demands total change immediately. The middle ground is rather occupied by what one could call a "shrewd" militancy, one that pushes opponents right up to the brink and knows how and when to stop a second before it is too late. Perhaps the word "shrewd" is offensive. Isn't the trouble with American society that we have had too much shrewdness, too much calculation? On the contrary, the real trouble is that we have had not nearly enough.

Senator McGovern was obviously caught in an impossible dilemma during the 1972 campaign. He could not have won the nomination without having the enthusiastic support of the political militants who coöpted for themselves the label "New Politicians" (what Norman Podhoretz calls "the new class"). On the other hand, the styles and the positions that he and his advisors deemed necessary to gain the enthusiastic support of the militants—particularly the younger ones—were bound to offend other Democrats, whose support he would certainly need after the convention. The classic example of his dilemma was his appearance during the convention in a hotel lobby session with radical young people, who were upset by the rumor that he was watering down his peace stand. From the point of view of the New Politics, this was a necessary and admirable symbolic gesture. From the point of view of the majority of middle-American Democrats who watched it on television, such an exchange was a demeaning compromise of the dignity of a presidential candidate. McGovern tried to expand the base of his support after the convention, to "move to the center," as his staff and supporters in the columns and on television announced. Undoubtedly some politicians could have shifted emphasis with a grace and elegance that might have attracted rather than offended those to whom he was turning, but McGovern's personal style and the self-righteousness with which he had behaved before and during the convention simply did not give him the flexibility he needed. In all probability he was himself too committed an ideologue to really believe in such a shift. The net result was that to a substantial proportion of the population he ended up looking either hypocritical or cynical. A coalition can be put together which includes professional politicians, labor union leaders, Catholic ethnics, young enthusiasts, and liberal left ideologues. But it requires more skill and flexibility to put such a coalition together than

George McGovern had. Perhaps the moral of this is that no man who wants to be elected president can afford to become too closely identified with just one faction of the party in his preconvention activity. If the only way he can get the nomination is to be identified with only one faction, he should perhaps use it as leverage for bestowing the nomination on someone else. Mr. Daley could tell him that certain advantages may be gained for the faction one represents by such activity. My own personal guess, however, is that a man with a more relaxed and flexible temperament than George McGovern could have obtained the nomination with the help of the liberal left segment of the party without permanently alienating other factions of the party.

There are four assumptions that set the social context of the political consensus in American society.

1. Americans consciously divide themselves into a vast variety of groups—social, occupational, professional, religious, ethnic, racial, age, and sex. Groups, both formal and informal, abound in our society. The typical American thinks of himself as belonging to many of these different groups even if he has no formal organizational affiliation with any of them. As Professor James Coleman has put it:

> *Individuals have many associations in a community, many roles to play, and many attachments to groups and individuals. If these attachments are spread throughout the community as a whole, then the individual has in a sense internalized many different elements in the community.*[2]

[2] James S. Coleman, "Community Conflict," monograph (Glencoe, Ill.: The Free Press, 1957), p. 22.

2. Most American social groups are represented by voluntary organizations (even if a considerable proportion of the eligible members do not in fact formally affiliate with such organizations). These groups vigorously pursue what they take to be the legitimate self-interests of their constituencies. In this competition they are occasionally able to mobilize considerable support from their members.

3. As Professor Coleman noted, most Americans tend to think of themselves as affiliated with many different groups, and, as I described in the case of the Polish surgeon, the pressure of these overlapping memberships can put an individual in an ambiguous situation. In Professor Coleman's words:

> *The individual who has attachments to many elements in the community very often finds himself pulled in opposing directions as the controversy broadens. One group of people to whom he feels close is on one side; others to whom he feels equally close are on the other. His friends at work feel one way; his social friends feel another. His fellows at the American Legion post are more on one side; the people on his Community Chest Committee on the other. Unable to commit himself fully to one side or the other, he either withdraws from the dispute, or, taking sides, is still beset by doubts and fears, unable to go "all out" against the enemy.*[3]

4. Finally, there is a strong vested interest in society for "keeping the rules" of the political, social, and economic competition—at least to the extent that you do not destroy your enemy or deprive him of what he takes to be his fundamental self-interest

[3] Ibid.

or make him a constant loser. There are two reasons for not liquidating your enemy: (1) The day may come when some opposing coalition may have the power to liquidate you and (2) today's enemy may be tomorrow's trusted ally. In the shifting game of political and social competition in the United States, the astute campaigner does his best to maintain friendly relations with those on whose support he may very well have to count in the next phase of the game.

The notion that one does his best not to put an enemy in a completely untenable position is widespread in American society, and it is particularly well understood and accepted by a leadership elite, including both politicians and the heads of the various voluntary organizations. The elites understand that if one wishes the game to continue, there must be a modicum of trust among the participants. Keeping the rules helps maintain that modicum of trust. If someone takes the fundamentally heretical position that the game ought to be abolished, most of the elite leadership group is baffled. Indeed, most of the rest of society is also baffled. They have the feeling that there really is no other way to run a society; if you abolish the game, you must start a new one, probably not very different from the old.

How exactly this American approach to government and society came to be is a fascinating subject. As I suggested in a previous chapter, it may well be that the religious and geographic diversity of the thirteen states necessitated a vast amount of political decentralization which, in its turn, created considerable "slack" in the governmental system in order to make both possible and necessary the emergence of unorganized, then organized, pressure groups. Since institutions charged with promoting the welfare of specific groups did not exist in the formal governmental agencies, these groups organized to promote their own welfare.[4]

This network of competing, overlapping, conflicting, and cooperating social groups does not mean that there is not considerable centralization of power in American society. Nor does it mean that some men do not have more power than other men. It does mean that there are a vast number of limited power centers spread about the United States and that society operates, in substantial part, through the interaction of these power centers.

The diffusion of social power into a large number of groups seems to many non-Americans to be incredible. Even in the political sphere, for example, most of us are governed not by one government but by many, all of which are more or less independent of one another. Thus I am protected from the possibility of a chaotic society by the United States of America, the State of Illinois, the County of Cook, the city of Chicago, the Metropolitan Sanitary District, the Chicago School Board, the Chicago Junior College Board, the Chicago Park District, the Cook County Forest Preserve District, and a substantial number of other governmental authorities, the total of which (the last time I bothered to count) was well in excess of twenty. This is, I suppose, indeed some protection from chaos, but one wonders how much. Even if there is room for a considerable consolidation of governmental power in administration, the competition-within-consensus model is an integral part of American culture. It would be very difficult to

[4] Even the emergence of government bureaus like the Department of Labor and Commerce did not reduce very much either the possibility or the necessity for organized pressure groups outside the government.

persuade most Americans to give it up and even more difficult to govern them in its absence.

The important thing to note is that the public is not called upon to exercise its franchise on a considerable number of issues. Most of the decisions are made by the leadership elite, which includes, of course, the heads and staffs of voluntary organizations, corporate and institutional, in the areas of business, labor, education, etc. These decisions must be made, however, with a wary eye on public opinion, since most political leaders and organization administrators can lose their jobs—the former more easily and more frequently than the latter. There is also always the risk that an opposition from within government, the organization itself, or a special interest group among the public may launch a campaign, either electoral or propagandal, to discredit or undermine public confidence in the organizational leadership.

The balance is a fairly subtle one. The public's control of the leadership is its right to change it periodically. The public's existence as a variable factor is a phenomenon that the leadership can ignore only at its peril.

The only alternative system of governing such a large complex system democratically is to call the public into formal session every time a decision of any consequence is to be made. Such a change in the American style would require far more energy and time invested in the political process than the typical American—at least the typical nonacademic American—is inclined to budget for. In other words, a plebiscite democracy as an alternative for competing-cooperating social groups is something that would have to be forced on the American public because it runs contrary to the American tradition and it would take more effort than the public has ever been willing to invest in politics. One would have to remove the citizen's freedom not to be a totally political man.

The radical who rejects the American pluralist model may fall back on Mao's model of permanent revolution. It is an open question whether permanent revolution works, and there is certainly no reason to think that it would be any more socially desirable to Americans than plebiscite democracy. In other words, like it or not, we are stuck with the system. The issue is not whether it can be abolished but how can it be made to function more effectively.

Radical critics think that pluralist politics models tend to be "conservative," because the people who construct them become so fascinated by the phenomenon of astonishing social complexity actually functioning as a system that they lose their ability to criticize the serious deficiencies of that functioning. Some critics denounce the whole "system" approach to social analysis as inherently reactionary because it underwrites the status quo.

The critics have a point. Social systems analysis can in some instances blind us to the weaknesses, inadequacies, and the failure of the system. We are so interested in telling how the system works and marveling that it does in fact work that we overlook ways in which it does not work. Furthermore, we become so engrossed with the complexity of the system we are analyzing that we find it hard to believe that it can be changed or at least changed very drastically or very rapidly. We tend to think of the model as being in "equilibrium," and we are hesitant about anything that will throw the equilibrium out of kilter.

It is appropriate, then, to acknowledge a strain toward a conservative bias in the pluralistic analysis of the American political system. But to say that there is a strain in that direction does not mean that it is irresistible. Because the pluralist model builders must exercise strong efforts so as not to lose sight of the inadequacies of the political system does not mean that they are incapable of exercising such efforts. It is required of them that they be wary lest they be seduced by the elegance of their own model, but there is nothing inevitable about succumbing to temptation.

On the other hand, those who are so ready to shout "Conservative bias!" ought to understand that however weak the pluralists' social criticism may have been at times, no one has come up with a better description of how the American political process works. If the pluralist must learn from the radical to be more aware of the deficiencies of American society, then the radical must be ready to learn from the pluralist how difficult and how inevitably limited will be even the most splendid plan for reform.

COALITION

America is a bargaining, coalition-forming society. It is probably the most sophisticated and complex bargaining society in the world. It is not merely that our government institutions are based on bargaining, but that bargaining permeates the whole of society. Indeed, political pluralism is probably more the result of social pluralism than its cause. Factions of corporation executives bargain with each other in intracorporation politics; priests and bishops bargain with each other in the Roman Church; students and teachers bargain; factions on faculty committees bargain; rivals and colleagues in trade unions sharpen their bargaining skills dealing among themselves; children bargain with their parents, and, increasingly, parents bargain with their children. The net result of all this is that in most sets of circumstance most people never get everything they want, yet they usually get enough to keep them reasonably satisfied. Although this is a fairly modest accomplishment, when one looks at some other societies produced in human history, it is an accomplishment not lightly dismissed.

The bargaining-coalition forming process has its failures. Among the most noticeable is its inability to provide sufficient social, economic, and political power for the nonwhite disadvantaged groups—a failure that goes back to prerevolutionary times. This failure is serious and could be catastrophic, but, as Gunnar Myrdal was neither the first not the last to observe, it is a failure not so much in the conception of the system as in its not honoring its own principles. A coalition-forming society, if it is to be true to itself and if it is to function with some effectiveness, must find means to facilitate the development of bargaining power among the nonwhite groups in its population. To say that this must be done does not mean that coalition formation is a total failure; it is, rather, that some groups have not yet been admitted as full participants into the coalition-forming game.

There are many different kinds of coalitions in the United States. There is first of all the long-range coalition, the most obvious of which is the political party (about which there will be more in a later chapter). In addition, there is the long-standing cooperation between certain segments of the Jewish community and certain elements of the civil rights movement. And, until recently, there was also a tradition of cooperation between the more progressive trade union leaders and civil rights militants. Another example would be the friendly attitude between social action leaders in the churches and the union movement—a friendship which continues so far as Catholic leaders are concerned but seems to be waning among the Protestants. Long-range coalitions do not preclude disagreement, but they do mean that most of the time one can count on one's partners in the coalition for support.

Short-range coalitions come into being to serve more limited purposes. They do not assume a broad range of common values. Sometimes short-range coalitions represent a temporary broadening of already existing long-range coalitions as, for example, when Everett Dirksen and his Republican supporters were recruited to pass the Civil Rights Act of the middle sixties. Short-range coalitions may be the beginnings of an alliance for which the participants think there may be long-range possibilities. The curious love affair between the Republican party and the South, for example, cannot, even after twenty years, be considered anything more than a short-range coalition.

Finally, there is the ad hoc coalition—a group of partners assembled for one particular purpose, with the understanding that with success the coalition will disband. Thus, a number of local community organizations may combine on an ad hoc basis to prevent a steel or utility plant from continuing to pour noxious smoke into the community. The nature of the human condition being what it is, such ad hoc coalitions have some built-in tendencies to perpetuate themselves, however, and the turning point is probably reached when the ad hoc group rents a Xerox machine.

Different kinds of strategies are required for those who are in some sense responsible for the different kinds of coalitions. A long-range coalition needs to be *tended.* Its leaders know they can assume continued support from the various components, but they also know that it is a mistake to take the loyalty of their colleagues for granted—a bit of knowledge that seemed to escape liberal Democrats during the 1960s on the subject of their white working-class colleagues in the party.

Short-range coalitions, as, for example, between white and black militants on campus, need to be *maintained,* which means that considerably more time and energy must be expended on servicing the coalition than would be required for the long-range model. Between goal-seeking and servicing activities, a much greater emphasis must be placed on the latter in a short-range coalition.

The ad hoc coalition must be first *convened,* then goals and strategies must be *negotiated.* In such circumstances, most of the energies of the leadership are going to be focused on the internal affairs of the coalition. One must discover who potential allies are in order to help push for what one deems to be mutually sought goals, then one must reason, persuade, argue, occasionally threaten, in order to win from the allies his commitment to join. The more obvious it is that his and your goals are the same, the less time has to be spent cajoling and negotiating toward union and the more time can be available for pursuing goals. On the other hand, the more reluctant he is to join the coalition, the less sure you can be that when the chips are down, you won't be deserted. Most coalitions designed to accomplish difficult and unpopular social change will have to face the fact that their allies are reluctant and ambiguous. Furthermore, they are likely to have much more moderate ideas on how far the opponents can or ought to be pushed. It does help, of course, in a fragile coalition to have persuaded your allies that your position in all its full rigor is the only one that possesses authentic moral worth. But morality as a glue for holding coalitions together has proven to be notoriously soluble.

Coalitions exist on the level of leadership as well as the rank and file, with the two levels interacting constantly with one another. Leaders are able to join coalitions with other leaders because they know that their followers will support them in this coalition, or at least not object too vigorously. On the other hand, sometimes the feelings and passions of the rank and file are such that a leader may well be forced into a coalition about which he has some reservations himself. We will say more in a subsequent chapter about political leadership, but it is worth noting here that it is an unwise leader who thinks he can habitually take positions to which his supporters are likely to be vigorously opposed. The endorsement, for example, by high-level church bureaucrats of certain racial policies (such as paying "reparations") to which their constituencies were vigorously opposed has resulted in a serious strain on the relationship between those bureaucrats and their constituencies. Unaccountably, the strain seems to surprise church leaders.

Coalition formation, then, and the bargaining that is part of convening, maintaining, or extending coalitions is the very lifeblood of the American political and social process. One may not like it, but he will be hard-pressed to change it.

It does not follow that the American political coalitions, past and present, have produced a society without flaw or blemish. On the contrary, there are obvious and ugly failures of the coalition system and if much social change has been made possible by forming coalitions, so has other social change been prevented by coalitions. There can be, in other words, "good" coalitions and "bad" coalitions. The secret for those who wish to reduce the amount of injustice and suffering in America is not to repudiate coalition formation but to form very powerful coalitions of their own.

COMPROMISE

"Compromise" is a dirty word in politics. In most other aspects of human living, the ability to compromise is thought to be praiseworthy. For example, a husband or a wife who is uncompromising in his/her relationship is viewed as stupid, harsh, and immoral. Parents are expected to compromise with their children and, save in the most advanced homes, children are expected to compromise with their parents. We compromise with our friends on where to eat or what movie to see; we compromise with our colleagues about the allocation of work; and we applaud when management and labor are able to compromise their differences to avoid a strike. In each of these sets of circumstances, he who refuses to compromise is the one to be castigated. But in politics it is just the other way around. There the compromiser is condemned as being immoral or corrupt and accused of "selling out." In politics (and until recently in religion) it is thought to be a sign of highest virtue to refuse even the slightest compromise. Of a husband and wife who get along well, we say in terms of praise, "They really know how to compromise." To accuse politicians of compromise is to suggest that they ought to be turned out of office for lack of principle and virtue.

But the politics of bargaining and coalition formation, which I am describing in this chapter, necessarily leads to compromise. One must settle for less than one wants. The articulation of goals within a coalition is enhanced by a sense of their absolute moral worth. Ideally, human beings never want anything more than they have a right to. Yet these colleagues of ours have goals of their own, fully vested with moral rectitude, which from our point of view are obviously immoral. When we tone down our goals to account for theirs, we clearly reinforce their immorality. To compromise, then, means to settle for less than absolute morality and legitimate rights.

It doesn't stop there. Not only must we be willing to accept the point of view of our colleagues within the coalition in order to form it, we must, to some extent at least, accept the other side's point of view as possibly having some validity. For we remember that in order not to disrupt completely the rules of the game, we must not destroy our opponent's fundamental self-interest. But how can we know what that is if we cannot put ourselves in his place to see things from his perspective? Then, of course, we risk infecting ourselves with his immorality, but we must do it for we may not risk destroying him completely. Thus, by joining a coalition we are forced to compromise not only with our colleagues within but with our enemies outside.

The capacity to understand another man's position without having to agree with it and without being threatened in one's own position is essential, I think, to political success. The phrase a Chicago Irish politician quips to an ally who finds himself constrained to be an enemy on a particular issue or campaign is, "Do what you have to do." The enthusiastic radical writes this off as a cheap political response designed only to evoke the possibility that the opponent may once more become an ally. It certainly does that, but it also indicates that he who speaks the words understands the complexity of the human condition and is capable of respecting the integrity of his opponents. The fact that respect for one's opponents and the capacity to learn from them and to understand their position "from the inside" are essential in politics is something that a professional politician takes for granted.

The willingness to compromise in politics, as in every other form of human endeavor, rests on the awareness that what is superior in pure theory is not necessarily and inevitably superior in the complex, ambiguous, and uncertain world of reality. If the world were simple, if human life were uncomplicated, if theoretical morality could produce practical solutions for every important social problem, then compromise is indeed corrupt if not insane.

But if the world is complicated, it seems to follow that what is morally superior is not that which is theoretically most desirable but that which comes closest to the desired goal without doing more harm than good—either by destroying the political fabric, by making the bargaining process impossible, or by even converting modest victory into complete defeat. And make no mistake about it. In a complex, uncertain pluralistic society like ours, modest victory is almost always the only alternative to certain defeat.

My argument, then, is that it is the skilled compromiser who is the most moral of political men while the intransient ideologue is the most immoral. To put the matter more bluntly, in the political game it is the greatest immorality to insist on something more than a modest victory, because more than that may turn opponents into implacable enemies; and, besides, the chances for complete success are minute at best.

This chapter is not designed to be an argument against radical criticism or political militancy. The society that lacks radicals and militants would be a very sick society. Rather, the argument here is that those who wish to change society, while they must heed the just demands of militants and listen to the insightful criticisms of the radicals, must also be sophisticated in the processes by which political power is amassed and exercised in our republic. One must have allies, and under most circumstances those allies may not be as impressed by radical rhetoric as we are and they may not be as sympathetic to the demands of the militants as we are. However, all that is required of them as allies is that they agree with us that certain changes are necessary and that they trust us enough to work with us to achieve those changes. And we must trust them enough not to demand that they become exactly like us. Coalition, consensus, compromise—not exactly the kinds of words that inflame human passions, but they are as indispensable for the human condition as passion is.

Pragmatism is an indispensable attribute for any American politician. How pragmatic one has to be, however, is to a considerable extent a function of the particular set of circumstances in which one finds oneself at a given time and place. For Democratic political leaders between now and July 1976, it would be very difficult to be too pragmatic. They are dealing with a coalition that has been badly fractured by a nasty ideological fight, the memories of which will take a long time to fade. To combine the gentle, sensitive, diplomatic skills of the peace-maker with the drive and the enthusiasm of a vigorous leader is no small task; but anyone who does not have these two characteristics should not apply for the job. The last thing in the world the Democratic coalition needs at the present stage of its history is a hard-line ideologue whose rigidity and self-righteousness prevent him from gently pasting the pieces back together—all the pieces.

WHERE HAS ALL THE POWER GONE?

The word "establishment" is inescapable in contemporary America. Almost no one will admit to being part of an establishment, and almost everyone is willing to attack it, though of course who belongs to the establishment depends generally on who happens to be doing the attacking. Is the vice-president, for example, a member of the establishment? How can anyone who attacks the *New York Times* be considered an establishmentarian?

The word has been misused and abused to such an extent that it no longer has any meaning at all, and while it makes good radical rhetoric, it makes very poor social analysis. But the question implicit in the "establishment" charge is still an important one: Who runs America?

Both scholars and ordinary citizens tend to split into camps on this question, and the camps don't necessarily follow the ordinary political lines. For both the extreme Right and the extreme Left are convinced that some shadowy force is running American society, whether it be Jewish Wall Street bankers or the military-industrial complex. In the one camp are all those who see power as broadly diffused in American society. The scholarly members of this camp are called the pluralists. In the other camp are those who see power in American society highly concentrated in a group of power holders, who either explicitly or implicitly conspire to control what happens in the society. The scholarly members of this camp are called the elitists.

The favorite spokesman of the elitists is the late Professor C. Wright Mills, who deftly traced the patterns of relationship between businessmen, government, and the military, arguing that the leaders in these three institutions were obviously the ones who held the power in society. If Mills were writing his

Power Elite today, he might very well add the university to his triad of power, since during the 1960s many members of that world began to move in circles of power with high-level corporate executives, governmental leaders, and active and retired generals and admirals.

The principal spokesmen of the pluralist viewpoint are writers like Robert Dahl and James Q. Wilson. These men suggest that Mills's analysis is deficient on three counts. First of all, it takes as typical a situation that was in fact more characteristic of the Eisenhower presidency than of presidencies before or since. Secondly, it assumes that because the communication networks make possible the existence of a power elite, it does in fact exist; and, thirdly, Mills and his colleagues offer rather little evidence to demonstrate that policy-making decisions are in fact the result of implicit or explicit conspiracy. Quite the contrary, the studies of community decision-making that the pluralists have done indicate that power is widely diffused in American society and is mobilized for specific decisions by the formation of various coalitions. Norton Long, one of the most original of the theoreticians of the pluralist school, argues that American society is a system of games: a political game, a corporate business game, a labor union game, a church game, an educational game, etc. The people who play these games generally play them out for their own purposes and according to their own rules. They enter into alliances with players of other and overlapping games only when these alliances are required by something that is seen as a challenge to or an opportunity to further their own interests.

As far as academic debate goes, the "pluralists" have had by far the better of the argument, though they have not won over the "elitists," who are still convinced that there "has to be" some sort of power elite actually running the society. They respond to the pluralists first by pointing out that certain groups are excluded from the power game. Secondly, the elite at least determines which issues are to be decided. Thirdly, many important decisions are made publicly enough but with practically no effective debate about them, because those who are concerned about them are not important enough or powerful enough to bring the debate before the public eye. Finally, if the data do not reveal the existence of such an elite, it is simply because the power elite is too shadowy and elusive to be trapped by data. It is still there and the elitists *know* that it is.

A number of writers, especially Theodore Lowi and Stanley Lieberson, have tried to combine the two viewpoints.

Theodore Lowi, in a lengthy review of a book called *American Business and Public Policy: The Politics of Foreign Trade* by Raymond A. Bauer, Ithiel de Soal Pool, and Lewis A. Dexter (New York: Atherton Press, 1963), emphasizes that power takes different shapes under different sets of circumstances, and that the various centers of power in a society modify their relationships to suit the circumstances. There are, for example, according to Lowi, three areas of possible relationships between government and business: distribution, regulation, and redistribution. Distribution represents some form of governmental patronage or subsidy, such as the rivers and harbors bill or agricultural price supports. Regulation represents the kind of government intervention that tariff policies or, more recently, highway safety standards constitute. Finally, redistribution is a direct attempt on the part of government to take resources from one area of society to give them to other areas of society—such as the income tax and the welfare programs.

In the area of distribution it is essentially the individual firm or the corporation that deals with government, and the relationship among the various firms is one of "noninterference." In the regulatory area, however, when issues of redistribution are at stake, the groups restructure themselves into associations, or what Lowi calls "peak associations" (such as the United States Chamber of Commerce, the National Association of Manufacturers), and instead of bargaining and coalition, their behavior in the arena of relationships with the government is marked by an ideology of class conflict with struggles between elites and counterelites.

To make this all a bit more concrete: If there is a government policy of subsidizing the construction of steel sea walls along the shores of the Great Lakes, the Practically Perfect Steel Company will cheerfully accept its government subsidy with no complaints from the labor union to which its workers belong; it will seek no cooperation from other companies. On the other hand, if the government is setting tariff policies that make it possible for Japanese steel to be used in the construction of the sea walls, Practically Perfect will join with the other steel companies in the country (the Iron and Steel Institute), and the members of its local union will join with the United Steel Workers of America. Both the union and the steel companies will form a coalition to protect themselves from a Japanese steel invasion. Finally, with industrywide bargaining going on, the government is likely to set the final terms of the contract. Practically Perfect and its employees will be locked into a battle taking place not in their own plant but in the negotiating rooms where teams from the steelworkers and the leading steel companies encounter one another and, at a higher level, in the lobbies of Congress where the Washington representatives of the AFL-CIO, and the NAM contend with each other in the name of their ideology and class position. Atomization, coalition formation, and class conflict, then, are to a very considerable extent the result of which political arena is currently being occupied by a given set of participants.

If the main attraction happens to be regulation, then the classical pluralist coalition formation is taking place; if, on the other hand, it happens to be redistribution, then one is observing a situation not unlike C. Wright Mills's power elite, with the important added dimension that in questions of redistribution there are usually two power elites in conflict. Which one happens to be the establishment at a given time probably depends on which political party is in power, which is to say that in a Republican administration, Practically Perfect Steel, the Iron and Steel Institute, the NAM are likely to have somewhat more influence in government than the local union, the Steelworks, and the AFL-CIO; in a Democratic administration, the reverse is more likely to be the case.

One of the major merits of Professor Lowi's brilliant analysis is that it stresses how complex the operations of power and the formation of coalitions are in the United States. It demonstrates that the analysis that sees establishmentarian devils lurking behind every bush has little to do with political and economic reality. Lowi forces us to ask not whether there is a power elite, nor who is running society, but rather what happens to be going on in society right now, and which arena currently contains the main event.

Stanley Lieberson attempts to resolve the question of pluralism versus elitism by investigating the famous military-industrial complex.[1] He points out that from the elitist side it can certainly be said that there has been a high level of military spending since World War II and that many of the largest American corporations depend heavily on such spending. However, through a complicated set of mathematical analyses, Lieberson demonstrates both that the economy does not require extensive military spending and that it is very probable that most corporations would be more prosperous if the government shifted to nonmilitary spending.

In attempting to explain this rather bizarre situation, Lieberson suggests that an advanced industrial society is "one in which a wide variety of interest groups are each attempting to balance an array of potential gains and losses in order to generate the maximum net gain." [2] In other words, military spending will be tolerated by other interest groups in the society when it does not involve heavy costs for them. Lieberson postulates four conditions necessary for a "compensating" power situation to operate; that is, a situation in which "the political system's output [fails] to reflect the interests of the majority without this necessarily meaning that a power elite controls the government:" [3]

> *First, power must be an exhaustible commodity such that each interest group has limited political influence. Second, the interests of the population must be diverse enough so that a given proposal will not have an equal impact on all segments.*

[1] Stanley Lieberson, "An Empirical Study of Military-Industrial Linkages," *American Journal of Sociology* 76, no. 4 (January 1971).
[2] Ibid., p. 577.
[3] Ibid.

Third, governmental actions that favor a particular interest group must not eliminate the disadvantaged majority's potential for other gains. . . . Fourth, legislation beneficial to a specific interest must not at the same time create too great a loss for the majority of other interests.[4]

In other words, in such a theory of "compensating strategies," high-level military spending is the result of a very high level of interest on the part of defense industries accompanied by a relative lack of concern by other segments of industry in the society.

The majority of industries disregard the small losses they incur from defense spending and turn their attention to other aspects of government policy that affect them more directly. Defense spending still influences the profits of dairy farmers, for example, but so too will other government policies such as price supports, marketing restrictions, exports and imports on dairy products, grading practices, trucking costs, and so forth. Accordingly, the area of government action with the most substantial direct impact on the goals of the dairy industry is probably not the military.[5]

Therefore, in a society with each group vying to generate the greatest net gain for itself, "a given policy need not be the product of simply the majority of interests, nor need it mean that a small set of interests is dominant. Rather, the policy may mean that the losses to a majority of interests are small, whereas the gains to some sectors are substantial."[6]

[4] Stanley Lieberson, "An Empirical Study of Military-Industrial Linkages," *American Journal of Sociology* 76, no. 4 (January 1971), p. 578.
[5] Ibid.
[6] Ibid., p. 582.

In a way it may be unfortunate that Professor Lieberson chose the defense industry as an example, because there are moral implications in defense expenditures that may cloud the point he is trying to make. His point, as I understand it, is that one need not assume a power elite to explain a social situation that is very advantageous to one group and disadvantageous to another. The explanation is far more likely to be that the net advantage to one group is very great while the net disadvantages to the other groups are perceived as relatively slight. A well-organized, vigorous, and skillful minority can have its way in a society in which power is widely diffused so long as the disadvantages experienced by other groups because of that minority's gains are relatively slight.

Under some sets of circumstances, then, it is not even necessary to form a coalition to achieve one's goal. The necessity for coalition formation is in direct proportion to the likelihood that one's gains are going to be perceived by a substantial number of other interest groups in the society as a direct threat to their own welfare. Indeed, the greater the threat, the larger the coalition needs to be.

While both Lowi and Lieberson attempt to steer a middle ground between the pluralist and elitist models, they are both on the side of the pluralists in three respects:

1. They see a wide diffusion of power in American society rather than its concentration in a small ruling group.

2. They see power as exercised either by relatively independent, diffused power centers or by power coalitions in conflict with one another.

3. They also see a constant shifting of alliances and coalitions in the power arenas. Some coalitions, of course, are stable but many others are not.

Both authors would agree with the elitists that power can be concentrated in elite groups, though Lieberson would add that power can also be exercised with telling impact quite apart from any linkage to a shadowy establishment. But they also agree with the pluralists that the distribution of power in American society is a very complicated matter, and that in most sets of circumstances the locus of power is at the periphery and not in the center.

It is important that all of us who are concerned about politics realize that only on occasion can we legitimately blame a vague and shadowy "them" for our problems. Admittedly, it would be much easier if we could; then we could just sweep "them" out of office and replace them with some of "us." But one of the melancholy results of a democratic society in which power is widely diffused is that "they" turn out in the final analysis to be "we."

Lowi and Lieberson are obviously far closer to the pluralists such as Long and Dahl than they are to C. Wright Mills. It is unlikely, however, that they or anyone else will shake the conviction widespread in American society that there are shadowy forces that control what happens; fighting these forces is extremely difficult if not impossible.

There is a good deal to be said for the elitist viewpoint, and anyone who approaches American society with the naïve notion that power is equally distributed in the population and that mere persuasive argumentation will mobilize the power in favor of social change is simply asking for trouble.

1. Some people have more power than others. The president of General Motors, for example, is likely to have more influence on decisions that are made in Washington than the assembly-line worker. The

archbishop of Chicago is likewise going to have greater impact on what the Catholic Church does than the parish priest. Compared to Mayor Daley or County President George Dunne or Governor Walker or the president of the Chicago Board of Trade or of Marshall Field and Company or the *Chicago Sun-Times,* I am relatively powerless about what happens in my native city. Indeed, a member of the United Steel Workers of America probably has more power than I do, because he is at least able to bring pressure on city events through his union that I am not able to bring because I lack some sort of intermediate pressure group standing between me and the city.

2. Because of the way power is distributed in American society, certain groups of men, either because of their position or because of the support they can command from large organizations, can have decisive power on specific issues, no matter what anyone else thinks. While it is rare that the combination of these powerful men can override the strongly felt convictions of a majority of the population, it is generally unnecessary for them to try. On most issues the majority of the population is relatively indifferent. Thus if the *Chicago Tribune* determines that there is to be a lakefront exposition hall named after their late beloved publisher, it is likely to succeed because it needs only the support of a few city leaders, and opposition to it is likely to be limited to a small segment of the population. A majority of Chicagoans probably don't care much one way or the other about the lakefront hall; if asked, they may be vaguely for it. It will be virtually impossible for the opposition to organize massive antagonism toward the idea among the general population.

3. Some extremely critical decisions are made in

American society by a handful of men. For example, the decision to go ahead with the Bay of Pigs invasion and the subsequent decision to respond to the Russian intrusion of missiles into Cuba by a blockade were made by a handful of men in secret. So, too, apparently, have most of the decisions in the Indochina war been made by a small group operating in secret. These men obviously do not make their decisions in complete isolation from the pressures of the wishes and opinions of the rest of society, and they also eventually run the risk of being ejected from political office if what they do displeases at least a majority of those who vote in an election. Nevertheless, most of us do not have much power in the making of foreign policy. Our influence on foreign policy is limited to what the political leadership thinks our limits of hostile response are and to our plebiscite on election day.

4. Well-organized pressure groups do exercise an influence on American society all out of proportion to the size of their membership and the representativeness of their opinions. Even though there is strong national support for gun control legislation, for example, the National Rifle Association has been successful in limiting gun control laws and in punishing senators who have dared to push too vigorously against the association. This is but one example of an incredible number of pressure groups that zealously watch social events to make sure that the well-being of their members—judged, of course, by the professional staff of the organization—is not harmed by what goes on among the political leaders.

5. David Riesman and others have called these pressure groups (which run all the way from the United States Catholic Conference to the National

Education Association and include the United Steelworkers of America, the American Chamber of Commerce, and a vast variety of other thoroughly reliable and respectable institutions) "veto groups," that is, their power is most effective in preventing things from happening than in causing them to happen. The American Medical Association, for example, has effectively vetoed national health insurance for several decades, but it has not displayed much power in getting positive legislation for its own benefit. The veto groups may occasionally join forces with one another and rally around some common cause, but under normal circumstances they are much better at saying no than at saying yes.

6. But when all these concessions are made to the accuracy of the elitist analysis, one is still faced with the fact that they miss the most critical obstacle to social reform in the United States, and that obstacle is not the existence of an establishment but the relative nonexistence of one. To put the matter somewhat differently, it is the lack of concentration of power that is the real obstacle to social reform.

Let us take two examples. First of all, if there were an establishment of business, military, intellectual, and political leaders who did in fact exercise political control over the country, they would have gotten us out of the Vietnam war long before they did. The war was bad for business, bad for education, bad for government, bad for everyone in sight. It combined inflation with recession, alienated the youth, split the college campuses wide open, and had a rending effect on the whole fabric of American society. Furthermore, American business did not profit from the war, American political leaders did not profit from it (they generally lost elections because of it), and the American people, whose sons were killed, did not profit from it. Almost all the influential national journals were against it, and even the military muttered that it was trapped into the war by intellectual advisors of the president against their better judgment. Nevertheless, though it may have been desirable for all concerned to get us out of the war, there never existed a powerful establishment that could convene itself and announce that the war was over. The young people who vigorously demonstrated against the war were frustrated and angry because they could not communicate with the establishment to make it end the war. They might have considered the possibility that if there were an establishment, it certainly would have ended the war. The reason they can't communicate with an establishment is that there isn't one.

One can also take it as well established that the best way to cope with housing pressures in America's large cities is to distribute substantial segments of the black population in the suburban fringe that rings these large cities. Political leaders, business leaders, research experts, community leaders, virtually everyone would agree that the desegregation of the suburbs is absolutely essential for coping with problems of urban housing. Yet there does not exist in American society a group of men powerful enough to enforce such a decision over the collective opposition of all the suburban veto groups. If there were an establishment with a base of power, we would certainly have blacks in the suburbs.

The implication of the previous paragraph is that an establishment should be capable of benign as well as malign activity. Many benign actions would be very much in the self-interest of any establishment worthy of the name. That these benign things do not get done is, I think, conclusive evidence that, alas, there is no establishment. Things would be much simpler and neater if there were.

Implicit in radical criticism of the establishment is the strategy that argues that if one replaced the existing establishment with a new one composed of radical elitists and representing "the people," then one could institute benign social reforms. Professor Mills was quite explicit about that. He did not so much advocate the abolition of the power elite as making it responsible—responsible to intellectuals. But obviously it could not be made responsible to all intellectuals, so Mills decided that the power elite should be responsible to those intellectuals who happened to have the same ideas on foreign policy that he did. The power elite, in other words, will become "responsible" when it is willing to do what C. Wright Mills and his colleagues tells it to do. On the whole, I am not sure I would have liked to be governed by Professor Mills or any of his successors. I very much doubt that we could have worked out an arrangement whereby they would have been willing to stand for reelection. It would be interesting to see what those critics of the establishment would do if they became it. They would discover, of course, as do all government leaders, how limited their powers really are. They would probably suspect some sort of conspiracy on the part of shadowy forces still existing in the society bent on frustrating their noble plans. Like most other Jacobins before them, they would probably use force to destroy the conspiracy, only to discover that even force has its limitations as a means of effective government.

The most important obstacle to social change in the United States, then, is not the concentration of power but its diffusion. If power was concentrated sufficiently, those of us who wish for change would merely have to negotiate with those who hold the power and, if necessary, put pressure on them. But power is so widely diffused that, in many instances, there is no one to negotiate with and no one on whom to put pressure. American society has been organized from the beginning around two premises: (1) "The central guiding trend of American constitutional development has been the evolution of a political system in which all the active and legitimate groups in the population can make themselves heard at some crucial stage in the process of decision." [7] The second principle is a corollary of the first: (2) The larger society cannot ignore for very long what a given group considers to be its fundamental self-interest. No group, in other words, can be expected to assume the role of the permanent loser.

Obviously, these two principles are not always honored in practice. Some groups are not big enough or not well-organized enough or not articulate enough to make themselves heard, and some groups have been losers, if not all the time at least most of the time. My point is not that these two principles are perfectly honored in American society; it is that to a considerable extent the structure of the decision-making process has been organized in such a way as to attempt to honor these principles. If there was strong centralized power with little in the way of veto groups capable of checking that power, social change, benign or malign, would be rather easy. But since power is widely distributed among a vast number of governmental, bureaucratic, business, labor, social, civic, educational, and religious groups, change on a matter that large seg-

[7] Robert A. Dahl, *Preface to Democratic Theory* (Chicago: University of Chicago Press, 1956), p. 137.

ments of the population deem important can only occur when the opinions of all these groups are listened to and at least in some fashion respected.

Again, let me emphasize that I am not saying that all groups within the population have the same power or that wins and losses are evenly distributed among groups. I am asserting that only on matters important to practically no one else can a group expect to win without engaging in bargaining. The more important the issue and the more widespread the interest in it, the more intensive the bargaining and the larger the coalition must be. The effective checks and balances in American democracy are not those that Madison wrote into the Constitution; they probably antedate the Constitution and arose from the wide variety of sometimes competing, sometimes cooperating, frequently overlapping, subgroups that have always existed in American society and which the American ethos has encouraged to organize.

Bargaining, in other words, is essential to the coalescence of power in American society. One bargains with individuals, with groups, or with individuals and groups. Sometimes one must bargain within one's group before a posture vis-à-vis other groups is declared. The individual or the group that is unwilling to bargain will simply not have power, at least not enough to achieve its goals, no matter how wealthy it is, no matter how important its connections, no matter how superior its morality, no matter how great its wisdom.

Professor Robert Dahl, using New Haven, Connecticut as a prototype political system, notes three characteristics of its operation: "there are normally 'slack' resources; a small core of professional politicians exert great influence over decision; and the system has a built-in, self-operating limitation on the influence of all participants, including the professionals." [8]

Dahl describes "slack" as being the great gap between the citizens' actual influence and their potential influence in the political system. He says, "In liberal societies, politics is a sideshow in the great circus of life." But, should the people divert their "slack" resources from nonpolitical to political purposes, "the gap between the actual influence of the average citizen and his potential influence would narrow." [9]

This "slack" permits elite leadership by both political and economic professionals to have a vast influence on what goes on in the society. It also imposes a severe limitation on their power.

> *If slack resources provide the political entrepreneur with his dazzling opportunity, they are also the source of his greatest danger. For nearly every citizen in the community has access to unused political resources; it is precisely because of this that even a minor blunder can be fatal to the political entrepreneur if it provokes a sizable minority in the community into using its political resources at a markedly higher rate in opposition to his policies, for then, as with the White Queen, it takes all the running he can do just to stay in the same place. Yet almost every policy involves losses for some citizens and gains for others. Whenever the prospect of loss becomes high enough, threatened citizens begin to*

[8] Robert Dahl, *Who Governs?: Democracy and Power in an American City* (New Haven, Conn.: Yale University Press, 1961), p. 305.
[9] Ibid.

take up some of the slack in order to remove the threat. The more a favorable decision increases in importance to the opposition, the more resources they can withdraw from other uses and pour into the political struggle; the more resources the opposition employs, the greater the cost to the political entrepreneur if he insists on his policy. At some point, the cost becomes so high that the policy is no longer worth it. This point is almost certain to be reached whenever the opposition includes a majority of the electorate, even if no election takes place. Normally, however, far before this extreme situation is approached the expected costs will already have become so excessive that an experienced politician will capitulate or, more likely, search for a compromise that gives him some of what he wants at lower cost.[10]

The model described by Professor Dahl is not one of a society where everything goes well, nor is it one where desired social change can take place rapidly, nor is it one where malice and stupidity do not stand in the way of progress. However, it is well to note that progress is frequently slowed much less by malice and stupidity than by the wide distribution of potential power and the long and difficult process of mobilizing it for change. The American political system that we are describing is in many respects dreadfully inefficient because it does its best to respond not only to the wishes of individuals but also to the vital interests of the wide, varied, and frequently overlapping subgroups within the society. A political leader, for example, who is trying to win the vote of the Polish doctor, described in an earlier

[10] Ibid., pp. 309–10.

chapter, would have to wonder which of the overlapping and competing memberships of that good doctor would be salient at the time he was courting his vote—and of course there is always the risk that he would make a decision quite independent of any group membership because, for example, he didn't like the looks of the candidate's wife.

One can fault this system of pluralism in two respects. First, one can say that it has failed according to its own principles; that certain disadvantaged groups are not given an adequate hearing or that society does not recognize its obligation to facilitate the development of political power in these groups. The criticism is certainly a valid one. The very nobility of the political ideal implied in American pluralism makes departures from it unfortunate and ugly, but if this is the only criticism one has to make, then the strategy is obvious: one must bargain to persuade the rest of society that its consensus must be broadened sufficiently to admit these other groups as valued and equal participants in the enterprise.

The second criticism is that given the complexities and difficulties of the modern world, the diffusion of power that exists in American society is dangerously inefficient. If one has to bargain with Polish surgeons, Latvian truckdrivers, red-necked farmers, Irish politicians, conservative black clergymen, Jewish garment makers, Swedish computer operators, Texas oil barons, Portuguese fishermen from Fall River, and cattle ranchers from Montana in order to win support for absolutely imperative social changes, then these changes will be delayed, perhaps for too long, while the evil and injustice continues. It is demeaning, degrading, and immoral to have to bargain for the elimination of clear and obvious injustice. Racism is obscene, war is obscene; both should go away without our having to bargain on the subject. A political system that distributes power so that bargaining is necessary to eliminate obscene immorality is in itself not merely inefficient but immoral. It is not proper that those who are moral and wise should be forced to negotiate with those who are immoral and stupid.

This is a logically and consistently coherent case; in effect, it advocates the abolition of the pluralistic bargaining, coalition-forming polity that we currently have. It advocates taking the slack out of the political system and placing it in the hands of a ruling elite that would be both virtuous enough and powerful enough to accomplish quickly those social changes deemed urgent or imperative. One supposes that a strong case can be made for issues like pollution, population control, and racial justice not to be made subject to the bargaining process, that wise and virtuous ruling elites should enforce by legislation and by police power, if necessary, the regulations that cope with these problems. The issues are so critical that there is no time to bargain with those whose intelligence and sensitivity is so deficient that they cannot see how imperative it is that action be taken with utmost speed. One can, I say, make a convincing case for such a political system, but let it be clear that it is an elite-establishmentarian system with a vengence, that it bears no similarity to what normally has been considered democracy, that it is completely at odds with the American political tradition, and completely objectionable to most Americans.

This chapter has been an attempt to take a middle position between those who see American society as dominated by an elaborate power conspiracy and those who think that power is evenly distributed throughout the society. The middle position was achieved by coming from the opposite direction. It was suggested that the real problem is not a concentration of power, but its diffusion. The diffusion of power does not mean that there are not certain groups in society that have amassed more power than they ought to have and more power than it is socially healthy for them to have. The ability of the gun lobby, for example, to block effective arms control, to center certain real estate groups to impede the enforcement of panic-peddling laws, constitute but two examples of widespread misuse of power in American society. But the misuse is, in most circumstances, the result of inordinate power in certain vital groups rather than in massive conspiracy among the power elite. It is worth noting again that if there were truly a power elite, both the gun lobby and panic peddlers would have been put out of business long ago, since those who are really wealthy and powerful in American society have much to fear from both hand guns and panic peddling.

If this model of American society is correct, the appropriate political strategy for those who wish to accomplish social change is not to tear down the establishment but rather to seek allies to form coalitions of various individuals and groups with some commonality of interest. These coalitions will represent an amassing of power that will be stronger than the power of those whose behavior we think is socially injurious. Thus, for example, a coalition was finally put together to force both safety and antipollution devices on the American automobile industry. It took a long time to put such a coalition together —indeed, much too long. Coalitions must be formed more rapidly if we are going to be able to cope with the critical problems that constantly arise in advanced industrial societies. The alternative to winning allies for one's cause is to impose it on the majority of one's fellow citizens whether they like it or not. Not only would this mean the end of political freedom, but it also might be extremely risky, because once we have begun to impose our will as a minority we run the risk that they may start counting noses and in full realization of our minority position, impose their will on us.

There was one thing clear in the summer and fall of 1972. Practitioners of the New Politics were as capable of misusing power as were the "corrupt bosses" whom they supposedly replaced. It did not, however, appear that they were substantially superior to the bosses in their capacity to use power intelligently. Indeed, a persuasive case could be made that as power brokers, the New Politicians were as inept as they were at everything else. Those who wish to rebuild the Democratic coalition can ill afford to be naïve about the position of power in American society. Neither can they afford the naïveté of raging against mythical dragons like "the establishment." There may well be certain concentrations of power in American society that the reconstructed Democratic coalition will want to break up, but it must first amass for itself a sufficient concentration of political power to be able to have a reasonable chance of winning an election and implementing its program. The builders of the new Democratic coalition must understand what their predecessors of 1972 apparently did not: One builds political power not by excluding people but by including them.

THE POLITICAL PARTIES

We Americans take our political party system for granted. Its confusions, complexities, and contradictions are almost as much a part of our lives as the air we breathe. It is a very instructive experience to try to explain the party system to an outsider, for by the standards of politics in almost any other country in the world—even in those few with two-party systems—American politics makes no sense at all.

The foreigner first asks if it is true there are no differences between the two American parties, as he has heard frequently both from his compatriots and visiting Americans. We respond that indeed their platforms are similar, but there are very substantial differences in the leadership of the two parties. It does matter whether you elect a Democrat or a Republican. In an intensive study of the attitudes of 1,788 Democratic and 1,232 Republican "leaders," three political scientists concluded that the parties were very different indeed.

Democratic leaders typically display the stronger urge to elevate the lowborn, the uneducated, the deprived minorities, and the poor in general; they are also more disposed to employ the nation's collective power to advance humanitarian and social welfare goals (e.g., social security, immigration, racial integration, a higher minimum wage, and public education). They are more critical of wealth and big business and more eager to bring them under regulation. Theirs is the greater faith in the wisdom of using legislation for redistributing the national product and for furnishing social services on a wide scale. Of the two groups of leaders, the Democrats are the more "progressively" oriented toward social reform and experimentation. The Republican leaders, while not uni-

formly differentiated from their opponents, subscribe in greater measure to the symbols and practices of individualism, laissez-faire, *and national independence. They prefer to overcome humanity's misfortunes by relying upon personal effort, private incentives, frugality, hard work, responsibility, self-denial (for both men and government), and the strengthening rather than diminution of the economic and status distinctions that are the "natural" rewards of the differences in human character and fortunes.*[1]

Even though this research is now more than ten years old, it is unlikely that things have changed very much since then. Some of the old issues have been replaced by new ones, perhaps; yet at least between the leaderships of the two parties differences persist.[2]

1 Herbert McClosky, Paul J. Hoffman, and Rosemary O'Hara, "Issue Conflict and Consensus among Party Leaders and Followers, in *American Politics,* eds. Stephen V. Monsma and Jack R. Van Der Slik (New York: Holt, Rinehart and Winston, 1970), p. 560.

2 Norman Nie has pointed out that with the increase in political participation since 1960 there has been an increase in the consistency of political viewpoints and suggests that the former has given rise to the latter. The rank and file is not of course as consistent as the ideologues but it is almost as consistent as the leadership was during the 1950s. At the present time the fascinating question is whether the decline of participation in the 1972 election (when large numbers did not vote) indicates a decline of political interest and a resulting lessening of political consistency. The Goldwater election of 1964 seems to have put a good deal more consistency into American politics than was there before. If the McGovern campaign of 1972 was an "ideological" campaign (one decided on issues) then we might expect the consistency level to be increased or maintained. If, on the other hand, it was a "personality" contest (which one was less unpopular) consistency may well have declined. We do not at this time (June 1973) have

"But then," our foreign visitor asks, "do the rank and file of the parties reflect these differences that exist between their leaders?" We have to answer, "Well, no." It happens that the three political scientists we mentioned before were unable to find anything more than moderate differences between the parties' rank and files on those issues that showed the greatest differences between the leaders. Being less involved with and less concerned about politics, the rank and files are frequently hard to distinguish from one another, particularly on questions which do not seem especially important at any given time. The party leaders seem to care about fundamental party differences and party followers do not, at least not nearly as much.

Our guest begins to think he understands. If there are no strong "ideological" correlates of party affiliation, then affiliation is not very important to people, and affiliation will not correlate with social-class position and can be readily shifted. To which we would have to reply that he's got it all wrong. Membership in parties is very important to Americans; it does correlate with social class, ethnicity, race, religion, and geographic region. It is acquired early in life and rarely changes. Then, concludes our visitor, there *are* ideological differences. One party is the one of the "haves," the other of the "have nots." We reply that neither party would accept such a definition and that, while Democrats tend to be more sympathetic to the underprivileged and Republicans to the privileged, the richest ethnic group in America (the Jews) are Democrats and some of the poorest

available the data to answer this question. Professor Nie is betting on the continuation of relatively high levels of consistency; I am betting on their decline.

(the mountain folk of West Virginia) are Republicans.

Our European visitor is sorry he raised the question, but he tries once more: "Obviously, those complicated, not to say confused, organizations must maintain tight organizational discipline if they are to survive for any length of time amidst such blatant contradictions." We must tell him he still doesn't have it right; that in fact American parties, as organizations, in a very real sense, don't exist at all. There are a number of inner-party structures that frequently compete among themselves and so lend little coherent structure in any national sense. There is first the national committee, which maintains a kind of housekeeping operation in Washington, then there are the congressional members of the party, who jealously watch the national committee. The state party leadership is very suspicious of anything that goes on in Washington. The local party organization, perhaps more efficiently organized than any of the other levels, is generally quite independent of those other levels and jealously guards its independence. There is the immediate audience, composed of those party followers who are deeply concerned about politics and who grant (it is hoped) the financial support that manifests their concern. Then there is the loyal voter who will vote for your candidate no matter who he is, the dubious voter who can be won away, and the swing voter whose behavior is quite unpredictable. Finally, for the party that controls the presidency there is also the presidential party. "Ah!" says the stranger, "He runs everything!" We say again, "Well, no. All he dominates is his own staff, his cabinet, and the national committee. The other party structures go on their merry way, though they are very careful to see that the president won't deprive them of any of their jealously guarded freedom."

"But American parties aren't really organizations at all!"

We congratulate him. He is beginning to understand the American political system.

"Then what are they?" our befuddled friend asks.

The only answer we can give him is that they are American political parties—a bit redundant perhaps, but there it is, and there is nothing quite like them anywhere else in the world.

In Germany, for example, a two-party system is beginning to emerge, but it still has much more in common with the multiparty ideological system of its past than with the coalitions peculiar to the American parties. (Indeed, Germany now is governed by a two-party coalition of Left and Right against the center.)

An American political party is an affiliation. It is something that Americans belong to with a greater or lesser degree of loyalty much as they belong to a religion. Indeed, a political party is something like a church and something like an ideology and something like an ethnic group. It is a map that guides one through the confusions of the bargaining, coalition-forming American political environment. Or to use the words of my colleague, Clifford Geertz, politics is a "culture system."

Man is an animal who survives by his ability to impose meaning on the world around him. Long ago in the evolutionary process, he left behind him the development of his instincts. Compared to other advanced animals, man has a rudimentary instinctual system. His fellow animals do not need to impose meaning on the phenomena of their lives because their instincts provide them with maps or "templates" with which appropriate behavior is determined. Lacking instincts, man must rely on culture; that is to say, on the explanations he can derive from and the meanings he can impose on the world around him. A man without culture, without a series of meaning systems, would not be a very high-level animal. He would be a pathetic creature without instincts who could not survive for very long.

There are many different kinds of meaning systems that constitute the culture man learns from his society: religion, ideology, common sense, science, art. Geertz describes in great detail two of these meaning systems—religion and ideology—and in the process develops more limited descriptions of science and common sense. Religion provides man with responses to the ultimate questions that could confuse him (the problems of final meaning of ultimate morality). It assures him of the fundamental interpretability of the universe; it enables him to deal with the unjust, the unexpected, the tragic, and, of course, the ultimate tragedy, death.

While every man must have to some extent a series of answers to the fundamental religious questions, ideology is less universal. It is required only in a society that has grown sufficiently complicated to be beset by serious social and political confusion. Ideology offers an explanation for the confusion, frequently a scapegoat to blame for it, and a plan to undo the confusion. Ideology, as Anthony Downs has said, is a vision of the good society together with a program for attaining it.

American political parties are not religions in the sense that they provide answers to the ultimate questions; nor are they ideologies in the sense that communism or socialism or monarchism are in European politics. The American political parties are not concerned with the fundamental restructuring of American society, as are the European ideological parties—at least in theory. But in common with ideology, the American political party does provide the means whereby system and order can be imposed by the participant on the world of political behavior. However, it is a world of political behavior that is not marked exclusively by class conflict; it is marked rather by the bargaining and coalition formation so characteristic of the American scene.[3]

The American political party, then, provides the citizens of this country with a perspective with which he can view political activity and impose some kind of order on the multifarious phenomena occurring in the political arena. There is some initial motivation to "join" a party for social and economic reasons (lower-income people are more likely to become Democrats). It is much more likely for the positions of Americans on specific issues to be shaped by the party they belong to rather than by an individual's stand on an issue determining party membership. Parties form attitudes rather more than attitudes form parties.

The political party is a super-coalition, composed of a wide variety of national, state, and local coalitions. The coalition is comprised of voluntary associations (such as trade unions), interest groups (civil rights organizations), strictly political groups (Cook

[3] I would like to distinguish between Sidney Verba's "civic culture," which I discussed in Chapter 3, and Geertz's "culture system." In the former, the context is the individual's habits and patterns of political activity within the polity and his attitudes toward it. In the latter, the context is the individual's activity and attitudes toward the development of systems (a political party is but one) as a response to the human strain for coherence and meaning within his culture. Important to Geertz's concept is the primordial human need for affiliation, to "belong."

County Democratic party), and major proportions of population groups (blacks, Catholics, or Jews). These coalitions came into being in the rather distant past (1860, 1893, 1932) because of decisive historic events. They have a long-term strain toward consistency despite temporary modifications under the impact of other historical events, which shake the political system to its base and may result in the formation of new coalitions or the shifting of old ones within the larger structures.

The shape of the two American coalitions has been fashioned by four critical events of the last century: the Civil War, the Panic of 1893, the immigration of the Catholic ethnic groups between 1860 and 1920, and the Great Depression. These coalitions persist for long periods of time, because altering them produces a severe trauma for individuals and society. If your political affiliation is a meaning system, you are strongly disinclined to give it up; it means having to cope with chaos within yourself and in the social order while proceeding to form a new interpretive scheme to make sense out of political behavior. As Peter Berger puts it:

> *"The meaninglessness" of so much of social life, currently decried as the source of so-called "alienation," is in fact a necessary condition for both individual and collective sanity. The currently fashionable left ideal of full participation in the sense that everybody will participate in every decision affecting his life, would, if realized, constitute a nightmare comparable to unending sleeplessness. Fortunately, it is anthropologically unrealizable, though the endless "discussion" that goes on in radical groups gives a certain approximation of the horror that its realization would sig-*

nify. It is one of the mercies of human nature that, finally, all participants and all discussants must fall asleep.[4]

When a great social trauma occurs that forces us out of our lifelong political affiliation, we are filled with anxiety. Political affiliation tells us who our allies are, which coalition colleagues we can normally count on. If political life becomes nothing more than an endless series of ad hoc coalitions put together on specific issues, we can only stand by anxiously to watch the dissolution of the political process.

So it is possible, then, to think of American political parties as maps that enable us to traverse the wilderness of bargaining-coalition with some confidence. Or to put it another way, a political party is a diagram of the principal coalitions that exist in our coalition obsessed society.

The American political party is not without a social class or ideological basis. Poor people are more likely to be Democrats. Democrats are more likely to be in favor of social change than Republicans, though there are liberal Republicans and conservative Democrats as well as rich Democrats and poor Republicans. But more important, the party functions as a scheme for coalition, made necessary by the fact that the United States was a coalition society even before it became a nation, certainly before political parties were born.

Why are there only two parties? The best answer is that no one knows for sure. Observers are even less sure why there continues to be a relatively even balance between the two parties. Professor V. O. Key, Jr. lists a number of possible explanations in a 1964

[4] Peter L. Berger, "Sociology and Freedom," *The American Sociologist* 6, no. 1 (February 1971): 4.

article.[5] Human institutions have a strong tendency to preserve their initial form. It may well be that the two-party division is the result of "two major conflicts of interest in the country" when the Constitution was being fashioned—the agricultural interests and the mercantile and financial interests—with the Democrats tending to represent the former and the Federalists the latter. The Democratic party has persisted since the beginning and has, more or less, consistently been against the "mercantile and financial" interest while the Federalists and their successors, the Whigs and then Republicans, have traditionally been more in sympathy with the shopkeepers, the merchants, and the businessmen. When the Catholic immigrants arrived on the scene, they gravitated toward the Democratic party (as did the Jewish immigrants later on), apparently because it seemed to be the party of the "underdog." The Civil War brought about a fundamental realignment in national politics. The South became Democratic and the North Republican. The Populist movement, culminating with the William Jennings Bryan campaign of 1896, moved the West more firmly into the Democratic camp while the East remained Republican. Finally, the Great Depression of the thirties assured the Democrats of the long-term loyalty of blacks, industrial workers, and intellectuals and the sympathy of many of the less advantaged farm groups. This outline is a very simplified version of the history of American political parties, but it does demonstrate the feasibility of the position of those who suggest that the fundamental cleavage between the two parties existed *before* the writing of the Constitution.

[5] V. O. Key, Jr., "The Two Party Pattern," in *American Politics,* eds. Monsma and Van Der Slik, pp. 504–9.

In addition, it is argued that single-member congressional districts (as opposed to proportional representation) and the winner-take-all nature of the presidency have also reinforced the existence of the two-party system.

Finally, the fact that the American political experiment began after a revolution, during which whatever existed of the European social structure of aristocracy and privilege was swept away, meant that American society would not be rent by the battles between the old regime and the new, which have been so prevalent in Europe in the last two hundred years. As Professor Key says:

> *Given this tendency for most people to cluster fairly closely together in their attitudes, a dual division becomes possible on the issue of just how conservative or how liberal we are at the moment. Extremists exist, to be sure, who stand far removed from the central mode of opinion, but they never seem to be numerous enough or intransigent enough to form the bases for durable minor parties.*[6]

Even in the 1968 election, in which the voices of the far right and the far left were louder than in many previous elections, George Wallace was only able to garner 12 percent of the votes in the country and 6 percent of the votes outside the South. According to the University of Michigan Election Survey, those who opposed the war in Vietnam and supported the tactics of radical movement war protest constituted no more than 3 percent of the population. In other words, even in 1968, some 85 percent of the American public was agreed on the fundamental na-

[6] V. O. Key, Jr., "The Two Party Pattern," in *American Politics*, eds. Monsma and Van Der Slik, p. 508.

ture of the political system. Under such circumstances, then, there is no reason for more than two political parties.

In addition, party structures provide the arena for much coalition formation. The bargaining among the various groups in voluntary organizations occurs *inside* the context of the party. In a nation like France, coalition formation takes place across party lines, while in the United States coalitions are formed within the party structures. Professor Arthur Stinchcombe has observed that this is likely to enhance support for the coalition's program. In France, one party is likely to be only moderately enthusiastic about the goals of its coalition partners; but in the United States, support for the positions of one's colleagues is likely to be stronger simply because they are colleagues who may support your goals later.

Finally, it must be emphasized that American political parties are "educational" institutions, at least in the broad sense of the word. The complex division of labor worked out between leaders and followers in the party is such that the leaders are expected to be well-informed on political issues, they are to make the deals, arrangements, bargains, and compromises required for coalitions; then they are expected to communicate to their followers the results of such arrangements so that they know what stands to take on issues and which candidates are best suited for their goals. It is as though the rank and file say to the elite, "We know that you are more interested in and more sophisticated about political and social issues. We also know you have more skills in coalition formation, and we are very well aware that you know more about possible candidates than we do. Therefore, we commission you to make decisions about issues, form coalitions, and choose leaders. But we, too, are interested in politics, so you better keep us informed. You had better not try to deceive us, because we may desert you for the other party."

In other words, the party system allows for some people to be maximally involved, others moderately involved, and for some to be minimally involved. It is an arrangement that does not yield absolute power to party elites precisely because considerable numbers of the rank and file are moderately interested in and moderately well-informed about politics. Also, they are rather skeptical about how far they should trust the leadership, at least in part because of a long-standing distrust in American life of the professional, full-time politician.

There are, one supposes, many things wrong with this political arrangement. Periodically scholars, radicals, revolutionaries, and other social critics arrive on the scene to denounce the two-party system, to call for ideologically consistent parties, to attempt to form third parties, and to deplore the apathy, laziness, and ineffectiveness of the typical American voter. One could argue with such critics that compared to the political systems of many other democratic societies, the American one works moderately well. Indeed, it works far better than it ought to considering the diverse and conflicting social forces in our country. And more than four-fifths of the American public seem quite content with the system as it is. The reformer either adjusts to the two-party system and learns to work within it or resigns himself to perennial defeat. It does seem sometimes that perennial defeat is just what the radical critic most desires. For him, maintaining moral purity is more important than winning. This is indeed a legitimate enough stand, but it ought to be clear that those who hold it are not really interested in accomplishing any notable change in American society.

To say that the American party system works moderately well is not to say that it is without fault. Some partners in the super coalitions have far more power than they should and others have much less. Furthermore, there are some groups in the society (one thinks of the old, for example) who have almost no representation in either coalition. Also, a division of labor between party elite and rank and file voters assumes that the leadership will take its educational role seriously and not merely tender to the biases and the ignorance of its followers. All too frequently party leaders are more interested in responding to pressure than in educating their rank and file. While there are limits to the amount of education the leadership can effect, it does not seem too harsh a judgment to observe that the educational function of party elites was not well exercised in the 1960s. Indeed, once they had assumed national power, some party elites not only did not educate, they also did not speak the truth. The American voter is profoundly skeptical about the honesty of his political leaders. (On the subject of the Vietnam war, skepticism turned out to be more than amply justified. Indeed, only in their most paranoid moments would Americans be prepared to believe that they were deceived as completely and as systematically as they were.) If the party system in the United States is going to continue to work in years to come, there simply will be no substitute for leaders who are willing to take on the educational responsibility of the party even and especially when it means telling the truth.

Because the liberal wing of the Democratic coalition is relatively small, it does not follow that it is unimportant. For it includes some of the most intelligent and dedicated—and also some of the wealthiest—members of the party. It is to the liberal intellectual and its youthful adjunct that the party must look for its ideas, its vision, its sense of morality, and its capacity for concerned social criticism. Under no circumstances could the Democratic party do without its liberal wing. But neither can the liberal wing do without the rest of the party—not at least if it hopes to implement its goals. Since 1930, incidentally, the liberal intellectual Democrats have been remarkably successful in selling large parts of their program to the rest of the coalition. Some of the liberal Democrats seem now to have despaired about selling anything more to their coalition partners. The data to be advanced in a later chapter indicate that this despair is unjustified. However difficult it may be for them to restrain their impatience with their less sophisticated colleagues, they simply cannot hope to force their programs down the throats of their partners. Many liberal Democrats are angry, impatient, and frustrated with what's wrong with the United States today, and they have every reason to be so, but it will be counterproductive if they allow a restless dissatisfaction to seduce them into arrogant disdain for their more slow-moving and less troubled coalition partners. The big city, trade union, and ethnic Democratic partners also need the intellectual liberals, but the need is mutual. That the partners would quarrel among themselves in a troubled and confused time is understandable, but if a quarrel leads them to tear the coalition apart, then no one will benefit. The burden of seeing things not only from their own perspective but also from the perspective of their coalition partners falls most heavily on the liberal Democrats.

But then that is what being a liberal should be all about.

How does one choose a party? A considerable amount of scholarly ink has been spilled on this question, and there are no absolutely satisfactory answers; but it does appear that childhood and early adulthood are the critical times. One is born into a political party in the United States much as one is born into a religion. There is a strong strain toward preserving the political tradition of one's parents.

The second important phase is young adulthood. If the political events that affect a nation are relatively serene, one is not likely to stray far from the parental orientation as one approaches voting age. If there are troubled or cataclysmic events during young adulthood, there is a strong possibility of political change. Part of the Roosevelt realignment was the fact that those who came to voting age in the 1930s were made Democrats by the force of events despite their inheritance. American blacks especially, but also substantial segments of the farm and white Protestant industrial working-class populations, left the Republican party of their parents behind. The New Deal won older converts too, of course, but its greatest gain came among those who reached political adulthood in the midst of the Great Depression.

After the young adulthood phase we apparently become fairly fixed in our political ways and tend to maintain the political alliance of our youth for the rest of our lives. Thus, as Philip Converse and his colleagues have pointed out, third parties, when they do appear on the scene, are especially likely to be successful among the young, because they are in the political decision-making stage. They are also the most likely to be resentful of the structures imposed upon them by their predecessors. A political loss of faith may be just as much a part of growing up as a religious loss of faith. Thus we ought not to be surprised that George Wallace's third party received considerable support from young people. The principal beneficiary of youthful restlessness, as shown in the recent polls, is not the New Left but the New Right. In 1968, outside the South, Wallace polled 6 percent of the white vote, 3 percent of which was over seventy years old and 13 percent under thirty. Wallace, like any third party candidate, found his greatest success among those who are at a politically volatile stage of life. Most of the Wallace vote, of course, came from the noncollege youth (although a slight majority of the college youth, contrary to popular myth, supported Richard Nixon in 1968, as apparently did the freshmen and sophomores in 1972).

The great realignments are found in either economic or political disaster. Moderate, long-range gains and losses of the party are caused more than anything else by changes in political affiliation during young adult years. Given the fact that the 1960s were turbulent rather than cataclysmic, we could expect not a major realignment but a substantial shift in patterns of party affiliation, as some young adults broke with those political traditions into which they were born. To some extent this has happened. As we noted in a previous chapter, many more young people are apt to describe themselves as "independent," which represents a drift away from the Democrats. However, it does not yet represent a drift toward the Republicans, largely, one suspects, because the Republicans have not been able to provide any sort of decent alternative for the dissatisfied young adult—be he of Wallace ilk or the New

Left. Roosevelt won over many young adults because he did have an alternative. Richard Nixon has not been able to persuade the young malcontents that he has. Realignment, then, does not seem likely now in the absence of either cataclysm or alternatives.[7]

Political affiliation, then, provides an interpretive scheme and a road map through a coalition-forming society. The party is a structure for forming coalitions and constructed in such a way that a division

[7] Realignment is a subject of great fascination to both political scientists and journalists. To the former, because it is absolutely the most exciting phenomenon in their business, and to the latter, because change is news and continuity is not. Hence both groups are prone to proclaim the existence of realignment on very slender evidence. During 1970, one political scientist (and a rather distinguished one at that) kept insisting to me that not only was there to be a realignment but that one had actually already occurred. Of course, the 1970 congressional election showed that it had not. If there is a realignment at all in the works in American society, it is one that most political scientists and journalists would not like—a realignment in which the Republicans become the majority party. The kind of realignment which most journalists and political scientists seem to think desirable is the emergence of an ideologically pure Democratic party.

The only major realignment that has occurred in presidential elections of the last twenty years—according to the work of my colleagues, David Greenstone and Norman Nie—is the shift of New England toward becoming permanently Democratic and the South toward becoming permanently Republican. These shifts tend to balance each other, so that a national realignment for presidential elections will only come about if the Democratic party insists on throwing elections away, as it did in 1972. Such a realignment would be curious indeed, for the Democrats would continue to be the majority party in state and congressional elections while becoming the minority party for national elections.

Political scientists and journalists will continue to announce impending realignments. Professional politicians would be well advised to be skeptical.

of labor between leaders and followers exists in which an economy of political effort is made possible. There is a strong tendency to maintain the political affiliation of one's parents, although the events of early adulthood may shake that affiliation and on occasion drastically modify it. The system seems monstrously illogical to an outsider, but most Americans are basically satisfied with it. He who wants to change society must accept this satisfaction and work within the context of the two-party system—at least most of the time.

There are three possible reasons for forming a third party:

(1) To replace one of the existing two parties. It is sobering to realize that this has happened only once. The Republicans did it during those hellish days leading to the bloody and costly Civil War.

(2) To bring pressure to bear on one or the other party in the existing system in an attempt to persuade it to modify a stand or to give a greater share to the third party adherents in shaping policy. Most third parties of the twentieth century have been of this variety. Surely the Progressive party of Theodore Roosevelt and, perhaps to a lesser extent, the party of the La Follettes were not seriously intended to replace the Republicans or the Democratic parties permanently. Similarly, one cannot imagine that George Wallace really expected to be president of the United States in 1968, and most of his supporters didn't think he could be elected either. But the Wallace candidacy and the support for it did bring serious pressure to bear on the other two parties. The Dixiecrat party of 1948 was nothing more than a serious attempt on the part of the South to reassert its power in the councils of the Democratic coalition. Furthermore, the so-called Conservative and Liberal

parties in New York for all practical purposes attempt to limit the power of their respective coalition partners—the one, of the progressive upper-class Republicans like Nelson Rockefeller and Jacob Javits, and the other, Tammany Hall and the Irish and Italian Democrats. The only third party that may have taken itself seriously was the Henry Wallace Progressive party of 1948. It apparently had an authentic mystical belief that it could become a major force on the American political scene.

(3) A third reason for founding another party is to establish an organizational base for the dissemination of a certain ideology. At two extremes were the Socialist party of Norman Thomas and the post World War II American Nazi party. These parties speak with the consistency of the ideologically pure. They speak to the moral conscience of the public (for good or ill), and may sometimes be the voice of the future, as was the program for social reform and justice so eloquently articulated by Norman Thomas when so much of it became law with the New Deal and the Fair Deal. One might establish an independent political party with the very realistic hope that if one gains any popular support, over the long run the party's ideas, if not the organization, will be absorbed by one of the other major parties.

The most unstable element in the Democratic coalition at the present time is the "ethnic" element, or, to put the matter more bluntly, the Catholic component. If the Democratic coalition, which has governed the nation for most of the last four decades and has presided over all the social reforms of that time, is to remain in political power for the rest of the century, it cannot afford to lose its ethnic members. If, on the other hand, the Republican coalition is going to become a permanent majority, it will have to win over the Catholic ethnics. And Kevin Phillips's "emerging Republican majority," to the contrary notwithstanding, this is not going to be an automatic process, and it will also not be accomplished by simplistic appeals to law and order or the race issue. The Democrats can afford to lose both the South and the intellectual counterculture group and still dominate American politics. The Republicans can pick up the South and still be a permanent minority party. Finally, whichever party is able to gain the support of the Catholic ethnic voter is also likely to win along with it the allegiance of the other sectors of middle American life.

Some enthusiastic McGovern supporters wrote off the Catholic defection of 1972 as the result of Nixon's romancing of Cardinal Krol, his promise of support for parochial schools, and his opposition to abortion. Such an explanation is characteristic of the New Politician's refusal to assume any responsibility for its own blunders. Cardinal Krol does not deliver very many precincts, if any. There is substantial evidence that Catholic attitudes on abortion are indistinguishable from Protestant attitudes. And while Catholics are concerned about support for their schools, there is absolutely no reason to think that this is now or ever has been a salient issue for Catholics in a presidential election. The Catholic defection from the Democratic party was a phenomenon that happened to Catholics—but not because they were Catholics. The Catholic voters were part of that middle American segment of the population that the New Politics deemed unessential for the new coalition they were putting together. Catholics were simply not part of that new constituency. They departed from the Democratic party in the 1972 presidential election for exactly the same reason that large numbers of other Democratics departed: there wasn't any room for them in the Democratic party of George McGovern and his supporters. It is still worth noting, however, that Catholics were substantially more likely to vote for McGovern than Protestants were. Approximately 48 percent of the Catholics in the country did vote for the senator from South Dakota. The one state he won has the second highest proportion of Catholics in the country, and the state he came close to winning (Rhode Island) is almost two-thirds Catholic. To put the matter differently, if the country were solidly Catholic, McGovern would have lost by only four percentage points.

The Republican party has not permanently captured the Catholic voter, but in another election like 1972, they might. Were that to occur, there would in fact be a new political realignment of the sort that happened in 1932. However, if the Democrats can reinforce the traditional loyalties of the Catholic ethnics in their party, the tradition begun with Franklin D. Roosevelt, a liberal Democratic national majority will continue.

Catholics gravitated to the Democratic party when they first arrived on American shores because the "mercantile" party, whether Whig, antislavery, or Republican, was more representative of the Protestant business "establishment," which would have been just as happy to see the immigrants go back to Europe. The Republican party's close identification with the militantly Protestant and the frequently anti-Catholic abolition movement plus the Rum, Romanism, and Rebellion campaign of James Blaine did little to persuade the majority of Catholics that the Republican party ought to be considered their friend. On the other hand, at least twice between the

Civil War and 1932, the Democrats made major mistakes in dealing with the Catholic partners of their coalition. The fiery, evangelistic style of William Jennings Bryan must have turned off the Catholic voters, though we lack the kind of precise data to analyze the precise nature of the resistance to Bryan. Woodrow Wilson seemed to have a positive genius for offending Catholics. His policy in Mexico, his statements about the inferiority of Italians, his lack of support for the Irish Republic, and his failure to protect Germany from the ruination of Versailles guaranteed that by 1920, Italian, German, and Irish Catholics would be firmly in the Republican camp. One wonders whether if Wilson might have modified his policies somewhat, the fate of the League of Nations would have been quite different. In any case, it was not until 1928 in the Al Smith campaign that the majority of Catholics were once again voting Democratic. The Catholic majority has persistently remained Democratic from 1928 through 1970. Only in 1956, did a majority of Catholics vote for Eisenhower. Even in 1968 Catholics were more likely to vote for Humphrey than for Nixon. The myth of the Catholic trade union vote going to Wallace was demonstrably false, no matter how many liberals are convinced of its truth.

While Franklin Roosevelt was certainly the architect who put the finishing touches on the Democratic coalition that has ruled the country for the last four decades, it should not be thought that there were no social trends in the United States before 1932 that contributed to the development of the coalition. The massive immigration between 1880 and 1920 was perhaps the most important of these trends, and the worried WASPS on the Dillingham Commission who were afraid that the immigrants would take political power away from them were quite correct in their fears. It took several decades for the ethnics to become naturalized citizens and then to form political blocs that gave them power in the polling places and the halls of government. John M. Allswang describes in massive and scholarly detail precisely how the ethnic political power in Chicago coalesced to make the city a permanent Democratic bastion.[8] But 1892 was the last year until 1928 that Chicago cast the majority of its votes for a Democratic presidential candidate. The city itself was bipartisan, first under Democratic and then under Republican control. During the 1920s, especially under the leadership of Anton Cermak, a Czech politican adept at knocking Irish heads together, ethnic political power coalesced. By 1932, it had become an important, indeed massive, building block for Franklin Roosevelt's coalition. (Paradoxically, Cermak was at first hesitant to support Roosevelt and then died in what may have been an attempt to assassinate the president-elect before his inaugural.)

There are a number of factors at work in creating this ethnic power base in Chicago. It had been building up in the early part of the century and had reached something of a height in 1918, to be dashed by the disastrous election of 1920 in which the ethnics finally broke with everything Woodrow Wilson stood for. But during the 1920s the Democratic party identified itself vigorously with the antiprohibition issue and then, in 1928, with the Catholic issue by nominating Al Smith. As a matter of fact, Chicago ethnics were somewhat more likely to vote for Smith than they were for Franklin Roosevelt. Furthermore, Cermak, who may have been the greatest ethnic po-

[8] John M. Allswang, *A House for All Peoples: Ethnic Politics in Chicago, 1890–1936* (City Press of Kentucky, 1971).

litical leader of them all (at least before Richard Daley), replaced the various Irish factions (which were more concerned with fighting each other and maintaining their own power than in making the most of the opportunities of a multiethnic organization) with a strong and well-organized ethnic coalition. After Cermak died, a new generation of Irish political leaders willingly took over the coalition and preserved it, managing even to forget the fact that it took a Czech to organize it for them.

In other words, after they had become naturalized Americans, there was still a period of "settling down" before many of the ethnic groups in Chicago definitively committed their allegiance to the Democratic party. Even before the Great Depression, however, the prohibition issue and the Al Smith nomination and the organizational genius of Anton Cermak were moving the ethnics toward a permanent Democratic affiliation. Roosevelt and the New Deal consolidated what was already in process.[9] Allswang suggests that something like the Chicago process may also have gone on in other cities with large ethnic populations, and that the Smith-Hoover election was a realigning election in many local areas that permanently and definitively won the Catholic ethnic groups for the Democratic party. Allswang's careful research would indicate that political realignment, when it happens, is not an instantaneous event caused simply by the importance of major political

[9] Curiously enough, the Czech community, which was Cermak's power base, has now for the most part moved out of Chicago. The Czechs are no longer an important factor in Chicago politics, although Cermak's son-in-law would later become Governor of Illinois and give his name to the famous *Kerner Report*. Whatever the other faults of the Irish political leadership in Chicago may be, they are at least capable of gratitude.

issues; it is something for which there are preparations, perhaps over a long period of time, at the political grass roots.

Particularly fascinating is the importance of the prohibition issue. Tony Cermak rode to political power in Chicago in part by being a vigorous "wet." [10] Prohibition has been dead for so long that we have forgotten the deep resentment of the ethnics over this attempt of the WASP elite to impose its morality on them.

Nevertheless, the time has passed when the Democrats can automatically count on majority Catholic support. There are two reasons for this:

1. The American Catholic population has finally "made it" in American society. While this is extremely difficult for many of the intelligentsia to realize, Catholic ethnics are no longer exclusively working class or lower middle class. Catholic young people are now more likely to go to college than Protestant young people. They are also more likely to go on to graduate school. While the image of the hard-hat Catholic enjoys a great deal of popularity, it is at variance with statistical fact that Catholics under forty are as successful socially and economically and occupationally as are Protestants, when one standardizes for city-size region of the country. Thus Catholics are increasingly caught in political cross-pressures. Their social class inclines them to the Republican party while their religious and ethnic background inclines them to the Democrats. However, it is difficult to sort out the two trends, especially since the departure of many Catholics to vote

[10] He also opposed the identification of Republican Mayor William Hale Thompson with the Capone syndicate. It is a fact of Chicago political history that rarely makes the national media that Capone's affiliations were Republican, not Democratic.

for Eisenhower and their return for Kennedy makes it difficult to assess the short-range and long-range trends at work in the fifties and sixties. As far as congressional elections are concerned, in most parts of the country the Catholic population is still on the Democratic side. Further research will be necessary to determine how much erosion has occurred and how much more is likely to occur from the Democratic base as a result of continued Catholic upward mobility. In any event, political cross-pressures generated by that upward mobility put into question the long-range commitment of many Catholics to the Democratic coalition.

2. While the Catholic upper middle-class is becoming suburban-professional, those Catholics who remain in the lower middle and working class find themselves hard-pressed by the new black militancy. They are apparently angered by what they consider to be the lack of concern about their problems on the part of governmental and social elites.

The Wallace campaign of 1968 tapped what might be considered to be the beginning of a neopopulist movement. While there was unquestionably an out and out racist component in the Wallace support, it may well be that some of the Wallace vote represented dissatisfaction with the perceived incompetence and inefficiency of big government and the lack of concern of big government for the "ordinary man." If, as is not unlikely, neither major party is able to respond to the inarticulate yearnings of the neopopulist revival, then nothing much will happen in American politics, and the instability that characterized the electorate in 1968 and 1972 will persist. In a later chapter I shall pursue the implications of this neopopulism and make some suggestions as to what an appropriate strategy for dealing with it might be.

It does not follow that the Democratic party is going to lose a substantial segment of its support to the conservative Republicans. Quite the contrary, the victory of James Buckley in New York in 1970 was something of a fluke; Democratic leadership around the country is not as suicidal as the Democratic leadership in New York. But the principal reason that Catholics will maintain their allegiance to the Democratic party is that the Republicans have thus far not been successful in providing any sort of alternative. While the Democrats *probably* won't lose very many Catholic supporters, they will not be able to count on Catholic votes in elections or Catholic support for policies with the same confidence such voter support was expected in the past.

Some Democratic leaders think they have a surefire way of recapturing Catholic defectors in 1976. If Senator Edward Kennedy is nominated, they argue, Catholics will flock back to the Democratic standard. Such a notion is as offensive to Catholics as is the idea that Cardinal Krol can deliver their votes or that parochial schools are the decisive issue for them in choosing whom to support in a presidential election. I am an incorrigible Cameloteer, but Senator Kennedy does have the Chappaquiddick problem, which may be more serious to Catholics than to others. However, the real problem for Kennedy with the Catholic voters is to persuade them (and not merely them—all the good Democrats who voted for Richard Nixon) that he is not a captive of the liberal left faction of the party like McGovern was. A Massachusetts senator can afford to be closely aligned with such a faction. Indeed, in Massachusetts a politician would have little choice. But a national Democratic candidate has to display more willingness to question the ideological rhetoric of the liberal left than Senator Kennedy has displayed in recent years. My own personal hunch is that it would be most unlikely for a Kennedy really to be a captive of any political faction, and should the senator choose to seek the presidency (and there are many understandable reasons why he should decide not to), he will emerge quickly as a national rather than a factional candidate. Nevertheless, it must be insisted that at this time, he still has the challenge of persuading the middle American majority that he will not only preach to them but that he will also understand them.

Periodically someone appears on the scene to announce that the American two-party structure as it presently exists is obsolete, that it must be replaced by ideologically consistent parties that would align all the "liberals" on the one hand against all the "conservatives" on the other. Of course the expert will determine who is liberal and who is conservative. Unfortunately American political leaders and American voters persist in ignoring the advice of such wise men. Furthermore, if the analysis of this book is correct, the tightly disciplined, ideologically oriented party may respond to the needs of certain kinds of intellectuals, but whether it responds to the needs of a complex, variegated, bargaining, coalition-forming society remains to be seen.

There is one other thing that must be said about the ideologically pure party. Outside of New York City, Massachusetts, a few congressional districts scattered around the country (particularly in the San Francisco Bay area), and some wards in Chicago, it could not elect a junior assistant dogcatcher.

Which brings us to the subject of realignment and new coalitions. On the Republican side realignment means that a combination of the "Southern strategy" and an appeal to Catholic ethnics on the race and law and order issues is supposed to guarantee a permanent Republican majority. On the liberal Democratic side, however, realignment and new coalitions take on a somewhat more mystical quality—a mysticism only possible among those who can't count. The new coalition, we were told in 1972, was made up of the young (by which was meant the counterculture and elite college young, who are a small minority even among college-educated youth), the intellectuals (of whom there are fewer than there are Teamsters), the blacks, the poor, and a curious group called "the suburban professional class." Frequently it was also said that the "working class" will also be part of this new coalition, though how this working class differed from the labor unions seemed to be a matter of some doubt; apparently, it meant the union members without their leadership.

Two things are immediately obvious about this so-called coalition. First, no matter how you count the votes, there aren't enough to win a national election. Second, it is substantially the same old Democratic coalition without the Catholic ethnic and the trade union membership (frequently the same thing). The blacks, the poor, the intelligentsia are already a part of the coalition. The overwhelming majority of well-to-do professionals are Republican, and those suburban professionals who are most likely to be Democrats are the Jewish and Catholic groups who have migrated to the suburbs and the upper middle class in the last two decades. While the suburban professional class may bring considerable numbers of votes to the Democratic camp in the counties around New York, they have been substantially less likely to do so in the other suburban areas of the country. How is the suburban professional class, say, in Cook and DuPage Counties in Illinois going to be recruited into the new Democratic party, and who will recruit them? The most likely suburban support for the Democrats is to be found precisely in the suburban segment of the Catholic ethnic population, which, by definition, has been thrown out of the coalition. In other words, the Democratic party was urged to give up the trade union and Catholic ethnic support in exchange for the miniscule youth vote and the highly dubious suburban professional class. It did not look like a particularly good bargain then, and after the McGovern disaster it looks even worse.

It is necessary, at this point, to ask a very delicate question: To what extent is there a latent and perhaps even not altogether conscious anti-Catholicism in some segments of the liberal left faction of the Democratic party? Many of my university colleagues are horrified at this thought and think that I am paranoid for even suggesting it. On the other hand, Adam Walinsky, a member of Robert Kennedy's academic entourage—who ought to know the liberal left wing of the Democratic party as well as anyone—was quite blunt in his charge, in an article in *The New Republic* on aid to parochial schools, that a virulent (though sophisticated) form of anti-Catholicism does indeed infect some segments of the liberal left. Through my own experience I have gained the same impression. I am not suggesting that the majority or even a large minority of left wing Democrats are semiconscious anti-Catholics, but I am suggesting that anti-Catholicism is by no means absent in the left wing Democratic circles. Indeed, the almost total silence of liberal left Democrats about the exclusion of Catholics from the list of "approved" minorities (and particularly eastern and southern European Catholics) ought to raise serious questions for self-examination among Democratic liberals. Any reconstruction of the Democratic coalition in which such self-examination does not occur is likely to be of uncertain strength and durability.

There is no such thing as a new coalition. It is either the old New Deal coalition (with or without the South), refurbished and reenergized, or it is a permanent minority coalition. Only someone who cannot add would think that a liberal coalition that excludes the Catholic and trade union voters who have loyally supported it for forty years has any chance of winning a national election. The real coalition is the same as it always has been, and the liberal elites in the Democratic party are going to have to live with unions and Catholic ethnics or resign themselves to being out of power for a long time to come.

Liberals, of course, need not and should not think that their trade union and ethnic partners are right in everything they do. It is not necessary to romanticize them as a class. One has only to live and work in an ethnic community to know that there is nothing very romantic or very splendid about them. The ethnics, like everybody else, are frail, limited, narrow, and sometimes very obtuse human beings. I shall attempt to demonstrate in a later chapter that they are no more prejudiced (and perhaps less so) than other Americans, but there is still a good deal of prejudice, fear, and sluggishness among working-class and middle-class ethnic Democrats. The liberal wing of the Democratic party need not "sell out" to their ethnic partners. But they will have to try to understand them, bargain with them, lead them—and sympathize with them and maybe even learn from them. The alternative is the permanent presence of a registered Republican in the White House.

A number of writers [11] have argued that America's two-party system is "decomposing," falling apart under the strains of the 1960s. The principal evidence they cite is the increase in the number of voters who describe themselves as "independents." However, Everett Carll Ladd and his colleagues [12] have analyzed data from both Gallup and the University of Michigan election studies for the last several decades and call into question the decomposition theory.

In 1946, 24 percent of the American electorate described itself as "independent" to the Gallup interviewers. Between 1950 and 1968 this percentage rose to 30. In the Michigan study, the percentage was 23 in 1952 and 28 in 1968. A change has certainly occurred, but it is a relatively small change; and even in 1968, seven out of ten Americans affiliated themselves with one party or the other.

Furthermore, the gains among the independents have been heavily concentrated among those under thirty. In 1968, 40 percent of those under thirty described themselves as independent as opposed to 32 percent in 1964 and 24 percent in 1960. If the independence of those who were under thirty in 1968 persists, and if succeeding age cohorts follow in the footsteps of those who are under thirty at the present, the independents will be more than half again

[11] See Walter Dean Burnan, *Critical Elections in the Mainsprings of American Politics* (New York: W. W. Norton, 1970); and Frederick G. Dutton, *Changing Sources of Power: American Politics in the 1970s* (New York: McGraw-Hill, 1971).

[12] Everett Carll Ladd, Charles Hadley, and Lauriston King, "A New Political Realignment?" *The Public Interest* (Spring 1971), p. 46.

as large as they were in 1946. But America will still be a country in which six out of ten adults describe themselves as affiliated with one or the other major party.

And there is some reason to assume that this will not happen. For as Ladd and his colleagues point out, in 1948, 27 percent of people under thirty described themselves as independent. In 1951, during the political unrest over the Korean War, that proportion rose to 35 percent, and by 1956, the percentage had fallen back to 24. As Ladd and his associates note:

> *The proportion of independents among young voters has been substantially higher than for the electorate as a whole, reflecting a lack of time to form strong party loyalties and a generally lower level of political involvement. And some of the big increase in the late 1960s can be traced directly to the intense dissatisfaction of many Americans, especially the young, with the positions on the Viet Nam war of leaders in both parties. This contributed significantly to a short-term deauthorization of party leadership. The Korean War did not produce nearly the same domestic storm, but there was still a significant short-term increase in independents.*[13]

As in so many cases, those who announce that a major social shift is occurring have a point. No one can think seriously about American politics in the 1970s without facing the fact that particularly among the young there has been a decline in party affiliation. But it is still true that most young people have party affiliation. In fact, 60 percent of those under

[13] Ibid., p. 61.

thirty do affiliate themselves with one party or the other. Nor does it follow that the sudden rise of independence is a long-range trend. It may be and it may not be. There is some historical reason for thinking that it may not be. Certainly one should not assume that the party system is going to go on into perpetuity exactly as it has in the past, but neither is there any evidence to justify sweeping generalizations about its imminent collapse. It may be more emotionally satisfying to proclaim radical change or total transformation, but it is usually more accurate to say that a given institution is going through significant and important changes, the implications of which cannot be ignored nor yet assayed.

Since the 1950s, the far left wing of the Democratic party has engaged in a kind of moral blackmail by threatening periodically to secede to form a third or fourth party. Even Senator McGovern hinted just before the Democratic convention in 1972 that if he were deprived of the nomination that was "rightfully" his, he might bolt. And Eugene McCarthy, that Don Quixote of the late 1960s, dropped hints of forming and leading a fourth party (which was about as likely as Mr. McCarthy's being elected pope). No one engaged in reconstructing the Democratic coalition can afford to take such blackmail seriously. Those liberals who would secede from the party would not carry many votes with them; indeed, it might actually help a Democratic presidential candidate. The Democratic party is the more liberal party, and it cannot win an election by pretending not to be liberal; but neither can it tolerate a situation in which its far left faction forces the party to take a stand that offends a large number of its potential supporters. A Democratic candidate has to be a liberal, but he cannot afford to be an ideologically pure liberal. This is an inescapable reality of the American two-party system as it presently operates. For the Democratic party to ignore this reality, simply means that it will continue to lose presidential elections even before the campaigns start. For liberals who want to influence American policy from the inside instead of criticizing it from the outside, there is not now and is not likely to be in the foreseeable future any alternative to the Democratic party.

VOTING

Party affiliation is lifelong, and since one party or the other tends to be the majority party for many decades, American politics ought to be a rather dull affair. The majority party should win every election by approximately the same majority of votes. But there are two reasons why such a phenomenon does not occur: (1) Voting rates go up and down from election to election, and (2) many voters do not always vote for the candidates of their own party.

Professor Angus Campbell argues that these two phenomena alone are sufficient to explain the "off-year" election in which the party winning the presidential election suffers losses in the next congressional election. The phenomenon may have nothing to do with dissatisfaction with the winning party's policies. In the presidential election, voting rates are higher. This brings into participation those who have less interest in politics; they are less likely to have clear convictions and strong party affiliations. Furthermore, those regular voters who are more weakly affiliated with a party are also more likely to be won away from their normal affiliation by the heightened excitement of the personalities and issues of a presidential campaign. The winning party in a presidential year attracts votes both from the weakly affiliated members of the other party and from those who do not vote in off-year elections.

Two years later, the issues and excitement are much less. The weakly affiliated party members vote for the party; those who were attracted to the polling booth by the presidential election stay home. Hence the party in power loses votes, and not necessarily because of a change in public attitudes. The off-year election, then, is a much more accurate barometer of party affiliation than presidential elections.[1]

There has been little change between 1958 and 1972 in the proportion of Democrats to Republicans in the House of Representatives (between 54 and 56 percent Democrats)—with the single exception of 1964 when the Democrats made big gains in the House, losing most of them in 1966. In 1968, the presidential election was close. Those who were attracted to the polling places by the excitement of a presidential election divided evenly, and the winning party earned no advantage in congressional representation. After 1968, for example, the Democratic proportion in the House fell from 57 to 56 percent and rose in state legislatures from 57 percent to 57.5 percent. In 1972, the Republicans routed the "New Politics" of George McGovern but made only trivial gains in the House and actually lost seats in the Senate.

In other words, the United States could go through the political tumult of the last decade—the

[1] Implicit in Professor Campbell's analysis is the assumption that those with the strongest political conviction and party affiliations are the most likely to vote. The so-called independents are those with the least conviction, the least amount of information, and the least inclination to vote. Most research evidence substantiates this assumption. However, it would appear, particularly from our study of college graduates cited in an earlier chapter, that a new brand of independent is beginning to appear, one who has strong political convictions and considerable political interest but does not affiliate with either party. However, instead of being between the Republicans and the Democrats, this new independent (at least in our college alumni sample) was somewhat to the left of the Democrats. What influence he will have on the future of American politics remains to be seen. See Angus Campbell, *Elections and the Political Order* (New York: John Wiley, 1966).

election of a Catholic, the assassination of a president and a presidential candidate, increasing black militancy, race riots, the Vietnam war, campus disturbances, the emergence of George Wallace, and the self-destruct proclivities of the New Politics—without there being much change at all in the distribution of votes in congressional elections. Richard Nixon almost won in 1960, despite the fact that the majority of voters were Democrats, because of dissatisfaction with John Kennedy's religion. He won in 1968 because of public dissatisfaction with the performance of the Johnson administration, and he overwhelmed the inept George McGovern in 1972. But the near miss of 1960, the close win of 1968, and the landslide of 1972 never made any permanent inroads on the Democratic voting pattern of the majority of American voters.[2]

The variety, then, in American elections comes from those short-run changes that are occasioned by a specific election, and these are changes in voting rates and in voting behavior, particularly of those who are more weakly affiliated to their parties. On the other hand, the stability through time is guaranteed by the consistent voting patterns of those who are strongly identified with their party and who are in fact most likely to vote, especially in off-year elections.*

[2] For a detailed analysis of the 1968 election, especially for a demonstration that it was generally *against* Johnson, not *for* Nixon, see Philip E. Converse, Warren E. Miller, Jerrold G. Rusk, and Arthur C. Wolfe, "Continuity and Change in American Politics: Parties and Issues in the 1968 Election," *The American Political Science Review* 63, no. 4 (December 1969): 1083–1106.

* Vermont Royster, the former editor of the *Wall Street Journal*, in an article in the June 1973 issue of the *American Scholar*, offers an alternative though by no means conflicting interpreta-

Professor Campbell presents a chart that shows how the country was divided in the 1956 election on the political continuum and how different segments of the continuum cast their votes.

Strong Democrats were 20 percent of the electorate, and 85 percent of them voted for Stevenson. Weak Democrats were 23 percent of the electorate, and 63 percent of them voted for Stevenson. "Independents" and "nonpartisans" were 27 percent of the electorate, and 73 percent of them voted for Eisenhower. Weak Republicans were 14 percent of the electorate, and 93 percent of them voted for Eisenhower. Strong Republicans were 19 percent of the electorate, and 99 percent of them voted for Eisenhower. Eisenhower, then, put together his 1956 landslide by taking all the Republican votes, approximately three-fourths of the independent vote, more than one-third of the weak Democratic votes, and

tion. He suggests that the New Deal coalition had by the middle 1940s lost the South, some of its farm supporters and also middle class northern support. It was still a majority coalition but not of the magnitude of the Republican majority of the last half of the nineteenth and the early part of the twentieth centuries nor even of the size that it had possessed itself in the middle '30s. The small advantage of the New Deal majority has made for unstable presidential elections since 1948 with the outcome usually close and frequently depending on the sort of personality factors which would be less relevant if either party had a decisive majority. Royster adds that while the New Deal coalition has been in trouble since 1946, the Republicans have not been successful in the last quarter century of putting together an alternative coalition (which, though Royster doesn't say it, is a political failure of monumental proportions). Hence the present relative unstability in presidential elections is likely to continue for some time to come—unless (and this is my addition to Royster) the Watergate affair puts the GOP out of business for a decade or more.

TABLE 8.1
The vote of Partisan groups in 1956

The Flow of the Vote

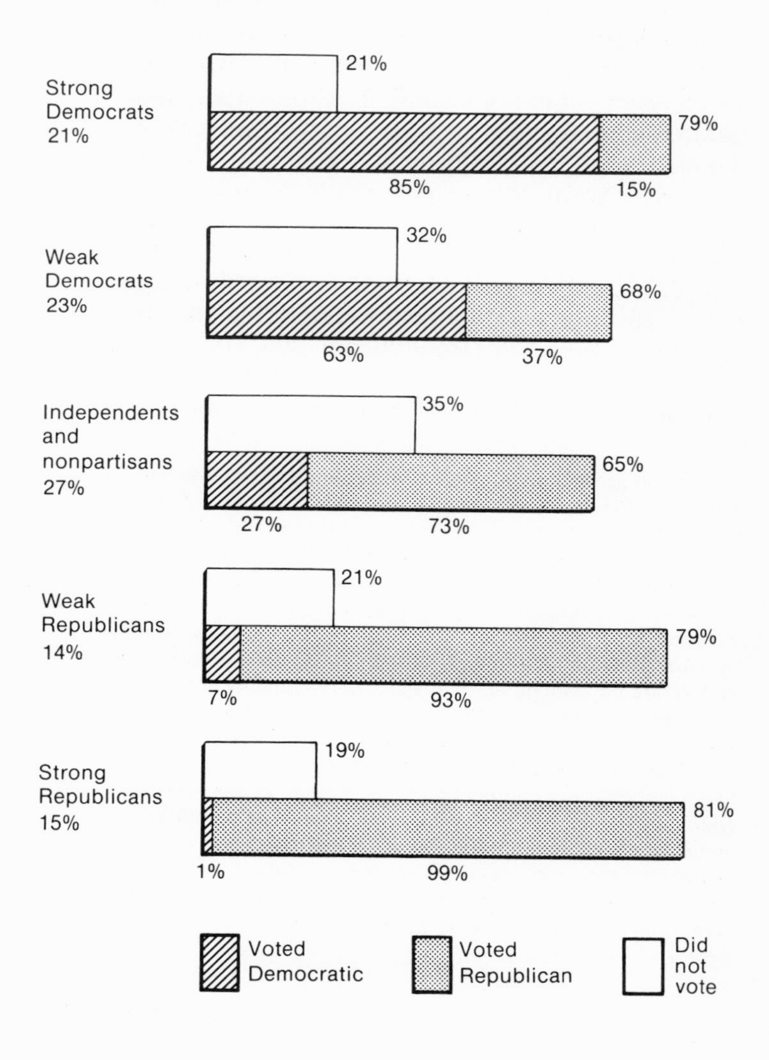

one-sixth of the strong Democratic votes. He held his own constituency, carried the independent constituency overwhelmingly (which normally tends to lean in the Democratic direction), and made substantial inroads into the Democratic constituency.

Professor Campbell points out that the retreat from the Democratic party in 1952 was to a considerable extent on the basis of issues. Those who changed from supporting Truman in 1948 to supporting Eisenhower in 1952 did so because of their dissatisfaction with the Democratic administration, the "mess in Washington," and especially the Korean war. However, in 1956, there were really no major issues dividing the parties. The failures of the Truman administration had receded into the background. The decisive reason for the Eisenhower landslide was the personality of the man himself. Whatever his qualities may have been as president, people liked him. The 1956 election was a vote of confidence for Dwight Eisenhower and not a victory for the Republicans, who were unable to make any appreciable gains in the Congress.

There are long-range and short-range factors at work in presidential elections. A long-range factor is the political affiliation of the electorate, which tends to be consistent. Short-range factors are the personalities of the candidates and the issues of the election. These personalities and issues are especially likely to sway the weakly affiliated voters and those who do not vote in off-year elections. The net result for presidential elections, then, is a calculus of long-range affiliation and short-range issues and personalities.

The late Professor V. O. Key argued strongly that the American electorate was not nearly so irrational or so ill-informed as many of its critics contend. Instead, he saw "an electorate moved by concern about central and relevant questions about public policy of governmental performance and of executive personality." [3] In other words, the short-range shift based on personalities and great global issues does indeed represent a response of the electorate to the political situation it perceives.

The weakness of Key's position is that the swing voters tend to be those with less political commitment and information. They are the ones who decide what is going to happen in a close presidential election. However, neither side is likely to win merely by appealing to the swing voters. If the Republicans are to win by anything more than a hair's breadth, they must win over substantial numbers of Democrats precisely on questions of issues and personalities. Thus in Key's model the American electorate, according to its own insights, is capable of not only responsible but also of of shrewd behavior.

Recent work by Professors Page and Brody [4] gives some confirmation of the Key model. When political candidates are relatively similar in their basic positions, voters are not sophisticated in catching the nuances of the differences that do exist. However, when the distance on issues between two political candidates is obvious, voters have no difficulty in recognizing which candidate stands for which position and consistently support the one whose position is most like their own.

The Republicans between 1952 and 1970 have had one personality, Dwight Eisenhower, and one

[3] V. O. Key, *The Responsible Electorate: Rationality in Presidential Voting* (Cambridge, Mass.: Belknap Press, 1966), pp. 7–8.
[4] Benjamin I. Page and R. A. Brody, "Policy Voting and the Electoral Process: The Vietnam War Issue," *American Political Science Review* 66 (Summer 1972): 979–95.

issue, a war, which have enabled them to win the presidency three times. In 1952, it was a combination of the Eisenhower personality and the Korean war; in 1956, it was strictly the Eisenhower personality; and in 1968, it was dissatisfaction with the Johnson administration and the war in Vietnam. (Why the Democrats persist in giving the war issue to the Republicans is a question beyond the scope of the present book.) In all likelihood it was the personality contrast between Truman and Dewey that redounded to the Democratic advantage in 1948. And beyond all doubt, it was the personality (that is to say, the religion) of John Kennedy that almost cost them the presidency in 1960. The principal impact of the Kennedy-Nixon debates in that year apparently was not so much to win Republicans over to Kennedy as to cut his losses from the Democrats.

In 1964, the Democrats not only maintained their majority, they actually increased it, to a considerable extent because Barry Goldwater's "shoot from the hip" militarism frightened voters with increased chances for involvement in war. The last minute surge of Humphrey's strength in 1968 almost turned defeat into victory for the Democrats.

The 1972 presidential race ought to have been a close one. Mr. Nixon had the advantage of being an incumbent candidate and the disadvantage of not being particularly popular. He was also saddled with a troubled economy, but probably was able to compensate for that by "winding down" the Vietnamese war and making two popular trips to China and Russia. An extraordinarily attractive Democratic candidate might have beaten Mr. Nixon, and a "neutral" candidate would probably have made the race close (losing by 4 percentage points, perhaps). In other words, the issues balanced out in the 1972 election.

The Democrats lost almost entirely on the basis of personality. Just how powerful a negative quantity Mr. McGovern's personality was becomes clear when one contrasts it with the proven unattractiveness of Mr. Nixon's.[5]

Despite the fact that the personality factor was running against it in 1960, the Democrats still managed to win the election, and despite the issue factor being against them in 1968, they almost won that election. In 1972, they simply threw it away. One concludes, then, that for the Republicans to have a sure majority in a presidential election they must combine issues and personality in a very powerful blend; otherwise, even in the best of circumstances, the best they can hope for is a very narrow victory. Of course, the other party may commit hari-kari again and leave the field wide open.

The issues in an election tend to be simple, with the two most important being war and the economy. The Democratic party has presided over three wars in the last thirty years. The electorate manifests considerable skepticism over that party's ability to avoid war. The Republican party, on the other hand, can claim credit for getting us out of the Korean war as well as the Vietnam war. There is a considerable paradox in this, of course, since "hawkishness" seems to be more characteristic of Republican leaders than Democratic leaders.

[5] This is a tentative observation, subject to correction when the Michigan survey team completes its 1972 analysis. I will be very surprised, however, if they contradict in any substantial measure my suggestions. Close elections like 1960 and 1968 are very difficult to analyze. Landslide elections like 1956, 1964, and 1972 are extremely easy. They indicate either that one candidate (Eisenhower) is extremely attractive or that the other candidate (Goldwater and McGovern) is extremely unattractive.

But the Republican party has established an image in the minds of the electorate of not being able to cope with economic problems. It was the economic disaster of the 1930s that cost the Republicans their permanent majority. It was the economic setbacks of the 1950s that restricted the gains of the Eisenhower era. Finally, Democratic resurgence in 1970 was certainly created by the economic condition of the country.

I strongly suspect (though as far as I know there is no evidence for it) that as long as the issues of peace and prosperity are pertinent to a given election, no other issues are very important. Whether the socalled social issues—race, crime in the streets, etc.—can swing a presidential election in either direction when the peace and prosperity issues are not pertinent seems to be problematic, though there isn't much doubt that a social issue can affect a local election. In other words, Republicans will not keep the Democrats from power in time of economic trouble by arguing a social issue. And they may not even be able to defeat the Democrats on the basis of a social issue when there is relative peace and relative prosperity. On the evidence of the last three decades, Democrats will lose presidential elections because of wars. In the absence of a war, they will lose because of massive dissatisfaction with governmental incompetence or because they nominate an unattractive candidate. Another way of losing elections emerged in 1972 when the Democrats expelled large numbers of their rank and file coalition members in a series of incredible policy and tactical blunders.

There are four kinds of American presidential elections:

1. Realigning elections. In the realigning election a major change takes place in the shape of American politics. The election of 1932 is a classic example of this form. In such an election there are not merely short-range gains for the winning party, there are permanent changes. Those who have changed from one party to another are likely to remain.

2. Maintaining elections. These are elections in which the party retains the presidency either because the issues and personalities neutralize each other or because the minority party is not able to exploit issues and personality sufficiently to give it victory. The elections of 1936, 1940, 1944, 1948, and 1964 represent maintaining elections.

3. Deviating elections. In 1952, 1956, 1968, and 1972, the minority party managed to capture the presidency because it successfully exploited issues and personalities. It did not succeed in capturing the permanent loyalites of those who converted to it to vote for president. While the Republicans did manage to win control of the House of Representatives in 1952, the Democrats have kept control of both houses ever since.

4. Reinstating elections. In a reinstating election, the majority party is able to recapture those voters lost in a previous deviant election to regain control of the presidency. The election of 1960 is the only example of this type in the last fifty years, so we are not able to say much about what happens in such an election, and John Kennedy's Catholicism made that election even more unusual. However, the University of Michigan researchers are firmly convinced that if Kennedy had not been Catholic he would have won by a far larger majority. At most, one can hazard a guess that in a reinstating election, the minority

loses its capacity to manipulate the issues and personality variables in such a way as to overcome its minority handicap. Those voters supporting the minority party because of dissatisfaction with the majority party or attraction for the minority candidate now return to their traditional voting patterns.

The fundamental difference between the two parties at the present time is that the Republicans must use issues and personalities to win converts, and the Democrats must use issues and personalities to maintain the loyalty of their faithful. Under normal circumstances it is much easier to do the latter. In 1972, the Democrats failed on both issues and personalities and turned what would have been a close election into a rout.

It is important to emphasize that issues such as Medicare, Quemoy-Matsu (1960), communism (1948), racial disturbances, crime in the streets (1968), and Watergate (1972) are not powerful enough to motivate sufficient voters to depart from their traditional alliances to swing an election. Under normal circumstances, there are two issues, perhaps three, strong enough to do that:

1. The economy. This is the most powerful issue, and the only one to cause a realignment in the last half century. I, personally, will believe only when I see it any realignment that occurs for any other reason.

2. War and peace. This issue may cause a number of voters to change their party affiliation for a given election, and, indeed, a military disaster could conceivably cause a realignment. Twice, dissatisfaction and weariness with war has caused enough Democrats to vote Republican and give the presidency to the Republican party.

3. Government incompetence. It seems that the Democrats lost in 1952 primarily because of the Korean war and in 1968 primarily because of Vietnam, but a case can be made for the general incompetence of the Democratic administration to deal with the problems the nation faced as a subsidiary cause for losing those elections. Communism and corruption in 1952 and racial and student disorders in 1968 symbolized the malaise of government. Without the two wars, it is problematic whether dissatisfaction with government incompetence would have been strong enough to defeat the Democrats. There have been no elections in the last fifty years with the issue of incompetence existing independent of a war, and so it is difficult to assess the strength of such an issue to swing votes away from the Democratic party in any great numbers.[6]

[6] See Philip Converse, et al., "Continuity and Change in American Politics," pp. 1083–1106 for a more detailed description of the evidence that it was dissatisfaction with the war that was primarily responsible for the Republican victory in 1968. It is interesting to note, for example, that the Michigan survey data show that two out of every three Americans thought that the Republicans were better able to avoid a larger war than the Democrats.

To say that people were dissatisfied with the war in 1968 and hence a sufficient number turned against the Democrats to defeat Hubert Humphrey is not to say that those who switched were necessarily ideological doves. One of the most serious mistakes the peace movement has made is to assume that a person who is a hawk is necessarily in sympathy with the war and will vote for the party that got us into it. As the research of my colleague, Sidney Verba, has demonstrated, many hawks were as dissatisfied with the war as the doves. They took their hawkish stand because they wanted to "get the war over with." Thus dissatisfaction with the war and the party who got us into it was by no means limited to the ideological dove. If the peace

Implicit in my reasoning thus far is the notion that the 1972 election was not an issue election at all. The war issue and the economic issue were uncertain and obscure. The government had displayed moderate incompetence, but not enough to get it into serious trouble. Thus, despite the brave announcements by both sides that 1972 was an issue election, indeed, the most clear-cut ideological election in a long time, it turns out that in fact that the voters did not consider it an issue election at all but a personality election. They chose, quite reluctantly, the candidate they considered to be the least unattractive. It is a tribute to the monumental self-destructiveness of the Democratic party that it managed to come up with a candidate that was even less attractive to the American voter than Richard Nixon.

movement had been flexible enough to recognize that many of the hawks also had a profound distaste for the war, it might have made many more converts than it did. Had it also realized that the anti-American stand of its youthful enthusiasts alienated further many of those who wanted to get the war over with and some of those who favored withdrawal, the peace movement might have had more success. Despite the Converse data that show that 70 percent of the Vietnam doves were opposed to the Chicago convention protest, the peace movement persisted in accepting three demonstrably false propositions: (1) All doves and potential doves approved of direct action and even violent protest, (2) all hawks were in sympathy with the war, and (3) all potential converts must subscribe to an "antipatriotic" position before they were permitted into the peace movement. I would suggest that all evidence shows that most doves, virtually all potential doves, and practically all hawks who wanted to get the war over with, rejected the strategies of the peace movement enthusiasts and were, if anything, driven off from the movement by the strategies of the flag-burners and the purveyers of liturgical gestures.

The lesser issues of communism, corruption, "getting the country moving again," "the missile gap," race, the mess in Washington, crime in the streets, are not important in a presidential campaign. They do affect voters, but in no presidential election in the last four decades have these issues been sufficient to affect the final outcome of the election. Indeed, in 1960, one of the most powerful of all issues besides peace and prosperity—religion—was not quite powerful enough to deprive the majority party of victory.

Social-psychological issues, such as anger at student protesters or black militants, are not enough to swing a national election. Political issues, such as Medicare or revenue sharing, do not have much power in that direction either. Party affiliation shapes our attitudes on an issue more than the issue affects our party affiliation. Most Americans, for example, do not understand and are not able to understand the complexities of the revenue sharing proposals. If the Republican party is for it, Republicans will support it; if the Democratic party is against it, Democrats will be against it. Some more sophisticated members of each party will take the opposite stand. On issues that deeply affect an individual, he may take his own personal position independent of the party stance. However, if an issue is not particularly salient for a given person, he will be strongly predisposed to assume the stand of his party, particularly if that party is represented by its leader. Similarly, if he knows neither candidate very well, the ordinary voter will be predisposed to see good things in the candidate of his own party and bad things in the other party's candidate. On both issues and candidates, political parties are a kind of mental shortcut. To use Professor V. O. Key's words:

They see parties as committed to the interests of their kind of people or of kinds of people with whom they sympathize, but they may have no clear understanding of the substantive policies that will advance such causes. For many others a more direct connection between policy preference and party identification prevails; they have views on policy issues and see their party as dedicated to the advocacy of those views. This connection may develop in either of two ways. Persons may first have policy preferences and then ally themselves with the party they regard as more disposed to promote those preferences. Or they may have a sense of identification with a party and adopt those policy views that they perceive to be the party line. To be sure, the reality of the process of relation of policy preferences to party identifications is more complex than this dichotomy suggests. Nevertheless, in one way or another correlations develop between issue opinions and party attachments, and the party becomes an instrument for the transformation of opinions into governmental action.[7]

There is, then, a subtle interaction between party and issue, party and candidate, and issue and candidate, with long-range voting trends shaped fundamentally by party orientation and short-range voting behavior shaped for a controlling segment of the population by issues and personalities.

I have assumed in this chapter that the perspective of political analysis developed by Angus Campbell and his colleagues at the University of Michigan is still a valid one. Nothing that happened in 1972 in-

[7] V. O. Key, Jr., *Public Opinion and American Democracy* (New York: Alfred A. Knopf, 1964), pp. 442–43.

clines me to modify this assumption. There is, however, one factor operating that necessitates an addition to the Campbell model. Ticket-splitting is apparently much more frequent now in American politics than it was in the past. In Campbell's frame of reference, the "independents" are usually the poorly educated, apathetic, politically indifferent potential voters. However, the "new" independents (and this is one of the only uses of the word "new" in contemporary political discussion that I consider to be valid) are well-educated, involved, and committed to political participation, who have persuaded themselves in an exercise of political maturity and sophistication to split their tickets. Voting for a candidate of one party for senator and of a candidate of the other party for governor is becoming increasingly frequent in American politics. Ticket-splitting in presidential elections began in the Eisenhower era when many Democrats voted for the hero general while at the same time voting for Democratic congressional candidates. It continued in 1960, when many Protestant Democrats voted against John Kennedy, and in 1964, when many Republicans voted against Barry Goldwater. In 1968, Mr. Nixon managed to capture sufficient numbers of Democrats who were dissatisfied with the war to eke out a victory. In 1972, he attracted a very large number of voters who cast their congressional and gubernatorial ballots for the Democrats. Ticket-splitting, then, has become a permanent factor in American presidential politics. It is worth noting that it is a factor that is a decided advantage for the Republicans, since the Democrats are the majority party and the ones most likely to benefit from straight party voting. In every presidential election since

1952, with the exception of 1964, the Republicans have benefitted from ticket-splitting. The Democrats have their work cut out for them if they are to keep their wavering members from drifting into the Republican camp. And since the waverers are likely to be conservative Democrats, the nature of the problem for the party becomes clear.

The new independents are those who are most likely to take their "cues" from the mass media. Research evidence indicates that the ticket-splitters are precisely the ones who make up their minds on the basis of newspaper and television editorials, the comments of tv news broadcasters and national columnists, and the campaign speeches of the candidates. They are for the most part moderately well-educated (or to use a less charitable phrase, half-educated). The very sophisticated, those who know their way around politics, are smart enough not to take their cues from the mass media. And the working class knows who its enemies are, and pays little or no attention to the media. It is precisely the ones inbetween, that is to say, those Americans who are naïve enough to think that a man's ability to be president can be judged by his performance on the television screen, who are most likely to be ticket-splitters—and also are the most likely to change their minds on political issues. The emergence of an ever increasing class of political pseudosophisticates is not a bright omen for American political democracy. What it will mean for the Democratic coalition, one fears, is that television "charisma" will become increasingly indispensable to hold the wavering Democratic voters. Heaven knows no one could accuse Senator McGovern of prostituting himself in a pretense of being charismatic (and I for one admire his refusal to do that). I shudder at the thought of a Democratic Ronald Reagan.

American politics is, as Scammon and Wattenberg have demonstrated, a politics of the center. The Democrats must retain the loyalty of that "somewhat right-wing" segment of its membership that might be inclined for reasons of issue or personality to be won over by the Republicans. The Republicans, on the other hand, must appeal to their own "left," that is to say, to those who do not think of themselves as Republicans but can be won over either by a global issue or by a candidate. When the Republican party moves from its own left to its right, as it did in 1964, it courts disaster. When the Democrats move from their right to the left, as they did in 1972, they drive the right wing into the arms of the Republicans (and in 1972, the Republicans embraced a good part of the center, as well). But the Democratic problem ordinarily is much less serious than the Republican problem. Since the Democrats comprise the majority party, they do not have to go as far to the right to win as Republicans have to move to the left to win. The Democrats also can afford to write off some of their own right wing. The Republicans not only cannot write off any of their left wing, they must move beyond it to convert Democrats.

Such talk of "right" and "left," of course, can be extremely misleading. There are many left-wing Republicans far to the left of right-wing Democrats. However, the left-right imagery gives at least some indication of the relative advantage the Democrats enjoy.

Scammon and Wattenberg are also correct when they say that the center is a floating center and that the rhetoric and policy that would appeal to the swing voter may change as the years go on. The general mood of the American public on the twin questions of isolationism versus internationalism and change versus social stability apparently does change. Minority group militancy, for example, may have had much wider support in the early 1960s than it does in the early 1970s. However, one must be somewhat suspicious of the concept of national mood. So far, the only two manifestations of national mood that have swung elections one way or the other have been national dissatisfaction with war and depression and national satisfaction with peace and prosperity. The other components and factors of national mood we know very little about, and we should be very skeptical when dealing with the concept.

But on one point I would go beyond Scammon and Wattenberg. Not only is American politics of the center, a center which "floats"; the center can be shaped. Given the fact that Americans are inclined to take their cues on political issues from their parties, and especially from the leaders of the parties, it is possible for the party leadership, particularly the presidential candidate, to determine by his choice of rhetoric and issues where the center is. That is, of course, not an absolute power, and I suspect that many liberal writers exaggerate enormously the educational power of the presidency. Nevertheless, the political leader is not merely the prisoner of where the center happens to be; it does impose some constraints on him. But from his position as the one who shapes the rhetoric and emits the cues, he can have considerable influence on where the center goes. The most important example in recent years of the role of political leadership in shaping public opinion is the changing attitudes of the American population on the racial question. Despite all the trouble during the 1960s, despite the riots, despite the Black Panthers and other forms of militancy, despite widespread dissatisfaction among whites with certain styles of militancy, there has been a rapid decline of attitudes of prejudice and bigotry. This decline is strongly related to the stance the political leadership has assumed on this issue. As Philip Mason said, "One cannot go too far beyond the 'consensus.' One can mold it and shape it." A political leader who departs too far from the "center" will lose. And so will the political candidate who becomes a prisoner of the center. The center may impose constraints on a candidate, but it also expects him to lead it from where it is.

If peace and prosperity are the only issues that really matter in an election, then it seems legitimate to ask why should there be any concern about other issues? This country has pressing social problems. More is required than merely the election of a candidate—Democratic or Republican—who is prepared to cope with the twin problems of war and inflation. It is also necessary that such a candidate be elected with a sufficient popular mandate to effect social change. More than that, it is also necessary that the next president be the kind of man who may restore confidence in the American experiment among some of those who have lost it. We do not need a miracle worker in 1976, but we do need an able and adroit and impressive political leader. The point of this chapter is that if the leader happens to be a Democrat, he has the distinct advantage of having the long run of political trends still in his favor. Perhaps the most encouraging sentence in this volume for those who wish to rebuild the Democratic coalition is that despite incredible ineptitude, the liberal Democrats still have more factors going for them than they have going against them. But the serious mistakes of 1968 and the cataclysmic mistakes of 1972 did not help matters. Politics is not baseball but the Democratic party would be well advised to avoid the third strike.

THE LEADERS

St. Teresa of Avila, the great seventeenth-century Spanish mystic, once announced that if she were forced to choose between a confessor who was pious and one who was learned, she would most certainly choose the latter. This is a sentiment with which Americans by and large agree. When it comes to their surgeons, their psychiatrists, their construction contractors, their lawyers, accountants, teachers, and scientists, Americans want professionals.

But in politics, as mentioned earlier, the virtuous and well-meaning amateur is not only highly regarded, he is frequently preferred to the professional: A military hero, a successful businessman, even a movie star, an athlete, an astronaut, and an intellectual are somehow thought to be more qualified for political office than the person who has made politics his full-time occupation. By most objective standards these amateurs are not very successful, and if they are, it is because they manage to professionalize themselves. But the public is rarely willing to admit that the amateur has not lived up to expectations. Suspicion of the professional politician is so powerful that excuses are made for an incompetent amateur that would never be made for a competent professional. Perhaps a residue of the Protestant ethic makes us suspicious of professional politicians because they don't "produce" anything; but most arguments center around the politician as dishonest or corrupt. Corruption in political life is in all likelihood no greater than in other dimensions of life in America, although the successful politician is probably exposed to more temptations than many other Americans. It does seem that the amount of political corruption in the country has decreased considerably in recent years, perhaps only because so many ways have been found for generally underpaid politicians to make money without violating the law.

The charge of dishonesty is a little more difficult to cope with. As we shall see in subsequent paragraphs, "telling the truth, the whole truth, and nothing but the truth, as seen by each person in political oratory would increase viciousness and hatred throughout the society." [1] The political leader, if he wishes to balance all the conflicting forces with which he is engaged, must use truth differently from which it is ordinarily used.

Thus, a party boss may tell three or four different men he thinks they would make excellent governors. Unless the men are as politically sensitive as the boss, each may deduce that he will be slated for governor. Of course, the boss never said that; he just said they would make excellent governors. Which one he decides to slate will depend partly on the political situation at the moment and partly on other factors, but by permitting each man to think he is at least being actively considered, the boss reduces the amount of conflict likely to plague his organization. He must have some other prize available for the disappointed gubernatorial candidates, but satisfying a rejected candidate after slate-making is much easier than containing interparty conflict before.

The political leader, then, is forced by the nature of the circumstances in which he finds himself to evade and avoid, to sugarcoat and to mislead more than the rest of us. He does so not because he is dishonest (though he may be), not because he likes to manipulate people (though it is very possible that

[1] Throughout this chapter I lean heavily on Andrew S. McFarland, *Power and Leadership in Pluralist Systems* (Stanford, Calif.: Stanford University Press, 1969).

he does), but because his role is essentially one of "conflict management." The conflict manager must be extremely careful of what he says and how he says it.

Even in the most authoritarian societies the political leader must restrain the forces of potential conflict that are at work among his people. In a democratic society, conflict management becomes a more serious proposition, because one cannot fall back on the use of force readily. In the United States, however, a political culture where coalition formation has become so advanced, a political leader must be a master of convening, tending, and maintaining coalitions. If he is out of office, it is his own coalition he must maintain; but if he is in office, it is not only the coalition of his supporters he must keep operating, he also must preside over the larger coalition that is the given community. He cannot afford to have the minority that did not support him feel completely alienated from the community.

The political leader, particularly if he is in office, is more than just a convener and maintainer of coalitions. He also is supposed to symbolize by his enthusiasm and commitment the goals of the party and to move the party toward political power by converting more voters to its cause. And if he is in office, the leader must "make things happen that would not happen otherwise." [2] The skilled political leader maintains a balance between making things happen and sustaining the coalition that supports him. If he tries to move too far beyond the coalition, he will lose the kind of popular support that gives him some control over events. If, on the other hand, he spends

[2] Andrew S. McFarland, *Power and Leadership in Pluralist Systems* (Stanford, Calif.: Stanford University Press, 1969), p. 245.

all his time maintaining the coalition, the community for which he is responsible is likely to drift and he runs the risk of being labeled a "do-nothing" leader.

The political leader is essentially a marginal man who manages conflict by being part of all the different major groups within his coalition. He is able to understand and sympathize with the principal goals of these coalition components. Professor McFarland, relying on the work of Karl Mannheim, summarizes on a fairly abstract level the ability of the leader:

> (1) *to partially identify himself with many individuals, groups, and classes and understand their different perspectives on reality;* (2) *to be open to the conflicts between these perspectives;* (3) *to retain a stance of detachment;* (4) *to attempt to derive a synthetic comprehensive perspective through the process of "dynamic mediation" among the various partial perspectives, which necessitates the avoidance of premature closure.*[3]

Obviously, it takes an extraordinarily secure and sophisticated person to absorb and synthesize the various demands of his constituency. The political leader is not trying to satisfy all of the people all of the time; but he is in a position where his occupational responsibility is to satisfy most of his coalition most of the time. Or as one black politician in Chicago said of the Cook County Democratic organization, "It doesn't give everybody everything they want, but it gives most of us enough of what we want to keep us happy."

The compromising, somewhat less than transparent language required to manage conflict within the coalition, puts the politician in the position where he

[3] Ibid., pp. 201–2.

is bound to look bad eventually to those who do not understand the nature of the political game. From the politician's viewpoint, the critical truth is that he can accomplish nothing unless he maintains his coalition. But to the outsider it seems that all that is required of a political leader is that he firmly and uncompromisingly take a stand in favor of Truth. Compromise and manipulation of the truth are seen by the outsider not as a necessary and inevitable part of the political process but as a sign of the weakness and corruption of the kind of men who go into politics. The outsider, of course, does not understand that if the political leader did take an absolute, certain, and uncompromising stand on what any given outsider considers to be the Truth, he would be swept out of office at the next election, never to rise politically again. For what seems Truth to one is Big Lie to another, and what is morally imperative action to one is down the road to hell to another.

In the popular mind, the political man who would rather be right than be president is a man to be admired and respected. He takes a firm, vigorous stand, he will not compromise, and he will sacrifice his political future because of his principles. What the outsider doesn't understand is that under most of the ordinary circumstances of political life, a refusal to compromise is a failure in the political process. In a country of coalition politics we have politicians because we need men who are able to arrange compromises. If everyone took a firm and uncompromising stand on what they believed to be the only right and moral course, Professor McFarland's prediction about the increase of viciousness and hatred throughout society would be all too frighteningly accurate, for as Professor McFarland shrewdly notes, "tact, or sugarcoated deception, (is) a response to conflict." [4]

It can be seen, then, that the politician is in a doubly ambiguous position. Not only must he manage conflict among the opposing forces within his coalition, he must also do so in such a way as to not appear to the larger society as engaging too frequently in compromise, which is frowned upon by much of the electorate. The politician may feel on occasion that like the ancient Israelites he must build bricks without straw.

The psychological stress in dealing with political conflict may produce great strain in the leader who is aware of the incompatibility of the demands made upon him. Professor McFarland remarks,

> *. . . Theodore Roosevelt, Franklin Roosevelt, Truman, Kennedy, and Johnson often regarded political conflicts, even those involving incompatible demands, as psychologically and physically invigorating up to a certain point. On the other hand, Taft, Wilson, Harding, Coolidge, Hoover, and Eisenhower seem to have had a lower tolerance for conflict; they found incompatible demands psychologically and physically depressing. Taft was a first-class judge and administrator but a poor manager of political conflict; Wilson had great political talent yet he propelled himself into tragically needless dilemmas, rendered insolvable by his own peculiar combination of principled moralism and stubbornness. . . .*
> *Coolidge escaped from conflict and complexity by sleeping twelve hours a day. Hoover, on the*

[4] Andrew S. McFarland, *Power and Leadership in Pluralist Systems* (Stanford, Calif.: Stanford University Press, 1969), pp. 212–14.

other hand, . . . was a magnificent organizer of resources toward agreed ends, but he was unable to deal with situations or people that contradicted his belief in laissez-faire liberalism. . . . He too was a man of tremendous ability who could not deal with certain situations of moral complexity.[5]

Dwight Eisenhower despised conflict. He thought of himself as a great conciliator. Conciliation meant that the conflicts had to be resolved before they got to him, and to this end he "established a formally organized system under the guidance of the assistant president, Sherman Adams." [6] Eisenhower may typify another response to complex conflict. McFarland quotes Richard Neustadt,

Robert Donovan supplies us Eisenhower's answer when it was suggested to him a few weeks before his heart attack that Congress might be called back for a special session in the fall of 1955: "He slowly twisted his head around to (Arthur) Burns and told him painfully that the cost of a special session might be the sanity and possibly the life of one Dwight D. Eisenhower." [7]

McFarland concludes, "Thus, in the solution of role conflicts, escape from the field and illness are important responses of politicians to situations where two or more groups make incompatible demands." [8]

Harry Truman, despite occasional fits of temper,

[5] Andrew S. McFarland, *Power and Leadership in Pluralist Systems* (Stanford, Calif.: Stanford University Press, 1969), pp. 212–14.
[6] Ibid., p. 215, quoting Richard Neustadt, *Presidential Power*, p. 165, citing Robert J. Donovan, *Eisenhower: The Inside Story* (New York: Harper and Row, 1956), p. 357.
[7] Ibid.
[8] Ibid.

seemed to enjoy the game very much. He is alleged to have remarked, "If you can't stand the heat, get out of the kitchen." In other words, he who does not enjoy the game of politics shouldn't play it; he who does not enjoy conflict-managing, force-balancing, coalition-convening and maintaining should find some other means of employment.

Of the presidents in the last fifty years, it seems that Franklin Roosevelt and John Kennedy were most skilled at and most enjoyed the political game. One would have expected Lyndon Johnson to be a skilled practitioner; however, the skills for a successful majority leader of the Senate apparently are not the same as those required to be president of the United States. Johnson was flexible and skeptical on matters of domestic policy, about which he was well-informed, but timid and rigid on matters of foreign policy, for which he felt unprepared. Then when the heat was on and he was subjected to tremendous cross-pressures generated by the Vietnam war, he lost his cool, refused to accept criticism from subordinates, cut himself off from dissenting opinions, and ranted about how the Washington and New York establishments rejected him because of his Texas background. One cannot imagine that cool and aloof Boston politician, John Kennedy, cutting himself off from dissenting opinion or losing his cool because, as a Catholic, he was an outsider.

Anger and temper tantrums lead to the kind of mistakes that conflict-managers and coalition-conveners simply can't afford to make. Richard Daley, for example, is one of the most astute urban politicians in the country, yet his inability to keep his cool with the press (demonstrated so clearly during the 1968 Democratic convention) has somewhat reduced his effectiveness, if not in Chicago at least nationally.

President Nixon apparently believes that his controlled use of anger is a political asset; but his peculiar kind of reflective self-consciousness displayed while merchandizing himself may well have produced a skepticism in the public about any show of presidential emotion. Political leaders can afford to have emotions, they can even be angry, but they cannot afford to lose their tempers, certainly not in public and only rarely in private and on matters of little moment. If a president wishes to rant and rave and scream and shout, use vile language and kick the desk because someone has mislaid a paperclip, no one should deny him that kind of therapeutic release.

A political leader cannot afford to see moral issues in terms of black and white. Reality is seldom that simple and one cannot just write off some of one's coalition partners as being immoral. It was Hoover's rigid moralism on economic matters that made him incapable of responding to the Great Depression. Woodrow Wilson's incredible Calvinistic stubborness prevented him from compromising with Cabot Lodge on the League of Nations. The political leader must see both sides of the question; that is to say, he must see how men on two different sides of the issue can with moral integrity, good faith, and personal sincerity be convinced that their position is the moral one. He must be aware that in the complex world in which we live, no single solution to a problem can claim a unique right to moral excellence, and that no large group of people, no matter how immoral their position may seem, can be disregarded without first making an attempt to see their problem from their viewpoint and to understand the very real situation that seems to them to make their position absolutely moral.

Most political leaders fervently wish that the tactic of claiming moral excellence for one's own position and assigning moral perversity to one's opponents would vanish from American politics (though they use it often enough themselves). The sophisticated and emotionally secure political leader knows, however, that few problems are solved by higher morality, and no problems will be solved by dismissing whole classes of people as sinners.

The wise politician knows that he has considerable but limited powers. From legal prerogatives of his office, from his role as leader of the coalition, and from his symbolic position as the "great educator," he emits the cues that enable his followers to judge what stand they should take on specific issues. The liberal press has repeatedly emphasized the moral and educational potentiality of the presidency. John Kennedy, in particular, was frequently criticized for not using it as a platform "from which to educate the people," which of course meant, "educate them the way we think they ought to think." Arthur Schlesinger notes that people like Lippmann and Alsop were attacking Kennedy for not using the educational power of the presidency scarcely months after he was in office. And James Reston wrote in "An Epitaph for John Kennedy," "He never really exploited his considerable gifts as a public educator." Schlesinger responds to these charges by saying that most of the criticism assumed that by stirring up the people Kennedy could bring pressure to bear on Congress to support his program. Kennedy argued that the effective social change is accomplished by not so much threatening Congress as by working with it. Given the narrowness of his own victory and the slimness of his congressional margin, stirring up popular emotions in an attempt to sway Congress would be foolhardy, self-defeating, and even dangerous.

In retrospect, Kennedy was obviously correct. The liberal myth that the president can force the public to move Congress if he preaches the true liberal doctrine to the public can be seen as one more of the rather simple-minded views of reality that afflict liberal journalists.

A political leader can, indeed, educate his people. He can broaden their vision and change their minds. The vast change in attitudes among white Americans on the race issue in the last twenty years is to a considerable extent due to the efforts of political leadership. But to say that over the long run a political leader can influence and change the minds of his followers is not to say that he can do it at will on specific issues and to such an extent that a torrent of public support will override congressional inertia. The assumption that he can is based on the notion that Congress does not by and large represent the country; a notion held by critics who live in the corridor between Boston and Washington and who know more about the mood of the country than do its elected representatives.

I once remarked to a distinguished pilgrim, who migrates back and forth between Cambridge and Washington, that having read Arthur Krock's memoirs, I was convinced that Mr. Krock felt that he knew far more about the nation and far more about how to be a president than any of the many presidents he had observed during his years in Washington. My friend replied, "But there were two principal differences between Arthur and the presidents. Arthur didn't have to run the country, and he didn't have to stand for reelection."

The American people are at the present time only

too ready to be educated by a political leader who will speak to them on the complexities and difficulties of the problems that face the country. Part of the appeal of Senator Muskie in 1968 and of his preelection telecast of 1970 was precisely that he was willing to play the part of a man who educated in the midst of complexity. Indeed, one of the functions of political parties and political leadership is precisely that they are expected to be specialists in political issues and provide information and cues for the rank and file to know what stand to take on any issue. But it is one thing to say that the political leader has an important educational role to play and another to say that he can use his educational position to produce immediate responses on specific issues. The best that any teacher can do is to take his students from where they are and patiently lead them somewhere else. The teacher who attempts by appeals to morality and, by the exercise of executive fiat, to transform his students instantaneously will have no impact at all. In this day and age he would be tossed out of the classroom.

The example of the political leader as educator is only one application of a more general principle. Political leaders do have a good deal of power, but it is much less than outsiders think (even those outsiders who happen to be national correspondents for the elite journals). In the final analysis, the authority of the government rests upon the consent of the governed. The political leader who moves too far beyond the consensus that supports him will have no meaningful influence at all no matter what the legal prerogatives of his office. The leader must keep his constituency pleased or at least in line when they are displeased. He must balance the needs, demands, and interests of his own special constituencies with the needs of the whole society. He must persuade, cajole, threaten, inspire, warn, entreat, exhort. At times he may even force, but he must not force too hard or too often or too much, because in the long run in a democratic society (and even in a dictatorial society in the longer run) one cannot govern by force alone.

All of which is a way of saying that the unofficial personal powers of the political leader, powers created either by his position as head of a coalition or by the characteristics of his personality, are more important than any legal powers that may come to him by his office. The informal exercise of the persuasive powers of leadership are likely to be much more effective than the formal exercise of its legal powers.

This is a truth that no professional politician of any experience will deny. His informal powers are more important than his formal powers. It is a truth of which most political amateurs and outsiders seem pitifully unaware. Politics ought to operate the way the old civics textbooks describe it. Decisions ought to be made according to processes described in the organizational charts. A politician ought not to have to rely on personality characteristics or off-the-record arrangements within his coalition. In other words, politics ought to be a clear, neat, rational business instead of the messy, obscure, frequently irrational business it is. The political leader, having been elected to office, ought to have the power to accomplish those things to which he has committed himself. He should not be forced to stoop to the degrading process of informal agreement, compromise, avoidance of the whole truth, and other political tactics so common in American government.

Bargaining and coalition formation have historically been of the essence of American political culture. The overwhelming majority of Americans are most instinctively committed to this style of politics, even though they do not understand all of its implications. We thus have the paradoxical situation that Americans want coalition politics and want leaders to preside over coalitions, but they complain when the leaders exercise the only skills that could possibly keep coalitions going. On the other hand, when a political leader arrives on the scene who threatens to govern in a style that is purely ideological or moralistic, he is likely to be soundly beaten. Americans may not be especially fond of political leaders who compromise, they may complain about their tendency to compromise; but they are even less fond of those whose styles indicate an unwillingness to compromise.

It is the political amateurs who most vigorously reject the coalition model of American politics. And here is the real danger of amateurism. The general public will not be taken in by the ideological or moralistic politician, but the amateur rejects the coalition model both as descriptive and normative; he is resolutely convinced that the man of pure integrity and ideological simplicity is the man the nation needs if it is to extricate itself from whatever quagmire it is presently trapped in. (Of course, American society has always been trapped in one quagmire or another. It has somehow always managed to get out of this quagmire and into the next one.) There is further in the mind of the amateur reformer the absolute belief that if a man of integrity and morality, honesty and conviction is offered to society, there is a vast hidden potential of support that will suddenly appear—from the woodwork. Republican amateurs who forced Barry Goldwater on the party in 1964 firmly believed this and probably still do. The fact that Goldwater was not the kind of man who could convene a coalition, manage conflict, and stand on the margins among various conflicting groups was a positive asset from the point of view of the Republican amateurs. They argued that the country had had enough compromising, enough conflict management; they would put a man of principle, integrity, and conviction into office. They turned out to be wrong.

The liberal amateurs share the Republican amateurs' view of reality. They push candidates of dubious political skills, because they deem such skills irrelevant. George McGovern demonstrated little or no ability at convening, tending, and maintaining coalitions. He became objectionable to certain important partners in the old liberal coalition and they left it. It did not matter to the liberal amateurs, because they admire a man who deliberately eschews political skills and takes a firm stand on morality, principle, and righteousness (so long as they agree with it). In other words, the liberal amateur says to us too, "In your heart, you know he's right."

If the amateur's candidate is to win an election he will have to win majority support, which he can do only if he can demonstrate latent skills at coalition formation. Even if he was deposited in public office by some fluke without having formed a coalition, he will have to acquire one quickly in order to govern (if only because his amateur supporters will soon break into feuding factions, thereby destroying any consensus). In other words, if we throw compromise and coalition formation out the front door, they will only come in at the back, bigger and stronger than ever. The amateurs who wish to eliminate compromise from politics will only be successful when they either eliminate people from politics or when they repeal human nature.

One can summarize the role of the political leader and the constraints on that role by attempting to codify the rules of the political game.

1. You do not destroy the losers, though you rejoice in their mistakes. You, too, may one day be a loser and you may need his support for implementing your policies. Today's enemy may be tomorrow's ally.

2. You do not drive out any group traditionally part of your coalition, nor do you exclude any group from the rewards of power and office that come with a victory. A forced break with a coalition partner should be done in such a way as to leave the door open for a resumption of partnership.

3. You may scapegoat any social group only very sparingly if at all. You know that most social problems cannot be blamed on any specific group in society. Scapegoating as a strategy is very dangerous; it drives social groups to the margin of the political consensus and to a feeling of desperation, where their behavior becomes at best unpredictable.

4. You do not attack any social group's vital self-interest. If forced to do so, you do it in such a way as to assure them that you do not threaten their existence and will stand by them with support in most circumstances. (John Kennedy, then, could become furious with U.S. Steel and force a price rollback, but then he quickly asserted that he did not really think all businessmen were sons of bitches.)

5. While you may support some redistribution of power and wealth, your strategy has to be one of enlarging the pie rather than cutting it up in different size pieces.

6. You do not select one particular social group as a special carrier of virtue or justice. On the contrary, you express respect for the rights of all social groups and sympathize with their problems.

7. You do not deceive the people, at least when the chips are down. Evasion, avoidance, procrastination are indeed part of the political game, but on matters of major public concern you cannot afford a credibility gap. You cannot permit the people to think that you are systematically deceiving them.

8. You try constantly to broaden the base of your coalition and the more general social consensus. You try to bring new groups into the consensus if not into the coalition. You realize how dangerous it is for a society to have some groups who are legally or practically excluded from the consensus.

9. You are loyal to your friends and keep your word to them—at least when that word is clearly and unequivocally given. As one Irish politician said:

> *"The only thing you have in politics is your word. Break your word and you're dead. The most successful politician is the politician who kept his word."*

10. You know how to lose. As Edward Kennedy put it, "If you don't know how to lose, you don't deserve to win." You may darkly hint that the other side has "stolen" the election; but you must not refuse to congratulate the other side on its victory, and you do not stalk away and sulk, and, least of all, you do not sug-

gest that the broader social consensus be broken up because you lost.

11. You do not engage in violence when you are defeated in the normal political processes.

12. You don't steal from the public fisc and you are very careful about your financial relationship with those who are seeking political influence. There is no more deadly a charge than that he has grown rich at the public expense. (The whole issue of the legitimate and legal means of money-making by public officials is one that is beyond the scope of this book, but once again there is a paradox: We run our American political life in such a way that only people with affluence can compete in it, yet we are very skeptical about the politician who is a financial success.)

13. You accept the good faith of others, though you may not agree with them or trust them.

14. You don't expect to accomplish everything all at once. You know how to wait and how to trust your plans for political progress in the social realities in which you find yourself at a given period of time. You know that while you can lead the consensus, you can't lead it beyond where it's willing to go.

These rules of the political game may seem unduly cynical, and it is perhaps easier for politicians than for most men to become cynics. Yet, in the absence of a list of tacit and implicit rules like the ones above, the American political and social process would quickly deteriorate into the chaos typical of so many Latin American republics. Such a set of rules evolved because it was understood long ago that such a variegated society as the American one could not survive for long unless there were such rules. From the point of view of the anarchist or the radical, the rules may seem corrupt and immoral. From the point of view of a study of comparative cultures, they seem some of the most impressive accomplishments of human political endeavor. The society as large and as diverse and as quickly put together as the American one ought to be beset by far more political strife than in fact has disturbed it. That we have had only one civil war may be an extraordinary accomplishment. The anarchist or the radical who wishes to eliminate the rules should ponder the possibility that the alternatives may not be Consciousness III or the glorious people's republic but an unending series of civil wars.

Of course, the radical and the anarchist do not care for order and stability. Peter Berger has some appropriate words for the apostles of disorder.

> *Children are our hostages to history. Consequently, to be a parent means (however dimly and on whatever level of intellectual sophistication) to have a stake in the continuity of the social order. As a result, there are limits not only to social disorder but to social discontinuity. Enthusiasts for violent change (most of whom, I have noticed, don't have children) fail to recognize this. Successful revolutionaries find out about the limits of disorder, usually to their dismay, as they must settle down to govern the society over which they have gained control. The experiences of the Soviet regime with the institutions of the family and of religion are instructive in this regard.*[9]

The accomplishments of the pragmatic, coalition-oriented, marginal man style of American politics

[9] Peter L. Berger, "Sociology and Freedom," *American Sociologist* 6, no. 1 (February 1971): 3–4.

has been very great indeed. One can only ask that the radicals who wish to destroy it be aware of what it is they are trying to destroy. One can only ask of the amateurs who wish to purify the political process that they first understand why the process works the way it does and secondly that they will have to come up with alternative methods of conflict management.

If the argument of this chapter is correct, the political leader, who by management and compromise, by education and informal agreement is able to maintain the American consensus and move it forward in constructive and healthy directions, is possessed of an extraordinarily important (and probably rare) human skill. I would argue that the successful politician is a man of great art and great virtue (though that virtue may not permeate his life). The problem of American society really is not that we have too many politicians; in fact, we have too few.

And unfortunately we do not seem to be able to protect the best of them from assassination.

A national political leader in the 1970s will have to possess extraordinary skills of bargaining and coalition formation. He must liquidate much foreign military involvement and still prevent the resurgence of isolationism. He must respond to legitimate demands of the militants and at the same time persuade other Americans that the demands are indeed legitimate. He must persuade middle Americans that the fundamental principles on which the society rests are not being destroyed but are rather growing and developing. He must restore confidence in the integrity and honesty of public officials. He must begin to find solutions to the technical problems of pollution, waste, and conservation of resources in an exceedingly complex and advanced industrial society. Even though he probably will not be able to convince some of the young, he still must realize that he has on his hands a whole generation that has every reason to be cynical about politics and politicians. Finally, he must find some way to end the peculiar economic situation where depression and inflation coexist and reinforce one another.

Is this the most serious set of problems that an American president has ever faced? Are we in a time of unprecedented crisis? The answers to such questions are not obvious. How does one compare one historical era with another? The situation in the republic was surely serious during the Great Depression. Is it more so now? It may not matter; it is serious enough, and only the most sophisticated political leadership, a leadership combining resources of intelligence with political skill, is going to be able to cope with the crisis.

We cannot, obviously, relinquish our world responsibilities, but neither can we afford another long and corrosive military adventure such as Vietnam. Even overlooking the moral implications of what the war did to Vietnam itself, the United States is simply not strong enough economically, politically, or morally to endure another such involvement. The internal social problems we ignored throughout the 1950s cannot be resolved unless the economy is prosperous and unless the public is better disposed to trust its government. A strategy of taking from one group—usually the working-class whites—in order to give to another group simply will not work. The tax money and the addition to the gross national product that are necessary to respond to the legitimate demands of minority groups will not be available unless we have a decade of sustained economic growth, which will be all the more difficult to achieve because now we must also be aware of the problems of pollution and resource depletion that economic growth generates.

John Kennedy's promise of 1960 to get America moving again was an exciting one that unfortunately was not fulfilled. Political leadership of the 1970s must make the same promise with the full realization that it will be much more difficult to live up to now. And 1976 is not far away.

THE AMATEURS

The remote ancestors of the New Politics, the "politics of style" and the "politics of love," were the "good government" reformers of one and two generations ago. This sincere, well-meaning, highly motivated group of people determined that American politics needed to be "cleaned up" and that the corrupt political bosses ought to be thrown out of office. The ideal of the reformers was clean, efficient, businesslike government, which is to say, government modeled on the ideal of the white upper middle class and aristocracy (or in New York, the Jewish upper middle class and aristocracy). The Catholic ethnic political leaders, who were the bosses, were ruling because of their patronage army and because of their corruption and because of their vote fraud. They were exploiting the people, and it was the solemn obligation of those highiy principled reformers to end this exploitation.

The reform movement failed by and large. When it did succeed in capturing control of the city it discovered that the social forces the bosses had to contend with did not simply go away when a clean, efficient Anglo-Saxon manager was installed. City-manager government, though it looked good on paper and represented an application of the business ethic to politics, somehow managed to lose contact with the social realities. The political science profession, which had enthusiastically supported the reformers, began to understand that the political boss did, after all, have an important role to play in society. He was a power broker who mediated among the various religious, ethnic, racial, and social groups of the city. He provided channels to power for the new immigrants that the official social and political structure did not provide. In the vocabulary of this book, what the reformers failed to understand was that American politics absolutely requires bargaining and coalition building. City managers are ill-equipped to do either.

In addition to the reform component of amateurism, there is what Professor James Q. Wilson calls, "the Liberal Audience." Wilson points out that during presidential elections there is tremendous pressure for the political party to move toward the center, but during the years between presidential elections, there are equally strong pressures moving the party away from the center. This pressure is exerted mostly by those volunteers who work hard for the party; they are much more deeply involved in politics than the average citizen and more apt to hold views further away from the center. It was the Republican volunteers or the Republican "attentive audience" (Wilson's phrase) that captured the GOP in 1964. Wilson asserts that the Democratic attentive audience was particularly influential during the 1960s. He describes it:

> *And the attentive Democratic audience is a liberal one, made up of volunteers and part-time public servants with discretionary money to spend, personal style to display, campaign skills to use, "interesting ideas" to propound, and influence in the mass media to wield. The importance of the members of the Liberal Audience has grown as the power and cohesiveness of the political party at the local level declined; as the bright young millionaires created by the boom of the '60s became interested in applying their social consciences to politics; as television acquired a power to bless or curse formerly reserved to archbishops; as organ-*

ized labor came to be scorned for its "middle-class values" (though courted for its working-class money); and as key posts in city halls, federal agencies, and even the White House were filled with brilliant young men fresh out of law school or sometimes even fresher out of college. To a substantial degree, at least on the East Coast, Democratic politics, when the party is out of power, occurs within this group and the several communications nets linking it.[1]

The liberal volunteers are serious, well-meaning, highly principled men, and they are absolutely convinced that the only kind of politics is the politics of precise policy position on a whole range of issues. The only kind of rational politics is issue politics. It is issues that should be used to get people involved in politics. It is issues that should distinguish one party from another and one candidate from another. Party affiliation, sectional, ethnic, and religious loyalties and personal identification with the leader are considered to be irrational and immoral means for deciding elections.

The amateurs have the intelligence, the motivation, and the time to devote to political activities, whether they be Democrats or Republicans. They are increasingly able to dominate the parties when a national campaign is not in progress. The Liberal Audience (as well as the Conservative Audience) rejects categorically the description of American politics I have presented in this book. It is hard to tell whether this rejection is normative or descriptive. Certainly, the "attentive audience" is convinced that

1 James Q. Wilson, "Crime and the Liberal Audience," *Commentary* 51, no. 1 (January, 1971): 73.

this is not the way politics ought to be. It also seems to think that this is not the way politics is. Whatever is left of the old ethnic coalition politics, the liberals argue, can be eliminated if only the well-educated, sincere, rational, and articulate sections of the population work vigorously enough and appeal enthusiastically enough to the people.

But Joseph Kraft's statement (quoted by Wilson) that the "disorder issue can be skirted or muted by personal appeal and stress on local needs such as pollution or housing" may encourage a politics of deception. An attractive personable candidate is expected to appear on the scene and "sell" the people on his personality. This seems to me to be some indication that the Liberal Audience wishes to hoodwink the voters into becoming liberals. Wilson's response to this strategy is most appropriate.

> *To say that charm and motherhood issues are the only alternatives to trying to "out-Agnew Agnew" is to misunderstand, fundamentally and tragically, both the needs and the mood of the electorate. Kraft must have forgotten what happened only a year ago to the most charming and appealing candidate in the most liberal city in America—John V. Lindsay.*[2]

This concern about image and charisma is precisely from those liberals who are outraged at the immorality of the "selling" of Richard Nixon. The truth of the matter is, of course, that with the possible exception of California and New York City, personal and political sex appeal have only limited political merit, and candidates cannot be

[2] Ibid., p. 78.

merchandized, at least not in the long run. The pertinent question is not whether a candidate has enough charisma to seduce the public into politics that are purely issue-oriented but whether he has enough political skill to reconvene the old Democratic coalition.

The Liberal Audience's approach seems to be that since coalition politics are immoral and corrupt, they are necessarily going to go away, and then a pure issue-oriented politics will make the country a far better place. One can only shake one's head in dismay when faced with such appalling ignorance as to what people and politics are really like. When the liberal reformer says, "Most people think . . ." what he means is "My friends and I think . . ."; and when he says, "People will no longer tolerate . . ." what he means is that the editorial writers in the journals that he and his friends read will no longer tolerate. The liberal volunteer is perfectly within his rights to hold his own position and to bargain vigorously and persuade others to adopt that position, but when he attempts to use his strategic influence in the mass media and the world of ideas to force others to accept his claims of moral superiority and to adopt not only his position but his political style, and when he seeks for candidates to mesmerize the people to accomplish this goal, he is engaging in political tactics which are, after all, pretty difficult to distinguish from those used by Adolf Hitler.

What the liberal amateur fails to understand is that, as Professor Wilson puts it, ". . . a strong case can be made that the function of political parties in the United States (and probably in most Western democracies) has been to convert "irrational" loyalties into political power so that leaders could govern without having to persuade 51 percent of the electorate to agree on all important issues." [3]

The trouble with the members of the Liberal Audience is that the only people they are in contact with politically most of the time are other members of the Liberal Audience. The "my friends and I" fallacy is a strong one, and the Liberal Audience of 1972 was no more immune from it than the Goldwater Audience in 1964.

The liberal amateur means well, but his issue-oriented approach to politics could have destructive effects. As Professor Wilson shrewdly observes:

> *The need to employ issues as incentives and to distinguish one's party from the opposition along policy lines will mean that political conflict will be intensified, social cleavages will be exaggerated, party leaders will tend to be men skilled in the rhetorical arts, and the party's ability to produce agreement by trading issue-free resources will be reduced. . . .*
>
> *. . It may be wondered whether these consequences of attempting to act in a public-spirited, disinterested way indicate a defect in democratic government. They are only defects if one believes that all aspects of society should be rationalized. In fact, no society, certainly no one as complex and dynamic as ours, can cope with its problems or even cohere* solely *on the basis of reason and concern for the public welfare: elements that are not reasonable and public-spirited must somehow help to hold it together and make it "work." A society must, in other words, depend to some extent*

[3] James Q. Wilson, *The Amateur Democrat* (Chicago: The University of Chicago Press, 1962), p. 357.

upon essential social functions being performed by accident, or, at least, without being intended, on the chance that motives that are not public-regarding will give rise to long-run, indirect benefits that will help maintain the society. To destroy in the name of reason and morality the mechanisms, the remote and indirect consequences of which may be indispensable to the maintenance of social order, might be disastrous.[4]

The liberal amateurs have an especially great power in American society, not because of their votes (they probably can deliver at the most somewhere between 3 to 5 percent of the votes outside New York City and Berkeley, California) but because of their large influence on the mass media and on the shaping of ideas in American society. I do not accuse them of any conspiracy, since no real conspiracy is necessary. As a point of fact, the Liberal Audience has powerful influence in the mass media and in the universities. When this influence is combined with its passionate sincerity and dedicated enthusiasm, it can even persuade political candidates that the way the Liberal Audience sees issues are in fact the issues. George McGovern was clearly so persuaded in 1972.

In recent years the academy has turned its considerable energies to the remaking of society, in particular to the causes of peace and racial justice. Many university intellectuals have become more deeply involved in politics. It would now appear that not merely have their efforts failed, they may even have become counterproductive for the very causes

[4] James Q. Wilson, *The Amateur Democrat* (Chicago: The University of Chicago Press, 1962), p. 358.

they tried to support. Surely the academic peace movement consistently reinforced the stand of the hawks in American society, and it may very well turn out that academic support for the so-called black revolution has slowed down rather than accelerated the pace of social improvement for American blacks.[5]

The root of the problem is that the "world outside" did not react the way it was supposed to, which is to say, the people who inhabit that world neither think nor behave like academics.

The crisis in the relationship between the academy and the world outside is not simply that the academic does not understand the world outside, not even that he does not think it worthwhile to attempt to understand the world outside, but in fact that he is only barely aware that the world exists. The attitude was summarized by the distinguished California philosopher who observed at the time of Ronald Reagan's gubernatorial victory, "I'm astonished the man won. Nobody I knew voted for him."

The academic is so dazzled by the brilliance of his analysis and expression that reflects the world he lives in that it is not difficult for him to ignore the existence of the rest of the world (save those social

[5] In this chapter, the word "academic" is used to represent that influential minority who sets the tone and the style and the fashion of the academy at any given time. I am not writing about all academics, a majority, or even a large minority. The "academic" in this chapter is rather the small but highly articulate group who are interested in remaking society without bothering to try to understand anyone else in the society but themselves. One must certainly include in this analysis the allies of the academy in the mass media who tend to feel guilty vis-à-vis the full-fledged academic, who presumably knows more and is more morally pure than the media huckster.

groups he sees as special carriers of virtue—youth and blacks at the present time, for example). Given the nature and the social functions of the academy such unawareness is not surprising. The academic is expected to be deeply involved in his own teaching and research. The rest of the world not only tolerates but encourages his isolation, because it has come to believe that the isolation is necessary for the academic to do what he is supposed to do. Whether the isolation is ever really desirable may be a matter for question, and it creates no serious problem until the academic discovers, usually with an overwhelming experience of guilt, that there are many things wrong with the rest of the world. Looking around and discovering the injustice and immorality in the rest of the world, he righteously decides something must be done about it and asks himself, "If something must be done, then who better than me to do it?" Perhaps the best possible answer to that question is, "Just about anyone." For when the academy decides to remake the rest of the world, whether the world wants to be remade or not, there is likely to be trouble abrewing, if only because the academic is but dimly aware of what motivates those human beings who are to be the object of his missionary zeal.

There are three underlying assumptions behind the academy's zeal:

1. It knows how to remake society.
2. The rest of society will fall into line and permit itself to be remade once the academy has pointed out the existence of immorality.
3. The rest of society will be willing to pick up the tab for the expenses the academy undergoes in its

process of fashioning that rest of society according to its own image and likeness.

But none of these assumptions is evidently true. Those who resist the academy's missionary zeal can point out that academics have an extremely difficult time keeping their own house in order, that academic departments in colleges are usually but one step removed from chaos, that there is no evidence the academy has been very successful in its own primary task of educating the young, and that it resolutely resists attempts on the part of those who are on the "outside" to evaluate its own performance. In other words, the academy, having been unsuccessful in its own specific function, now assumes that it should be permitted to appropriate the functions of a number of other social institutions. Having failed to run the university well, it now assumes, as a matter of right, that it should be permitted to run the rest of society.

Hannah Arendt disposed neatly of the basic academic-politician assumption—the assumption that society will sit idly by and permit itself to be remade.

> *Self-interest, when asked to yield to "true" interest—that is, the interest of the world as distinguished from that of the self—will always reply, "Near is my shirt, nearer is my skin." That may not be particularly reasonable, but it is quite realistic; it is the not very noble but adequate response to the time discrepancy between men's private lives and the altogether different life expectancy of the public world. To expect people, who have not the slightest notion of what* res pub-

lica, *the public thing, is, to behave nonviolently and argue rationally in matters of interest is neither realistic nor reasonable.*[6]

To put the whole matter more directly, the academy is not the place to develop the skills required for political action, for persuasion, for coalition formation, for development of consensus. Indeed, the academy is not even the place where most men can expect to acquire the skills that are necessary for dealing respectfully with those who have the temerity to exist beyond the boundaries of the academic grove.

To the world outside, the academic missionary looks intolerant, reactionary, authoritarian, hypnotized by his own rhetoric, and ignorant. When faced with the involvement of such a man in politics, the world outside reacts first with laughter, then with a call to a psychiatrist, perhaps, and finally, with a summons to the police or the national guard.

I do not wish to exclude the amateur from politics and especially the academic amateur. The problems of American society are so complicated that they simply cannot be solved without the help of the dedicated. Nevertheless, if the scholar comes into politics, by the very principles of his own scholarship he should suspend judgment until he learns how the system operates. He should not attempt to destroy the ongoing political process until he has asked himself whether its destruction might not do more harm than good. He should not write off vast masses of people without trying to understand them or to sympathize with their positions.

[6] Hannah Arendt, *On Violence* (New York: Harcourt, Brace and World, 1969), p. 78.

Fading off to the left from the Liberal Attentive Audience are the Politicians of Style. They share with the reformer the conviction that American politics is essentially corrupt. They share with the Liberal Audience the conviction that politics ought to be issue-oriented. But it is not enough, according to the Politics of Style, for people to endorse the right side of issue questions only, they must also endorse them in the *right way.* Substantial majorities of the American population do in fact support the liberal side on the critical issues facing the country, but this is not nearly enough for the Politicians of Style. That the American voter, including the white ethnic voter, is strongly in favor of the guaranteed annual wage and racial justice is not enough. He must also be ready to support woman's lib, gay liberation, the Black Panthers, legalized abortion and marijuana—all in ways specified by the Politicians of Style. Nor is it merely enough that the American voter was against the war in Vietnam. He must be against it in the way and for the reasons approved of by the Politicians of Style. He must be ready to burn American flags, to denounce the American society as corrupt, imperialistic, and to give every evidence that he hates the United States as much as the sons and daughters of the Anglo-Saxon and Jewish aristocracy who attend Yale hate it.

Nor does it suffice that the American voter is deeply concerned about the pollution issue. He must combine his concern with pollution with sympathy for obscenity, free love, long hair, and dirty bodies. If he does not admire the late Ho Chi Minh or Jerry Rubin, then his political position is relatively unimportant.

And it is not merely enough that the voter is willing to support candidates and legislation that would dramatically change American society. He must also be willing to confess his guilt and make reparation for his own past offenses and those of his ancestors, even though the ancestors of many American voters were still on the plains of Galicia, the mountains of Sicily, or the bogs of County Mayo when those offenses were committed.

Finally, it is not just enough that the American voter realize there are serious problems facing the society. He must be ready to write off the society as corrupt, immoral, racist, sexist, imperialist, and indeed whatever other category is popular in the lexicon of the Politicians of Style. He must give up his nine-to-five job, his two cars, his suburban home (or his urban home, for that matter) and drag himself off to Woodstock, or turn on with acid or pot, or join a hippie commune, or listen to rock music all day long. In other words, for the American voter to become moral he must stop being straight.

Obviously, the Politician of Style has even less chance of winning an election than the messianic academic. But then he is not really interested in winning an election; he is not really interested in changing society. As Father Daniel Berrigan is alleged to have remarked, "There is no reason to be hung-up on practicality." Coalition formation is not what counts; winning allies is not what counts; creating majorities for a candidate in favor of social change is not what counts. All that really counts is that one assume the appropriate stance, engage in the proper liturgical gestures, and be warmly applauded by the appropriate audiences. Let us take, for example, the Chicago convention demonstrations, in which the Politicians of Style were so warmly sympathized with by substantial segments of the Liberal Audience. No one in his right mind thinks that the Chicago protesters could possibly have had an impact on the outcome of the convention. Nor does anyone seriously argue that if they did have such an impact, the things they stood for were representative of how the majority of the Democratic party in the nation felt. It is argued that the protesters came to register their dissatisfaction with the Vietnam war, but surely no one believes that. Their behavior before, during, and after the convention is ample evidence that they did not intend merely to protest, and they did not have the slightest reason to believe that they could change the outcome of the convention. Their principal reason for coming was to disrupt the ordinary political processes of the nation and, if necessary, to disrupt the life of the city. They did not succeed with either of these goals, of course, but thanks to the lack of discipline on the part of some members of the Chicago police force and the willing cooperation of some of the mass media, they managed to get a great deal of free publicity for themselves; they made a considerable impact on at least the Liberal Audience if not the nation as a whole. Philip Converse's finding that three-quarters of the 1968 doves approved of the way the Chicago police handled the convention demonstrations indicates how politically effective the strategy of the protesters really was. But then no one would ever accuse David Dellinger or Rennie Davis, or Tom Hayden, Abbie Hoffman, or Jerry Rubin of being the kinds of persons who were out to win allies. They were out to make a show and to attract attention, and they were extremely successful. For them, that is apparently enough.

The Politicians of Style are politically irrelevant and the Politics of Style is a deliberate self-conscious pursuit of political irrelevance. The burning of draft records and the pouring of blood on government files, *pace* the Brothers Berrigan, gets a good deal of media coverage and wins all sorts of warm applause from some segments of the Liberal Audience and particularly from upper-middle-class would-be radical Catholics. If people wish to engage in this sort of behavior, it is their privilege, so long as having done it, they don't appeal to some higher morality to protect themselves from the law. If they wish to do these things in the name of principle or morality and as a prophetic judgment on the rest of society, that is their privilege, too; but if they argue that what they engage in is serious political and social action aimed at modifying American society and politics, it must be said of them that they are both wrong and foolish. For everything we know about American politics and everything we know about the dynamics of public opinion would indicate that the liturgical gestures of the Politics of Style are counterproductive.

Not all political amateurs, be they reformers, New Politicians, academic liberals, the New Class, or Politicians of Style, substitute enthusiasm and principle for competence and understanding. But enough of them do to make political amateurism a very uncertain component of the American political process at the present time. It may well be that the romanticism of the 1960s will give way to a sophisticated pragmatic realism of the 1970s, in which case the dramatic increase of political amateurism of the 1960s will represent a political bonus for American society. But if the amateurs are unable to become more sophisticated politically, in the words of the famous song from their most popular university, "They will pass and be forgotten with the rest."

Most political amateurs are *not* narrow ideologues. On the contrary, most of them are generous, committed American citizens who believe in our political processes and wish to make them work more effectively. The amateurs I describe in this chapter are rather special kinds of political personages for whom politics becomes something of a religion. Within the McGovern movement there were large numbers of volunteers, especially young ones, who did not share the narrow, ideological views of those who dominated the television screen in July 1972. But of course the television camera seeks out not the ordinary but the unusual, not the average but the abnormal, not the typical but the bizarre. Neither Rick Stearns nor Shirley MacLaine—much less Bella Abzug or Jesse Jackson—is a fair example of the amateur political movement. Arrogance and ignorance were responsible for the Democratic debacle in 1972, an arrogance that laid claim to superior morality and understanding and an ignorance that misunderstood the American political process and the response of ordinary Americans to political stimuli. But tens of thousands of McGovern volunteers were neither arrogant nor ignorant, and many young volunteers who went into the campaign as amateurs came out as semipros at least. Many of the young people who earned their political spurs in the McGovern campaign will be of decisive importance in rebuilding the liberal Democratic coalition, and some of them will go on to become major political figures before the century ends. The major deficiencies of the youthful volunteer movement, it seems to me, came from the fact that the young volunteers carried around in their heads pictures of the political process that they absorbed from the mass media and from their college teachers. But I have the impression that a considerable number of them began to reevaluate their pictures in the rough and tumble encounter of political campaigning and to question their assumptions. American politics has not heard the last of them.

There was considerable talk about the New Politics and the New Politicians in 1972, although it was difficult to extract a precise definition of the terms. If the New Politician is a man who is aware that there are new political issues, new political audiences, new styles of communication, and new political expectations, then the more of them we have the better. But if a New Politician is one who thinks that ideological enthusiasm is a substitute for political bargaining and coalition formation, then he is not likely to be very effective as a political leader. On the other hand, if the "Old Politician" is one who is caught up in the issues of the 1930s, 1940s, and 1950s, and is unaware of the impact of television on political campaigning and political leadership, then he will soon be extinct as the Neanderthal man. But if the Old Politician is one who can apply skills of bargaining and coalition formation to the solution of contemporary problems, while at the same time attracting the enthusiastic support of a new generation of committed amateurs, then the old politician is likely to be around for a long time to come.

The Democratic coalition will not be rebuilt by an amateur. On the contrary, it is a job for the most skilled, sophisticated, and sensitive political professional. But that professional will have to know how to work with amateurs and how to educate and train them so that they may become professionals like himself. The professional politician who does not know that the volunteer movement is here to stay and that volunteers can be an immense asset for a political leader is a failure by his own standards. A professional who cannot integrate amateurs into his coalition is inadequate.

THE NEW ISSUE

American politics are changing, not as poor George McGovern would have had us believe, but changing nevertheless. It is not one that is destroying the political context described in the previous chapters. The change is, rather, the introduction of a new element in that context. A new issue has arisen that is not yet as powerful as the peace and prosperity issues, though it is related to both of them. It may very well never be as powerful as those two issues, so in wartime or depression the New Issue may well recede into the background. At the present time, this New Issue is not powerful enough to move the Republican minority to a majority position in American society, but with a political candidate as popular as General Eisenhower able to exploit it sufficiently, there might be a fundamental realignment.

The New Issue is certainly powerful enough to revivify the ailing Democratic coalition, which seems to me its legitimate heir, in any event. The New Issue is something like the Social Issue of Scammon and Wattenberg, though I think it is both broader and deeper. In Chapter 7, I called it "neopopulism," because it is somewhat similar to the populist movements of the past,[1] though there may well be

[1] There was a good deal of talk about "populism" in 1972. The McGovern movement claimed to be populist, although in fact its policies advocated more big government rather than less, and real populism is profoundly suspicious of government power. Mr. Nixon is making something of a populist appeal, without using the word, in his current campaign to decrease the power of the Washington bureaucracy. My hunch is that neopopulism is more opposed to arbitrary, irresponsible, and unresponsive government power than it is to government as such. The one truly authentic populist speech—in the grand populist tradition —in the 1972 Democratic convention was that of George C. Wallace. One can disagree with Governor Wallaces's stand on

more differences than similarities. It could be called the "participation movement," since it manifests itself in increased political participation; but this does not mean that it represents a yearning for participatory democracy of the sort sought by the New Left or those virtuous paragons of Consciousness III.

It could be called the "respect issue," because it certainly demands on the part of those who are concerned about it that they be respected as full human beings. And it could be called the "meaning issue," because it is especially important for those who are seeking more meaning in life. But it involves more than participation, more than respect, more than meaning.

Some will call it the "revolutionary issue." It

race and foreign policy and still understand that of all the major political leaders of America, he is unquestionably the strongest contemporary exponent of the ancient American political tradition of opposition to concentrated power. If there is anyone in American politics who is *really* against the Establishment, it is Governor Wallace. In a contest between the "liberal-intellectual Establishment" and the "corporate-Disneyland Establishment," Wallace spoke for the vast number of Americans who cannot conceive of themselves as belonging to anything that is powerful or important. His political style is not to be imitated, his political goals are not to be admired, his political prejudices are not to be accepted; nonetheless, he says something important about how many Americans who are neither racists nor hawks feel.

I am personally uneasy about the classical populist tradition. It was frequently anti-Catholic and almost always anti-intellectual. The neopopulism described in this chapter represents a major transmutation of that tradition. Just the same, when George Wallace denounces concentrations of wealth and power, I cannot help but think that other more enlightened and sophisticated politicians should listen very carefully to what he says, because he is speaking for many Americans who are unhappy, not about social change, not about racial integration, but about the concentration of power.

surely represents an important change in the structure of American politics. However, it is not revolutionary in the sense that most of those who would be moved by the issue want out of the society. On the contrary, those who are moved by it want in. It is not fundamentally a sign of pathology in the society, but rather a sign of abundant health. The New Issue may never tear American society apart, not at least by itself, but if the political leadership does not find a way to cope with the issue, it is one that will keep society disturbed for a long time to come.

One of the reasons that it is so hard to describe this issue is that it has yet to assume definite shape and form. It exists in a rather vague series of discontents. One of the challenges to political leadership in the decade ahead will be to give it shape and form. The New Issue is that people do not want to be excluded from the political and social decision-making process.

There are many reasons why they wish to be dealt into the political process. Increased leisure means that they have time for politics. The increase in education means that they know more (or think they do) about how politics works. The increased power of government bureaucracies causes them to want more control over the governmental decision-making process. And not least important is the desire to see that the costs of social policy are equitably distributed. The disadvantaged groups in society want in, I suspect, in order that they might cease to be disadvantaged. The advantaged groups want in (or to stay in) because of guilt or responsibility or desire for power or generosity or altruism. The vast majority of Americans, who are somewhere in between the advantaged and disadvantaged, are politically concerned not so much to prevent the improvement in the lives of the disadvantaged as to make sure that they are not stuck with paying the major share of the cost. The American political creed says that improvement for the disadvantaged occurs either from an enlargement of the pie or from reslicing the pieces smaller—all the pieces, not just the neighboring one. Despite the environmental pessimists, I am inclined to believe that there is no reason why most of the resources necessary to eliminate poverty and discrimination in American society cannot come from an increase in the size of the pie. However, the most appalling mistake of American liberals in the 1960s was their failure to realize that without even thinking about it they imposed disproportionate costs for social change on precisely that segment of society that was least able to pay. It was the homes, jobs, schools, property, and the lives of lower-middle- and middle-middle-class Americans that seemed to be placed in jeopardy by the changes of the 1960s. When these segments of the population protested, they were written off as racists. It was only when the quota system and "affirmative action" (which is merely a disguise for quotas) began to pinch the upper middle class and especially the university intellectuals that public outcry was raised. By 1972, then, neopopulism not only says, "We want to participate," it also says, "Stop screwing us!"

It does not follow, however, that the neopopulists I am describing are opposed to broader participation in American life by members of minority groups. I have noted in previous chapters that many Democratic voters were turned off by the members of the "new constituency" they saw on their television screens at the Democratic convention. But I would insist that their objections were not to the fact that there were more blacks or more young people or more women or more Spanish-speaking people at the convention. On the contrary, I suspect that most Americans would rejoice at such a change. The neopopulist objection, as I understand it, would take the following forms:

1. "I don't mind their being there, but I do mind that we were kicked out to make room for them."

2. "Who says that they really represent the people they say they do?" (How many women elected Bella Abzug? How many blacks elected Jesse Jackson?)

3. "They're all better educated and make more money than I do. How come they claim to be the oppressed minority? If my country has been good enough to them so that they could get educated, make money, and be elected to the Democratic convention, why do they hate me?"

It is very difficult to explain the world view and the assumptions behind such questions to the well-educated liberal left intellectual. Either you understand instantly what people mean when they say such things, or, I'm afraid, you will never understand it. But the Democratic coalition will only be rebuilt by those who do not write off such questions as a sign of racism and bigotry.

The neopopulist does not want to be excluded or victimized. The negative form of the statement is deliberately chosen. It is clear that an increasing proportion of people want to be actively involved in the decision-making processes, far more people than those who want to be actively involved in politics. In an earlier chapter I argued that on the basis of the data of Almond and Verba, what counted for Americans was not so much that they had, in fact, been personally involved in political activity as they knew they could be if they wanted to. I suspect that in the narrow sense of traditional political activities, most Americans still feel they have access to politics. Government, however, plays a much bigger role in our lives today than it did even thirty years ago, and the large corporations (business, labor, education, etc.) are also far more important in our lives than they were in, let us say, the 1920s. Life has grown immensely more complicated. Even though man has been able to control some of the forces of nature, the new organizational technological forces that have been released seem to make life more capricious, arbitrary, and uncertain than ever before. The neopopulist issue, in short, represents a vague and inarticulate demand on the part of a considerable number of Americans that the organizational society be made controllable.

If my concept of the New Issue is correct, it explains much of what has happened during the 1960s. My colleague, Norman Nie, has pointed out to me that between 1952 and 1968, the proportion of Americans who engaged in one or more of four campaign activities—working for a party or a candidate, donating money, attending rallies, and joining partisan organizations—has doubled from 9 percent to 18 percent. Nor can this increase in participation be explained merely in terms of an increase in the educational level of the population. When one holds education constant, the participation increases, and the absolute rates of participation are higher for blacks than for whites. While Professor Nie's research does not yet enable him to offer any definitive explanations, it is clear that the increase in participation is not just the result of the fact that the population is better educated now than it was twenty years ago.

There is also the emergence of the various special group protest movements—black protest, student protest, welfare rights protest, woman's liberation, and the Wallace candidacy. While there are many differences among them, there are some striking similarities. All of them demand more concern for violated rights and more control over their own destinies. Each of the protest movements fairly screams at the rest of society, "Don't you dare forget about us!" In the complex world of the organizational society, each of these groups seems to feel that it is being bypassed, and unless it protests vigorously, it will be forgotten completely.

To a considerable extent all the protest movements have failed. While black militancy won many concessions before 1967, protesting strategy has been generally much less successful since then. All the other protest movements have made only minor impact on the social structure despite all the attention they have received from the mass media. Even though there is widespread sympathy, I think, for the goals of black militants and among women for women's liberation, the leaders of the various protest movements have been unable to capture much organizational support from its supposed constituency. No one presumes that woman's lib speaks for more than a tiny handful of even women college graduates; and it is clear that the black militant movements cannot deliver votes on election day.

The movement leadership can appropriately argue that it doesn't really need active majority support, and that if it continues to engage in its strategy of consciousness raising, that is to say, lifting the level of consciousness of its constituency, it will eventually acquire a wider and much stronger organizational base.

But at the present writing, most of the protest movements seem to have lost most of their vigor—with the possible exception of the women's movement. It is also clear that many of those who are basically sympathetic to the goals of those movements that claim to represent them are completely turned off by the strategies and styles of their leadership. Most of the movements have failed, in fact, precisely because, while the leadership discovered a superb political issue, its own ideology and rhetoric prevented it from presenting the issue in such a way as to be able to exploit potential support available in the society. It is not, I think, that the overwhelming majority of Americans are moderates who do not like revolutionary rhetoric and posturing; it is that the movements' leaders do not seem to be able to articulate adequately the problems that their potential followers feel. The rhetoric of the leaderships has been of separation, conflict, confrontation, and destruction of the established order. However, as I understand the New Issue, it represents the desire of people not to tear apart the social structure, but to find a more human and respectable place in it, a place where one has the capacity to exercise some control over what is happening.

It is not surprising that the first generation of movement leadership should miss the point. For when inarticulate and vague dissatisfactions begin to coalesce into an issue, the first leaders who charge into the fray are likely to have preconceived and ideologically defined views of both the questions and the answers that are pertinent to the New Issue. The failure of the protest movements of the 1960s can be traced to a very considerable extent to the fact that first-generation leadership had the answers to the wrong questions. Whether a second-generation leadership will appear on the scene that will be able to articulate the New Issues in a more satisfactory way and evolve a strategy with wider popular appeal remains to be seen. Even if they do, of course they will not gain anything like 100 percent or even 50 percent of their potential constituency, but they will have much larger organizations than the movements can presently command and much larger political impact. If there is an effective second-generation leadership, the first thing it will do is to eliminate the word "revolution" from its vocabulary, a word likely to be no more acceptable to their potential constituency than to their opposition. Indeed, when "revolution" is eliminated, it will be a sign that the period of inception is over and effective development can begin.

The New Issue, though it is still an inarticulated feeling on the part of an increasing number of Americans, is that people's destinies and the course of society ought to be more controllable than they are, that decisions which affect their lives and the lives of their children ought not to be made by vague and shadowy bureaucrats over whom they have no control. To put the matter somewhat differently, many Americans are suspicious that their society is drifting toward Plato's Republic, and they damned well want to make sure that the philosopher kings are held accountable.

And here is where the credibility issue, which has plagued the Johnson and then the Nixon administrations, becomes so important. The public increasingly suspects that the experts and the bureaucrats are not telling the truth, perhaps on occasion not even telling the truth to the elected political leaders. The American public, for example, was never permitted to make a decision about the Vietnamese war; indeed, the American Congress was not permitted to make that decision. Without going into all the details of the Tonkin Gulf resolution, it is still evident that most congressmen did not know what they were voting for, and it is also at least possible that they were deceived about the incident that gave rise to the resolution. Furthermore, the decisions to expand the war were made in secret and were disclosed to the public only gradually, frequently in an aura of half-truth in which people began to suspect that what was vigorously denied one week would be a matter of public policy the next.

The public was deceived about the Vietnam war. The philosopher kings can be turned out of office eventually in a national election, and with them go the Walt Rostows and the Henry Kissingers. But who gets rid of the army officers in the Pentagon who lie to their civilian superiors and to the U.S. Congress about the nature and extent of their activities? What can we do about the rude bureaucrats at the Board of Education or the Internal Revenue Service or the Social Security Agency?

What has happened is that the major problems facing the society—peace, racial diversity, the economy, and the environment—have now become so complicated and so enmeshed in the organizational bureaucracy that experts and administrators can appeal to either their expertise or their bureaucratic code as a pretext for being free from popular control. The New Issue says, in effect, that these men must once more be subjected to popular control, or at least to popular review. And the administrator must have some kind of administrative code if there is not to be chaos. Nevertheless, the new populism insists that these men are not to be a law unto themselves, that they must not lie to the people. They must be responsible to the people, whose servants they are after all.

Despite present economic problems and the squeeze that middle America finds itself in between inflation and taxes, neopopulism is to be found in groups that are economically and socially better off than ever before in history. With affluence comes the time and the education necessary to ponder their position vis-à-vis the rest of the world. It was no accident that the black sit-in movement began on the black college campuses, for it is only when a society has enough money to provide college educations for its most depressed minority group that the minority group is likely to have a leadership articulate and sophisticated enough to begin its protest. The economic affluence that has produced the bureaucratic structure of the organizational society has simultaneously produced the kinds of people who will demand an improvement of their position in the society and a greater voice in controlling what goes on there. Only an affluent society is likely to have generated a vast structure of expertise and administration that is such a marvelous target for protest.

Obviously black protesters want better jobs, better housing, better education. Obviously, too, they want to be treated with respect and dignity. But they are making these demands precisely against experts and administrators who seem indifferent to them as human beings and who are not ready to yield any right of review or control. The political leadership of the country is a secondary target for black protest, a target only so far as the protesters can blame the political leadership for the insensitivity of the bureaucracy. *Mutatis mutandis,* the same could be said of all the other protesters. Whatever the protest leaders are saying, their potential constituencies say, "Let us be part of the system," or, more specifically, "Give us some share in the control of the system." The day of the great alliance will dawn, perhaps, when the protesters discover that nobody else thinks they have control of the system either.

It must be emphasized that those who would rally to the New Issue are not demanding control over every decision made by the Internal Revenue Service or every shift of American foreign policy. Some might be more interested in direct participation and decision-making review than others; and certainly the point is not to make policy by majority vote. People must feel, however, that the expert decision-makers and administrators are subject to some kind of control and review where they are responsible and responsive. It is enough for the average American to know that he can become active in politics if he wants to and that his activity, with that of his compatriots, will have some impact on government. At the present time he does not have that assurance.

The American public is far more advanced in its thinking than the political leadership seems to understand. The problem is not to obtain public consent for the kinds of policies necessary to ensure peace or racial harmony or a more balanced relationship with nature. It is to persuade the public that these policies will not be implemented by arbitrary, arrogant, and autocratic bureaucracies, bureaucracies that in the long run will prove to be as incompetent as the Pentagon with all its expertise—and every American who ever had military service knows just how incompetent that is.

The New Issue, then, is an issue of personal control, or at least the option of personal control, and personal respect rooted in the fact of personal control. Those who are influenced, however inchoately, by the New Issue are not about to accept solutions imposed without their consent and without their control by leaders, bureaucrats, administrators, or academic experts. Those intense men who write their intense little articles for *World* about the restrictions and regulations that must be imposed on the rest of society for its own good are the ones most likely to stir the new populists into fury. And those bearded youthful revolutionaries, who with frequent use of such words as "like," "I mean," and "you know" lay down their simple-minded orders about how society must remake itself, are not likely to obtain a sympathetic hearing either. The neopopulist is quite ready to be virtuous, but he will be so on his terms, not someone else's. He will arrive at his virtue by free decision. He will also want to make sure that the virtue to which he is being exhorted does not impose upon him the burden of disproportionate and inequitable sacrifice. He will not be persuaded that virtue that singles him out as the victim of social change is virtue at all.

It will be argued that the demands of the neopopulists simply cannot be satisfied. A policy in which liberation is imposed on women is much easier to achieve than one in which the corporate structure is forced to respect a woman's right to control her destiny and to be liberated or not liberated, as she chooses. Segregation imposed on the black militant or the white racist, or integration imposed on the white liberal are relatively easy to produce. It is much more difficult to force a bureaucratic structure to respond to the individual black as an individual human being and to provide him with the option of living in a white neighborhood, a black neighborhood, or an integrated neighborhood, or wherever he wants to live, which would be to give him some control over the bureaucratic structures that dominate the housing market.

There is ample evidence that the American public is bored and weary with the American leader who has the simple magic answer. Adlai Stevenson II may have been before his time; it may not have been appropriate in the mid-1950s to speak of complexity to the American electorate. On the other hand, perhaps Stevenson's problem was the attractiveness of his opponent rather than his insistence on seeing things in their gray tones instead of black and white. I think the American people do not have to be told that issues are complicated and that there are no easy solutions. A considerable number of them at least know this as well as most of the political leadership. The public would be delighted to hear a political leader who would now acknowledge that things are complex and that he is not ready to promise anything more than progress toward solutions. The public even may have become so sophisticated that it is aware that he who promises much may well deliver nothing, and he who promises limited progress may deliver something more. It will not be necessary for the political candidate to promise solutions so much as to indicate that he is aware of the problem and intends to make some progress toward a solution. One of the attractive aspects of Senator McGovern's personality was that in the early phases of his campaign, he appeared to be a sensible, sober man, aware of the difficulties and limitations of policy making. I suspect that one of the secrets of his early success in the primaries was that he made neither demagogic charges nor sweeping promises. Unfortunately, as the primaries wore on (and the Harvard intellectuals began to feed him complex economic schemes), he began to propose sweeping programs that he did not understand himself. Then, after the convention, he began to make strident charges against his opponent. I am persuaded that he was caught in a trap prepared by his own personal rigidity and by extraordinarily bad advice. It is a shame that his calm, matter-of-fact Middle Western pragmatism was blotted out by his fundamentalist preaching. To turn Art Buchwald on his head, the old McGovern was much more appealing than the new one.

My hunch—and it is only that—is that fire-eating is finished in American politics, and not merely because Professor McLuhan has persuaded us all that television is a "cool" medium. The American public is now sophisticated enough to be able to see through a candidate who is trying to substitute charisma for intelligence and manipulation of the public for sympathetic understanding of it. The neopopulist, I would bet, will expect respect from only a reasonable and softspoken man.

Respect from and control of the corporate bureaucracy are not as pressing as war and unemployment, indeed as long as these other two issues exist, the New Issue will stay in the background (although no candidate will be hurt by addressing himself to it today). In the long run, if peace and prosperity are achieved, the principal political and social issue facing American society will not be revolution; it will be providing a sense of both control and respectability for an ever-increasing portion of the population who are demanding these as their right.

If the New Issue is not going to be decisive in the 1976 election, then why should one bother with it? It is important for a number of reasons. In a close election it could swing victory one way or the other. While it may have more impact on local politics than on national politics now, it is likely to grow more important nationally as the decade goes on. Finally, even if the issue is not decisively important in the 1976 election, it does summarize the present crisis of American political and social life. The political leader who wishes not only to get elected but to govern must address himself to the New Issue after his election, certainly, if not before.

And why not before? A political campaign geared to the New Issue could be an extraordinarily effective campaign. For there is nothing un-American about the desire to participate. On the contrary, wanting to be part of the system, to control and govern one's own destiny, is a desire that is quintessentially American. Nor is there anything un-American about the desire for an equitable distribution of the costs of social change. The political leader who can interpret the turbulence of the times in terms of the American political tradition and respond to it with the rhetoric that says the desire to participate is a sign not of the collapse of American democracy but of its growth and expansion will have tremendous popular appeal.

The New Issue is not at variance with the American political tradition. Indeed, the desire to participate and to be treated with respect and dignity is very much in harmony with the traditional American patriotic rhetoric. I do not think that such a formulation of the New Issues is false. It may not appeal to some of the elite groups in the country who are not moved by the traditional American rhetoric and who might be more sympathetic if the desire for more participation was expressed in revolutionary terms. However, most Americans are not revolutionary.

The so-called reforms in the Democratic party in 1972 were obviously a well-meaning attempt to broaden participation in American political life, but as these reforms became the tools by which the liberal left enthusiasts seized control of state delegations and eventually the national committee and convention, they led not to an increase in participation but to a decrease in it. The old line political leaders were displaced in power—though many of these, having been elected to public office, had a more legitimate claim to represent the American voters than did those who replaced them. But any political reform that increases the income and educational level of a convention can scarcely be said to have produced a "more representative" convention. Because there were blacks, women, and young people on the convention floor, it does not follow that blacks, young people, or women are represented by them. If a black was elected from a predominantly black district, then in fact he represented a certain segment of the black population. If there were special constituencies for women and for young people, then those elected from such constituencies would truly represent women and young people. But most of the women, blacks, and young people at the convention were self-anointed, self-appointed spokesmen for such constituencies. Their credentials as representatives were virtually nonexistent. The quota system made the Democratic convention *look* more representative. It gave the *appearance* of greater political participation. In fact, such representation was sheer tokenism. No number of symbolic blacks or symbolic young people or symbolic women can possibly indicate greater real participation by women or blacks or young people in the convention or in the party. Real participation only exists when those who allege themselves to represent a specific group have in fact been elected by and are responsible to that group. Some black and Chicano and Puerto Rican delegates were in fact selected by such constituencies, but not a single woman or youth delegate was so selected. Young and female delegates to a convention will only speak for their own constituencies when American politics are reorganized into districts based on sex and age—an event that one devoutly hopes will never occur. The more youthful or female delegates at political conventions the better; but let it be clear that they are representing the people who elected them—young and old, men and women.

The balanced ticket is almost as old as American politics, and what I take to be the neopopulist opposition to quotas (or at least the way the Democratic party chose to interpret them) is not opposition either to broad representation or to a balanced ticket. It is that I object to the rigid, ideologically motivated imposition on the Democratic process of systems that guarantee political power to certain individuals who have appointed themselves as representatives of broad constituencies for which they have in fact no legitimate right to speak.

Did the seating of Jesse Jackson (and the unseating of Cecil Partee) mean more or less participation for Chicago blacks in the 1972 Democratic convention? Did Democrats from the city of Chicago have a greater participation in the 1972 convention because Alderman William Singer was there and Mayor Richard Daley was not?

The "reforms" were an attempt—and probably an honest one—to broaden participation, but the net result was that many Democrats who had previously felt included in the party now felt excluded. Some of those who are now supposed to be enjoying greater participation (women and young people) were not in fact adequately represented at all. As a technique for broadening participation, then, the Democratic reforms were a disastrous failure. Make no mistake about it: quotas exclude more than they include. Neopopulism is likely to be an implacable foe of quotas. Curiously enough, the balanced ticket rarely stirred up much animosity. Even more curiously, the very ones who insist on imposing quotas were not so long ago the very ones who denounced the balanced ticket as "ethnic" politics.

A political campaign, designed to respond to the issue of participation, as well as the problems of peace and prosperity, ought to be extraordinarily effective, particularly for a candidate who is looking for an effective rhetoric. This with a program that combines such diverse partners as the liberal Left, discontented minorities, the ethnics, the big city political leaders, and the unions can hardly fail.

No one can deny that some of the youthful population want out instead of in, but it would be a mistake to think that the youth counterculture is characteristic of even most young people, to say nothing of the other protesting groups within the society. The well-to-do psychedelics and revolutionaries and communards have already decided that American society is beyond redemption. Their family experience and their education have caused them to write off the possibility of the New Issue being taken seriously. Fortunately, or unfortunately, most other Americans are not inclined, indeed cannot afford the luxury, to join a commune or to wait for the Consciousness III eschaton. The opposite of social despair is not mysticism or drugs; it is certainly not bomb-throwing; it is coalition politics, which, for whatever reason, is beneath the dignity and intelligence of the precocious youth of the counterculture. They are, of course, perfectly within their rights if they want to leave the rest of American society behind. But the political leadership and its intellectual advisors who thought that the youthful counterculture was the issue and ignored the widespread desire of American citizens not to get out of society but to get into it are not only missing the point, they are guilty of political folly.

If the economy is in trouble, or if there is an international crisis, or if the Republican administration has made a mess of things, the New Issue will not be decisive in 1976, but those who are interested in putting the Democratic coalition back together again can hardly afford to take such a chance. An attempt was made to broaden participation in the Democratic party in 1972. The attempt backfired and in fact turned the party over to a very narrow segment of its membership. While this segment was unquestionably the most enthusiastic and most committed group in the party, such qualities on the part of a few does not mean broader participation of the many. The Democratic reforms, designedly or not, turned control of the party over to those who were most disposed to be politically active. Those who work and give time and energy to politics have every right to more influence, but when that influence becomes dominant, the nonactivists will surely conclude that their own participation has diminished.

No leader of a rebuilt Democratic coalition can

permit amateur activists to dominate the party. For if he does, he will turn the neopopulist current against himself. Nor can he permit the party's profound concerns about involving the disadvantaged in the political process to cause those who are only moderately advantaged to feel that they have been excluded.

The secret of rebuilding the Democratic coalition is to create a situation in which *all* Democrats feel that they have greater representation at the political conventions and in the councils of the party. The whole "mini politics" system of reform and caucuses will have to be abandoned, to be replaced by some kind of direct election by the voters of convention delegates within the context of some sort of informal agreement among party leaders for the necessity of balanced tickets.

As long as it is saddled with its present "reforms," the Democratic party is in no position to take advantage of the neopopulist political current. The McGovern campaign claim that the base of political participation had been broadened in 1972 must have seemed a cruel joke to many Democratic voters who in fact felt that they had been excluded. The 1972 convention utterly destroyed the possibility of the Democrats exploiting the New Issue. Those who are laboring to rebuild the Democratic coalition will not be able to exploit the issue in 1976 unless they can find ways to persuade all their potential constituents that they are respected and are included and are wanted and are part of the party. From the point of view of most Democratic voters, those well-meaning enthusiasts who seized power in the Democratic convention of 1972 represent a narrower and more unrepresentative establishment than the political bosses ever did. It is precisely against such an establishment that the neopopulist current is running. "Who do they think they are?" ask the neopopulists.

It seems a fair question.

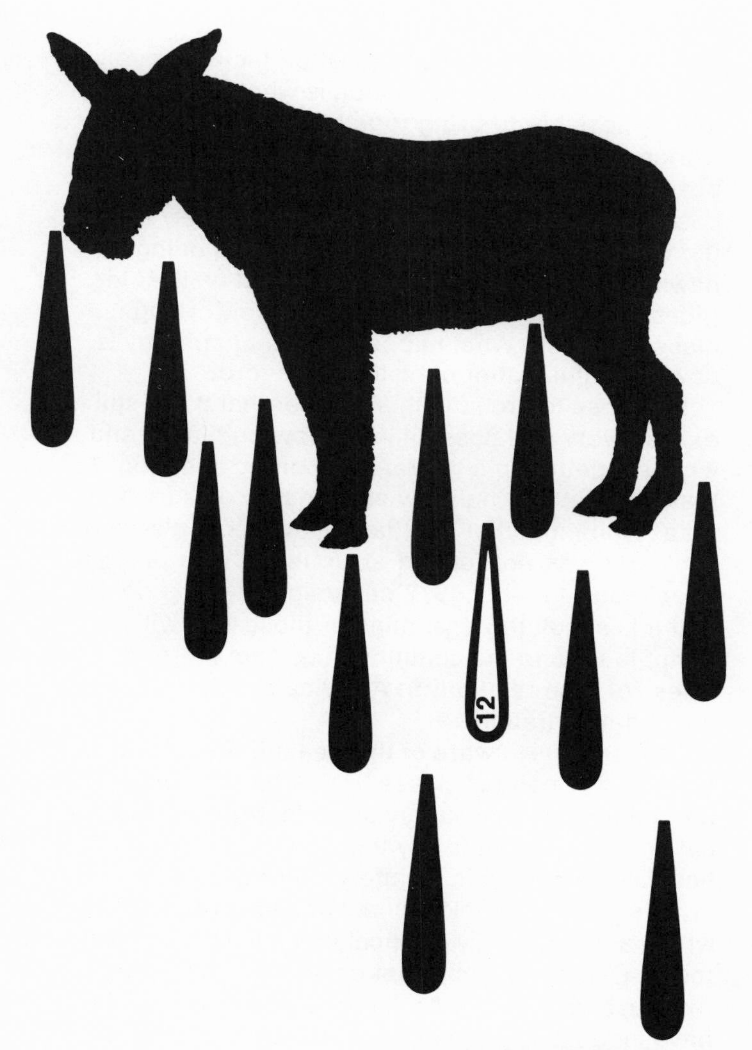

FACTS IN BLACK AND WHITE

The most serious political question facing those who will rebuild the liberal coalition is whether it is any longer possible to bring together enough blacks and working-class whites to win an election. The implicit premise of the New Politics in 1972 was that success in such an effort would be most unlikely (since the working class was racist—as well as being hawks). The New Politicians depended on the "legions of the young" to make up for the working class defection. What happened to that strategy is now a painful matter of historical record.

I propose to argue in this chapter that there still exists a very real possibility of drawing blacks and whites together in a liberal Democratic coalition. To make my case, I shall rely very heavily on survey data. While much of this data is available elsewhere, it clearly was not looked at by those who designed —or reported—the 1972 campaign. I would contend that it is absolutely essential for those who will attempt to rebuild the coalition to correct their "pictures" of race relations in America by examining these data carefully.

I am certainly aware of the weaknesses of survey data, and I shall not pause at this point to attempt to defend the national survey as an instrument of political analysis except to say that it is the only tool we have available and is infinitely superior to the "what my friends and I think" school of social research on which a good deal of political commentary is based today. One of the important contributions that sensitive observers of middle America like Robert Coles have made is to emphasize that people, even the uneducated, are complex, and that a given individual can give voice in the course of a five-minute conversation to both a violently racist attitude and a profoundly sympathetic problack opinion. Political situations can be fully as complicated as the people involved in them, and it is the function of political leaders—at least those interested in maintaining a healthy democratic society—to appeal to the best that is in the personalities of their constituents. I contend that the national survey data show that there is a good deal more potential good will and acceptance to which the sophisticated political leader could appeal in American society than those who dismiss middle America as incurably racist or hawkish are prepared to believe.

However, I have no intention of minimizing the difficulty in solving the political, social, and economic problems that face the United States. It is true that a majority of white Americans are ready to pay a 10 percent increase in their taxes for social reform that would prevent further race riots, and it is true that American blacks still have a good deal of faith in the American system and optimism about their chances of succeeding in it. Yet these attitudes need to be voiced by a political leader who can maintain a coalition between blacks and whites. This leader (whoever he may be) will not find it easy to devise practical programs that will not put his coalition under severe stress, nor will those practical programs necessarily resolve the problems to which they are directed. To say that the raw material for coalition exists does not mean either that the coalition will be a successful one or that it will never come apart; it simply means that it is possible to form a coalition.

Nor does it follow that because there is raw material for a moderate coalition, extremists of one variety or another will not be a problem. A little more than 10 percent of American whites voted for George Wallace in 1968. A little less than 10 percent of American blacks say they would join a riot if one occurred in their vicinity. Approximately 10 percent of American college students are profoundly alienated, and approximately the same number of noncollege youth in the North under thirty voted for Wallace. While 10 percent is a relatively small percentage, it still represents millions of people. And only a tiny handful of the 10 percent extremist factions are potential candidates for guerilla warfare of Right and the Left, but still there are enough of these far-out types around to make American society a fairly dangerous place. Nevertheless, it is remarkable, I think, that given the turbulence of the last decade, the extremists and revolutionaries are still so relatively few in number. Even though moderation represents the feelings of some seven-eighths of the population, there is no absolute guarantee that it will carry the day. All one can say at the present reading of the survey data is that the moderates are still the overwhelming majority and that therefore there still remains a chance to accomplish major social change in the next decade—perhaps a better chance than is enjoyed by any other country in the world.

The present chapter will be divided into two sections. In the first part I shall discuss the changing attitudes toward racial integration of white Americans in general by region, age, and education. In the second part I shall discuss the black component of the Democratic coalition.

CHANGING ATTITUDES ON RACIAL INTEGRATION[1]

In the last ten years, the United States has experienced what is probably the most acute crisis in race relations since the end of the Civil War. City after city exploded in violence. The riots in Watts and Detroit captured national headlines and prime-time media coverage for more than a week. Martin Luther King, Jr., the apostle of nonviolence, was assassinated, and another spasm of violent riots shook the land. King was replaced on the television screen by a far more militant brand of black leader who spoke ominously of violence. The popular press carried accounts of blacks arming for guerrilla warfare. Stokely Carmichael, H. Rap Brown, Eldridge Cleaver, and Bobby Seale became national personalities. The Black Panthers appeared on the scene, and shootouts between the police and Panthers occurred in numerous cities. Violence among street gangs in major cities was so frequent that it no longer rated even a casual notice from the press. Black mayors were elected in major cities, college campuses the country over were swept by unrest, part of which at least had racial overtones. Robert Kennedy was assassinated, and the 1968 Democratic convention occasioned a donnybrook in front of the Conrad Hilton hotel in Chicago. Columnists, editorial writers, and political experts publicly worried about a "backlash." George Wallace did extremely well in many primaries in 1968, and in the presidential election he

[1] This section of the chapter is adapted to a considerable extent from the article by Andrew M. Greeley and Paul B. Sheatsley, "Attitudes Towards Desegregation," *Scientific American* (December 1971).

led the most successful third-party attempt in many decades. In 1972, he made a strong bid in Northern urban states for convention delegates. Any assessment of his impact in the 1972 election was forestalled by the assassination attempt of late summer.

Nevertheless, despite the turbulence of the late sixties, attitudes of white Americans toward desegregation continued to change almost as though nothing was happening.

For a period of almost thirty years, the National Opinion Research Center (NORC) has been sampling attitudes of white Americans toward the position black Americans should occupy in American society. The sample consists of about 1,500 people, about 1,250 of whom are white. With a sample this size it is possible to test for opinion by age, region, income, occupation, education, religion, and ethnic origin.

Two questions dealing with integration in public transportation and schools ("Generally speaking, do you think there should be separate sections for Negroes in streetcars and buses?" and "Do you think white students and Negroes should go to the same schools or separate schools?") were asked in 1942, 1956, 1963, and 1970. In 1942, 44 percent of the American public was willing to endorse integrated transportation (Table 12.1). Twenty-eight years later, this proportion had doubled, rising from 44 to 60 percent in the fourteen years between 1942 and 1956, and from 60 to 88 percent in the fourteen years between 1956 and 1970. In the South, the change has been even more dramatic. Only 4 percent of white Southerners accepted integrated transportation in 1942, a little better than 25 percent in 1956, slightly more than 50 percent in 1963, and 66 percent in 1970.

TABLE 12.1
Changing Attitudes on Integration in Public Transportation and Schools
(Percent of White Population Taking a Prointegration Position)

Transportation	1942	1956	1963	1970
National	44	60	77	88
Non-South	57	73	89	94
South	4	27	52	67
Schools	1942	1956	1963	1970
National	30	49	63	73
Non-South	40	61	73	84
South	2	14	34	46

The integration of transportation, then, is virtually no longer an issue in the United States. In retrospect, it may well be said that the right of blacks to ride in the same seats and buses that white people use is not, after all, a very important right; obtaining it does not notably improve the welfare of black people. From the perspective of 1970, such an assertion is certainly true, but from the point of view of what attitudes were in 1942 or even 1956, the change is striking. In a little more than a decade and a half, since Martin Luther King's historic boycott in Montgomery, Alabama, transportation integration has ceased to be an issue in American society.

However, integration of schools is still very much an issue, even though now in the North more than eight out of every ten respondents endorse it. In 1942, only 2 percent of whites in the South were sympathetic to school integration. In the ensuing fourteen years, this proportion increased by but 12 percentage points. However, since 1956 (two years after the famous Supreme Court decision), the proportion of Southern whites accepting school integration increased by thirty-two percentage points, so that now almost 50 percent of Southern whites are in favor of it, and almost 75 percent of the total national population believes in integrated schools.

An interesting pattern emerges in Table 12.1. The proportion of the Northern population supporting integration at one point in time is very close to the proportion of the total population accepting integration at the next point in time. The figure in the second row of each column, in other words, is almost the same as the figure in the first row of the subsequent column. Thus, one could hazard the guess that if trends recorded in Table 12.1 are to continue, by 1977, most of the American population can be expected to accept integrated schooling, perhaps as many as 60 percent of Southern whites. In NORC's 1977 report, it may well be possible to say that the desegregation of education is no longer an issue in the United States.

Table 12.2 presents the percentage of white Americans taking prointegration attitudes on five items of NORC's eight-item scale devised in 1963. It is noteworthy that three of the items on the original scale have been retired, simply because virtually all Americans now accept without question integration in jobs, public transportation, and public facilities.

Between 1963 and 1970 there was an increase of eleven percentage points in sympathy for school integration and an increase of twelve percentage points between 1970 and 1972. Acceptance of a Negro at dinner increased from 49 percent in 1963

TABLE 12.2
Attitudes on Integration 1963, 1970, and 1972
(Percent Prointegration)

Item	1963	1970	1972
"Do you think white students and Negro students should go to the same schools, or to separate schools?" ("Same schools.")	63	74	86
"How strongly would you object if a member of your family wanted to bring a Negro friend home to dinner?" ("Not at all.")	49	63	70
"White people have a right to keep Negroes out of their neighborhoods if they want to, and Negroes should respect that right." ("Disagree slightly" or "Disagree strongly.")	44	49	56
"Do you think there should be laws against marriages between Negroes and whites?" ("No.")	36	48	59
"Negroes shouldn't push themselves where they're not wanted." ("Disagree slightly" or "Disagree strongly.")	27	16	22

to 63 percent in 1970 and to 70 percent in 1972. And so forth.

By assigning each respondent to the survey a score of five to zero, depending upon the number of prointegration responses he gave to the five items in Table 12.2, we can readily compute the average scores for various subgroups of the population. The five items form what is known as a Guttman scale. If a person rejects one item on the scale, the odds are extremely high that he will reject all items below it. For example, someone opposed to integrated schools is not likely to welcome the presence of a black at his dinner table, and even less is he likely to approve of integrated neighborhoods or racial intermarriage. A person with a score of 4 can be assumed in the great majority of cases to take a prointegration stand on the first four items of the scale. Tables 12.3 through 12.7 show these scores on the Guttman scale of the five items in Table 12.2.

Much of the change that has occurred in the last two years has been concentrated in the South. Indeed, we observe in Table 12.3 that the movement toward sympathy for racial integration in the South between 1970 and 1972 is as extensive as that in the North between 1963 and 1972. White Southerners still lag behind in support for integration, but in 1963, the typical white Southerner was just barely willing to accept integration in the schools. In 1972, he was willing to accept integration in the schools, a black at the family dinner table, and has made some progress toward accepting the right of blacks to live wherever they wish.

Much of the change in racial attitudes in the past has been concentrated among the young. White people under twenty-five have always had more tolerant racial attitudes than their elders, and between 1963 and 1970 this generation gap was increasing (Table 12.4). But since 1970, the largest gains on the prointegration scale have been registered by the two groups of people aged twenty-five to forty-four and forty-five to sixty-four. Thus not only is the South catching up with the North; these data suggest that the middle-aged are now beginning to catch up with the young.

The greatest change in the South is taking place among the young. Table 12.5 shows the prointegration scores by both region and age group. One can see that in the last two years there has been little or no change in attitudes among young Northerners but striking changes among those in the South under forty-five. If the years between 1972 and 1974 show

TABLE 12.3
Prointegration Scale by Region

	1963	1970	1972	Change 1963–1970	Change 1970–1972	Change 1963–1972
Non-South	2.45 (887)	2.88 (911)	3.16 (1010)	.43	.28	.71
South	1.11 (331)	1.47 (352)	2.17 (342)	.36	.70	1.06

TABLE 12.4
Prointegration Scale by Age

	1963	1970	1972	Change 1963–1970	Change 1970–1972	Change 1963–1972
Under 25	2.38 (218)	3.26 (121)	3.62 (161)	.88	.36	1.24
25–44	2.32 (545)	2.71 (453)	3.16 (515)	.39	.45	.84
45–64	1.93 (400)	2.27 (402)	2.69 (474)	.34	.42	.76
Over 65	1.53 (184)	2.05 (281)	2.19 (199)	.52	.14	.66

TABLE 12.5
Prointegration Scale by Region and Age

Non-South	1963	1970	1972	Change 1963–1970	Change 1970–1972	Change 1963–1972
Under 25	2.93 (80)	3.76 (82)	3.78 (123)	.83	.02	.85
25–44	2.66 (401)	3.11 (341)	3.39 (399)	.45	.28	.73
45–64	2.26 (283)	2.66 (283)	2.91 (347)	.40	.25	.65
Over 65	1.90 (120)	2.41 (201)	2.55 (138)	.51	.14	.65
South						
Under 25	1.37 (37)	2.23 (39)	3.08 (38)	.86	.85	1.71
25–44	1.19 (131)	1.52 (112)	2.37 (116)	.33	.85	1.18
45–64	1.06 (107)	1.36 (119)	2.08 (127)	.30	.72	1.02
Over 65	.82 (56)	1.11 (80)	1.34 (61)	.29	.23	.52

continuing changes of the magnitude registered during the past two years in both the North and the South, there will be virtually no difference in sympathies for racial integration between Southerners under forty-five and their Northern counterparts. We could project that by 1974 both Northerners and Southerners under age twenty-five will have a score close to 4.0 on the scale, which means that both groups will accept school, residential, social, and marital integration. For typical white Americans between age twenty-six and forty-five we could project a score somewhere between 3.0 and 4.0, which means that in the North and South alike typical whites in that age group will be able to accept educational, social, and neighborhood integration.

Even if we grant that NORC's integration scale is, like all survey instruments, an imperfect device and that it may to some extent measure what people think they ought to say instead of what they are in fact prepared to accept, the change in these expressed racial attitudes in the South over the past decade must still be classified as one of the most impressive social accomplishments of modern times. Given the South's past and the immense resistance to integration that once existed there, the changes reported in Table 12.5 and not unreasonably projected into the future would not have seemed possible ten years ago.

If changing racial attitudes in the past two years have been particularly concentrated in the South and especially among younger Southerners, they have also been mostly likely to occur among better educated whites who have graduated from college (Table 12.6). Prointegration attitudes have always been highly correlated with education, but since 1963 the college graduate group has shown by far

TABLE 12.6
Prointegration Scale by Education

	1963	1970	1972
Grammar school	1.32 (355)	1.69 (281)	1.98 (238)
Some high school	1.88 (315)	2.23 (242)	2.50 (247)
High school graduate	2.32 (376)	2.57 (413)	2.98 (453)
Some college	2.73 (193)	3.06 (189)	3.32 (245)
College graduate	3.15 (130)	3.48 (135)	3.97 (168)

	Change 1963–1970	Change 1970–1972	Change 1963–1972
Grammar school	.37	.29	.66
Some high school	.35	.27	.62
High school graduate	.25	.41	.66
Some college	.33	.26	.59
College graduate	.33	.49	.82

the highest rate of change. This finding has important implications for the future, as the proportion of our sample reporting college graduation increased from 9 percent in 1963 to 14 percent in 1972. At the same time, the proportion who failed to complete high school, who are the least tolerant of blacks, dropped from 49 percent of our sample to 36 percent over the same period. Again, should these trends continue, the average scale scores are bound to increase in future years.

When the influence of education and region on prointegration attitudes is considered simultaneously (Table 12.7), it is clear that the effects of education are consistent in both the North and the South. In both regions it is the college graduates who have shown the greatest amount of change in both the last decade and in the last two years. The gains in the South vis-à-vis the North have come primarily from the high school graduates and those with some college. White Southerners who did not graduate from high school still lag far behind their Northern counterparts in acceptance of integration, and the gap has narrowed very little in the last decade.

To sum up, in the last two years changing attitudes toward integration have occurred most notably in the South among the young and the college educated. To the extent that there has been change in the North in the last two years, it has been most notable among those who have graduated from college.

The apparent change in racial attitudes in the South forces us to raise the question of whether the Democratic coalition can afford to assume that it must write off the South, as it has done for the last decade. The South has been a convenient scapegoat for American liberals who have simply been uninterested in trying to understand, much less sympathize with, the problems the South experiences as it goes through a whole series of powerful social changes of which racial integration is but one. Might it be possible for a skilled and sensitive Democratic coalition builder to win back large numbers of

TABLE 12.7
Pointegration Scale by Education and Region

Non-South	1963	1970	1972	Change 1963–1970	Change 1970–1972	Change 1963–1972
Grammar school	1.73 (207)	2.09 (176)	2.34 (155)	.36	.25	.61
Some high school	2.27 (208)	2.74 (164)	2.84 (186)	.47	.10	.57
High school graduate	2.60 (263)	2.85 (311)	3.14 (358)	.25	.29	.54
Some college	2.99 (121)	3.36 (149)	3.51 (174)	.37	.15	.52
College graduate	3.48 (86)	3.77 (108)	4.09 (136)	.29	.32	.61
South						
Grammar school	.68 (112)	1.03 (105)	1.31 (83)	.35	.28	.63
Some high school	1.01 (84)	1.17 (78)	1.64 (61)	.16	.47	.63
High school graduate	1.36 (72)	1.75 (102)	2.47 (95)	.39	.72	1.11
Some college	1.42 (33)	1.95 (40)	2.76 (71)	.53	.81	1.34
College graduate	2.00 (30)	2.33 (27)	3.12 (32)	.33	.79	1.12

Southern white votes, which together with the ever increasing number of black voters in the South might return the South to "solid" Democratic status? The Republican "Southern strategy," which appeals fundamentally to the conservative and segregationist mentality of the South, has been successful perhaps only by default. The new breed of moderate Democratic governors elected in Southern states should serve notice on the national Democratic party, particularly its intellectual elites in New York and Boston. There are possibilities in the South that we cannot afford to ignore.

There is, then, a broad consensus in American society in favor of racial integration, but it does not follow that there is universal acceptance of policies advocated to achieve racial justice. One need only read the daily newspapers to know how strong opposition to busing is even among those who are sympathetic to the general principle of racial integration (and among many whose children do in fact attend integrated schools). The strength of the opposition to busing is obvious from Table 12.8. Only among four population categories does the percentage in favor of busing rise over 20 percent: persons under twenty-five, college graduates, those who attended graduate school, and Jews. But even in these four categories more than three-quarters of each group are not in favor of busing.

Neither is the black attitude on busing at all unanimous (Table 12.9). While a little more than half of the blacks in our sample (and the relatively small number of blacks makes us cautious about generalization) are in favor of busing, almost half of the black respondents are not. The strongest support for busing among blacks is to be found among the oldest and among those with only grammar school edu-

TABLE 12.8
Attitudes on Busing among Whites
(Percent in Favor of Busing Negro and White School Children from One School District to Another)

Region		*Religion*	
South	6	Protestant	11
Non-South	15	Catholic	12
Age		Jew	24
Under 25	23	*Ethnicity*	
26–44	14	Anglo-Saxon	7
45–64	11	German Protestant	13
Over 65	9	Scandinavian Protestant	16
Education		Irish Protestant	9
Grammar	11	Irish Catholic	10
Some high school	13	German Catholic	11
High school graduate	11	Italian Catholic	6
Some college	13	Slavic Catholic	9
College graduate	20		
Graduate school	24		

cation. Perhaps the younger and better educated blacks are somewhat more in sympathy with the separatist positions taken by their more militant spokesmen.[2]

How can one reconcile the overwhelming sympathy for integration with almost equally overwhelming opposition to busing? It is tempting (and not all ob-

[2] The data in Table 12.9 obviously should be taken with considerable reservation because of the rather small number of black respondents on which it is based. Incredibly enough, there is no systematic effort to study large national samples of American blacks every year, a deficiency of American research enterprise that staggers the imagination. One would think that it ought to be high on the priority lists of the rebuilders of the liberal coalition to see that such surveys are taken routinely.

servers have resisted the temptation) to dismiss the support for school integration as hypocrisy, indeed covert racism, unless it includes support for busing. However, such a simple solution may not do full justice to the complexity of social reality, and certainly it does not explain the lack of black unanimity on the busing issue.

There are at least four possible explanations for opposition to busing:

1. Racism, explicit or implicit, that wishes to protect its children from attending school with blacks.

2. Fear of danger or resentment of the inconvenience of busing.

3. Commitment to the neighborhood school as an important social institution.

4. Doubt as to whether "racial balance" would in fact achieve much improvement in the quality of education for blacks.

It is not the purpose of this chapter to discuss the pros and cons of busing. However, it must be noted that on the last three explanations the evidence to support or deny those objections seems to be inconclusive to most experts.

It may very well be that busing is absolutely essential to achieve racial justice in American society, but the evidence in favor of this position has not been made in such a way as to convince educational specialists. Hence, one cannot, at least on *a priori* grounds, write off popular opposition to busing as pure racism. Unquestionably, there is racism involved in some of the opposition to busing, but with the tools presently available to us we are not able to sort out the purely racist opposition from opposition based on fear of the risks of busing and skepticism about its effectiveness.

TABLE 12.9
Attitudes on Busing among Blacks
(Percent in Favor of Busing Negro and White School Children from One School District to Another)

Region		*Education*	
South	52 (81)	Grammar school	60 (52)
Non-South	55 (57)	Some high school	48 (19)
Age		High school graduate	55 (31)
Under 25	54 (21)	College	52 (15)
26–44	51 (42)		
45–64	51 (47)		
Over 65	62 (28)		

The difference in attitudes on racial integration, as a general principle, and busing, as a specific policy to achieve integration that is perceived as socially necessary, illustrates what seems to me to be a decisive change in the racial issues that face us in the United States. Until relatively recently, a large segment of the American population was unwilling to accept the principle of racial integration even though that principle was an obvious deduction from the American creed and even though the nonacceptance of the principle created what three decades ago Gunnar Myrdal called "the American dilemma." Now, on the verbal level, the principles have been accepted, the creed is honored in theory by most of the population, and the American dilemma has been resolved in theory.

The problem has shifted from the acceptance of the principle of racial integration to the question of the practical policies that most effectively will achieve racial justice. Contrary to opinions of a generation ago, there is now no question that segregated schooling enforced by law is a violation of the American creed, but there can still be considerable question as to what are the most effective means of achieving racial justice in education. In the last decade a subtle shift has taken place from questions of general social principle to questions of concrete social policy. Necessarily, the latter issues are more complicated and less certain.

We suspect that if the elites in American society hope to obtain broad consensus for certain major social policy changes to achieve racial justice, they are going to have to demonstrate why a given social policy is absolutely necessary to implement the new theoretical consensus. Data presented in Tables 12.10 and 12.11 suggest that the overwhelming majority of whites and a very substantial minority of blacks have not yet been persuaded that busing is an indispensable prerequisite for racial justice.

The NORC integration scale does not have many years of life ahead of it. It will shortly be retired with the observation that as far as theoretical principles are concerned the overwhelming majority of Americans are committed to racial integration. New and more elaborate measures will then have to be devised to discover what policies for achieving racial justice are likely to obtain broad consensus and what kind of arguments in favor of these policies are likely to be the most effective. Not only are the social issues more complicated and less clearcut, the problems for social researchers are going to be far more difficult than they were in the days when 70 percent of the American whites were against school integration.

I emphasize that we are dealing only with expressed attitudes and that we are measuring these attitudes with very imperfect tools. It is quite possible that our respondents are giving the answers they think are socially desirable—although even that prointegration answers should become socially desirable represents a change of a sort. Furthermore, survey items are but crude indicators of a complex personality orientation involved in racial tolerance and racial bigotry.

Nevertheless, the data reported in NORC's monitoring of American racial attitudes amply documents the capacity of Americans to change. In 1952 only 30 percent of the population accepted school integration. In 1956 the figure had risen to 49 percent; in 1963 it was 63 percent; in 1970, 74 percent; and in the spring of 1972, 86 percent. To say that such change is a remarkable social accomplishment is to suggest neither that the American nation should rest on its laurels nor to conclude that the sin of racism has been exorcised from the land. If any pride is to be taken in the accomplishment of attitudinal change in the past three decades, it is the kind of pride that imposes an obligation to work for those policy changes that will be attuned to the new attitudes.

Attitudes are not necessarily predictive of behavior. A man may be a staunch integrationist and still run when his neighborhood is threatened. A man with segregationist views may vote for an integrationist political candidate if the salient issues of the election do not involve the candidate's integrationist position. And again, responses to NORC's interviewers may well indicate not what an American really feels but what he thinks he *ought to say*.

And while a change of attitude does not necessarily predict a change in behavior, nevertheless, attitudinal change can create a context in which much behavioral change becomes possible. Increasing support for school integration, for example, makes it somewhat easier for official policies of school integration to be pursued. The increase in support for integrated neighborhoods may facilitate at least tentative solutions to that vexing problem of changing neighborhoods in Northern cities in the decade to come. Changing attitudes, then, even the dramatic sort monitored by NORC in the last thirty years, do not represent by themselves effective social reform; but it is possible to see them as a sign of progress and as creating a context for reform.

How promising the context for reform really is can be found in data collected for a study at the Survey Research Center at the University of Michigan in 1968 for the Kerner Commission. The majority of whites in fifteen Northern cities agreed that there was discrimination against blacks in jobs, promotion, and housing. About two-fifths agreed that police are unnecessarily rough and disrespectful of blacks and that they themselves are better off than blacks with comparable education. More than three-fifths think blacks have a right to live anywhere, and about half would not mind a black family next door. Two-thirds would be in favor of a law against discrimination in job hiring. Almost seven-eights would not mind working for a qualified black. Only one-third would object to their children having black friends. Three-fifths would vote for a qualified black mayor, and two-thirds are in sympathy with the government's spending more money for jobs, schools, and housing in order to prevent riots. Fifty-three percent of all the respondents were willing to pay a 10 percent tax increase for such programs.

Approximately the same proportion (54 percent) think the best way to prevent riots is to improve conditions for blacks. Only 16 percent think that tighter police control is the most effective strategy.

The Michigan researchers summarized their findings as follows:

> *1. There is a willingness among the white population of these Northern cities to see government play a strong hand in helping bring about improvement in the conditions of the cities. This opinion is not unanimous; there is a substantial minority who oppose the suggestion of such programs. But there is a consistent majority on all these proposals who accept the necessity of governmental assistance and this approval is not reduced when the purpose of the assistance is specifically related to the needs of the Negro population and the prevention of riots.*
> *2. The superficially simple solution to the problem of urban riots—more rigid police control of the Negro areas—is not generally seen by white urban residents as an adequate answer. The large majority of these people accept the proposition that there must be an improvement in the condition of Negro life.*[3]

It is worth noting that the Michigan data was collected during the time of great racial unrest in American cities. It would seem on the basis of these data that there existed more support at that time for

[3] Michigan survey, 1968, p. 98.

the kinds of solutions recommended by the Kerner Commission than the political leadership of the country seemed to comprehend. Obviously, there are major problems in translating such positive attitudes into concrete political and social programs. When one's own job or one's own neighborhood seems threatened, one may act much less enlightened than would appear in a response to a survey questionnaire. Nonetheless, the recommendations of the Kerner Commission, supported by the Michigan data, would suggest that American political leadership has not recognized the existing resources of popular support or has chosen not to mobilize them. Whether America is or is not a "racist" society is largely, one supposes, based on a definition of the terms. It surely is a society in which there are still built-in disadvantages for minority groups —especially nonwhite groups. It is also a society in which substantial numbers of the white population are anything but enlightened. However, the Michigan data would indicate that it is a society in which there is strong popular support for the kinds of programs that might eliminate many of the serious effects of racism, past and present. To ignore this support and to indulge in fantasies about racist middle America, or to issue repeated demands for abject confessions of guilt as a substitute for constructive social policy is to engage in the most foolish sort of romanticism.

To suggest that there has been a change in American attitudes is also not to suggest that all is well in American society. Presumably, no one will argue that the fact of change should go unrecorded because it may lead to the diminution of motivation to work for further change.

It has been argued that American politics are politics of the center, albeit a floating center. Without in any way wanting to deny the utility of such a model, it still must be said that at least on the matter of racial integration, the American center has floated consistently to the *left* since 1942, and that this shift has not been impeded—nor accelerated—by the turmoil of the last seven years. To put the matter more concretely, the political leader who adjusts his style to an antiintegration backlash is, on the basis of our data, adjusting to something that does not exist. On the other hand, the leader who is convinced that American society contains the raw material for leading the center even further to the left on the subject of racial integration would find strong support for his strategy in the NORC and Michigan survey data. While we cannot say with any degree of scientific precision that it is the sustained pressure of the leadership elites that has produced increasing support for integration since 1942, it nevertheless does seem to me to be reasonable to argue that if every president since Franklin Roosevelt had not endorsed an integrationist position, the change of attitude our surveys have monitored might not be nearly so impressive. By the same token, it is reasonable to argue that if the present and future administrations present the case for integration more forcefully, they will find basic attitudinal support among the white population of the United States.

THE BLACK COMPONENT

If the white component of a rebuilt coalition cannot be ignored, neither can the black component. On the contrary, black political leadership is becoming much better organized, much more sophisticated, and much more insistent. It will increasingly demand the right to insist that its participation cannot be taken for granted. The Democratic party is probably going to have to face during the 1970s the critical question of whether it dares to nominate a black vice-presidential candidate. If it does not, it may very well lose its black partner either through the formation of an independent black party or, more likely, from a temporary withdrawal of the blacks from the political process.[4]

But blacks do not want to withdraw from American society. On the contrary, the overwhelming majority of them want to be more involved in society rather than less. But now they want to be involved on their own terms, which is to say they want the rest of society to accept their right to dignity and to respect while maintaining a cultural heritage of their own.

I shall rely on data collected during the 1960s, most of it by the National Opinion Research Center.[5] The most recent data available for this chapter were collected for the Columbia Broadcasting System by the Opinion Research Corporation of Princeton, New Jersey, in 1968 after the death of Martin Luther King and before the election of Richard Nixon. With the

[4] More Americans say that they would be willing to vote for a qualified black presidential candidate at the present time than said they were willing to vote for a qualified Catholic candidate in 1960. Indeed, according to a recent Gallup poll, almost three-quarters of the American population would accept a qualified black candidate for the presidency. Democrats could probably get away with nominating a black vice-presidential candidate in 1976. Indeed, a black vice-presidential candidate on a "national unity" ticket could well represent one of the most brilliant political ploys of the century. Whether the Democrats are brave enough to try it seems to be very doubtful.

[5] It should be emphasized that in most cases the survey interviewers were themselves black, and all studies (with the exception of the Michigan 1968 study, which was limited to fifteen cities in the North) were dealing with national samples.

TABLE 12.10
Black Attitudes Toward Separatism and Integration
(With Two White Comparisons)

	Percent Agree	
	Black	*White*
A separate black country (definitely or probably a good idea) [1]	6	
It would be a good idea for blacks to have a completely separate country of their own, made up of some of the states of the United States [2]	3	23
It would be a good idea to have a completely separate country somewhere else [2]	5	33
Prefer to live in an integrated neighborhood [3]	80	
Willing to move into an integrated neighborhood, even if there might be some trouble [3]	46	
Would choose an integrated club [3]	63	
Belong to an integrated church [3]	38	

[1] NORC, 1963. [2] CBS, 1968. [3] NORC, 1966.

exception of certain Gallup questions, no more recent data are available for analysis here, although preliminary results of an NORC study conducted in the spring of 1972 and not yet available for presentation show that there is no need to change the basic themes of this chapter.

First of all, American blacks continued to be integrationists rather than separatists (Table 12.10). In 1963, only 6 percent thought that a separate black country would be a good idea, while in 1968, 3 percent approved of a separate black country made up of states within the United States, and 5 percent thought it would be a good idea to have a separate country elsewhere. Interestingly enough, white sym-

TABLE 12.11
"Would you personally prefer to live in a neighborhood with all Negroes, mostly Negroes, mostly whites, or a neighborhood that is mixed half and half?"
(In Percent)

All Negro	8
Mostly Negro	5
Mostly white	1
Mixed half and half	48
Makes no difference	37
Don't know	1
	100

pathy for a black nation is much stronger than black sympathy for it. Twenty-three percent of white Americans are willing to give blacks their own states, and as many as a third are willing to give them a completely separate country somewhere else. In other words, white Americans are apparently more ready to get rid of blacks than blacks are ready to leave.

Four-fifths of American blacks would prefer to live in integrated neighborhoods; almost half of them would move to improve their housing even if there might be some trouble. Almost two-thirds would choose an integrated club rather than an all-black club, and two-fifths belong to an integrated church.

In 1968, blacks living in the fifteen cities surveyed by the University of Michigan research team displayed the same attitudes toward residential integration (Table 12.11). Thirteen percent said they wanted to live in neighborhoods that were all or mostly all Negro, and 37 percent said that it made no difference where they lived.

TABLE 12.12
Percentage of Negroes Favoring Separatist Response to Each of Ten Questions

Believe stores in "a Negro neighborhood should be owned and run by Negroes"	18
Believe school with mostly Negro children should have Negro principal	14
Prefer to live in all Negro or mostly Negro neighborhood	13
Believe school with mostly Negro children should have mostly Negro teachers	10
Agree that "Negroes should have nothing to do with whites if they can help it"	9
Believe whites should be discouraged from taking part in civil rights organizations	8
Prefer own child to go to all or mostly Negro school	6
Believe close friendship between Negroes and whites is impossible	6
Agree that "there should be a separate black nation here"	6
Prefer child to have only Negro friends, not white friends too	5

The findings of Table 12.12 show that while 18 percent agreed that stores in "a Negro neighborhood should be owned and run by Negroes," only 14 percent thought that schools with mostly Negro children should have Negro principals, and only 10 percent thought that these schools should have mostly Negro teachers. Only 8 percent wished to exclude whites from the civil rights movement, only 6 percent believed that close friendships between blacks and whites are impossible, and only 5 percent would prefer their children not to have white friends.

We are frequently told that the majority of older blacks are still integrationists, and it is the young people who are much more likely to be separatists. The data on the Table 12.13 show that indeed the younger blacks, particularly younger black men, are

TABLE 12.13
Percentage in Each Age Category Showing Separatist Thinking on Five Questions

Negro Men	16–19	20–29	30–39	40–49	50–59	60–69
Believe stores in "a Negro neighborhood should be owned and run by Negroes"	28	23	20	18	14	18
Believe school with mostly Negro children should have mostly Negro teachers	22	15	13	6	5	15
Agree that "Negroes should have nothing to do with whites if they can help it"	18	14	6	12	4	13
Believe whites should be discouraged from taking part in civil rights organizations	19	12	8	6	3	5
Agree that "there should be a separate black nation here"	11	10	5	5	4	10
Negro Women						
Believe stores in "a Negro neighborhood should be owned and run by Negroes"	18	16	16	15	13	8
Believe school with mostly Negro children should have mostly Negro teachers	11	9	6	5	5	12
Agree that "Negroes should have nothing to do with whites if they can help it"	11	7	7	8	5	7
Believe whites should be discouraged from taking part in civil rights organizations	11	7	7	5	7	3
Agree that "there should be a separate black nation here"	9	3	2	6	4	3

more likely to take a separatist stance than their elders; nevertheless, the overwhelming majority, even of those under nineteen, reject a policy of separatism. As the Michigan researchers note:

> *If we were to assume that the younger people will hold to their beliefs, then in a little more than a generation separatism would rise noticeably over the whole population.* Even then, *however, it would remain a distinctly minority position with the Negro community. Instead of being represented by five or ten per cent of the Negro population, it would characterize 15 or at most 20 per cent of the adult Negroes in these fifteen cities. The majority would still have to be described as "integrationist" in goal and sentiment.*[6]

On the other hand, as Table 12.14 shows, there is very strong sympathy for an emphasis on black cultural identity to the extent that two-fifths of the respondents think that black school children should study an African language.

Interestingly enough, this sympathy for studying an Africa language does not seem to show any special relationship to age but some association with *lower* education (Table 12.15). The Michigan researchers note:

> *This is somewhat puzzling and suggests that the item represents not so much a new idea, but more an appeal to rather long-standing needs within the Negro community. Its greater attraction to the less-educated may also indicate that its importance is mostly symbolic, since those least able to add such an extra language burden to their education are most willing to approve a proposal to*

[6] Michigan survey, 1968, p. 18.

TABLE 12.14
Percentage of Negroes Approving Each of Four Positive Cultural Identity Statements

"Negroes should take more pride in Negro history"	96
"There should be more Negro business, banks, and stores"	94
"Negroes should shop in Negro owned stores whenever possible"	70
"Negro school children should study an African language"	42

do so. It may also indicate that the item appeals especially to those in the Negro community who are furthest from having achieved a middle-class American way of life.[7]

It would appear, then, that for most American blacks an emphasis on black pride and black culture can coexist with a commitment to racial integration. Those white observers who equate black cultural emphasis with separatism are making a leap that most American blacks are not willing to make. But then one can understand it in terms of the American melting pot myth, which has always assumed that he who wants some freedom to be different from the rest of society obviously, inevitably, and logically wants to be separate from it. The black demand for cultural identity is fundamentally no different from the demand of other immigrant groups for the right to maintain some of their own cultural traditions.

Our study did uncover unexpectedly strong support for a kind of cultural pluralism symbolized by the study of Negro history and of African lan-

[7] Ibid., p. 28.

TABLE 12.15
"Negro School Children Should Study an African Language"
(Percentages for Men and Women Averaged)

	Age 16–19 *	*Age 20–39*				
		8th Grade or less	9–11 Grades	12 Grades	Some College	College Graduate
Approve	44	54	41	39	43	28
Disapprove	46	33	47	46	44	61
Don't know **	8	7	11	12	12	9
Other	2	6	1	3	1	2
	100	100	100	100	100	100

	Age 40–69				
	8th Grade or less	9–11 Grades	12 Grades	Some College	College Graduate
Approve	43	44	38	33	33
Disapprove	37	38	51	49	42
Don't know **	17	17	10	18	24
Other	3	1	1	0	1
	100	100	100	100	100

* This group combines all educational categories.
** The "don't know" category is quite large and probably of substantive importance in indicating uncertainty, hence it has been distinguished from other miscellaneous responses.

guages. This seems to turn not so much on the rejection of whites as on the acceptance of things black. It involves a commitment to the development of Negro identity as a valid basis for cultural life within a larger interracial and if possible integrated society. Such a movement from race to ethnicity may help Negroes in a number of ways, but it does not promise quick relief to problems of perceived discrimination and unfair treatment.[8]

The official policy of mainline America has been to reject in practice if not in theory a demand for cultural pluralism from the white immigrant groups; now it would appear that some segments of American society are willing to tolerate pluralism for American blacks, but they interpret it as cultural separatism. The data shown throughout Table 12.15 indicate strongly that blacks do *not* interpret it as separatism.

It would appear from Table 12.16 that American blacks can combine a conviction about the desirability of integration with sympathy for protests, demonstrations, and even riots, although most of them reject violence as a means of obtaining their rights. In 1963, 90 percent of American blacks thought that protests were helpful. A year later, 56 percent thought that civil rights demonstrations had helped, and almost half thought they would like to see more demonstrations. Approximately 60 percent of the respondents in that year thought that violence would never help blacks obtain equal rights. By 1966, half of the black respondents thought that riots like the one in Watts helped the Negro cause as much as hurt it, and 77 percent thought that in the absence of demonstrations the government would do very little about civil rights. In 1968, 34 percent of the black Americans thought that the urban disturbances had helped the cause of blacks and another 11 percent were willing to state that they helped at least as much as they hurt the black cause, indicating a

[8] Michigan survey, 1968, p. 27.

TABLE 12.16
Black Attitudes Toward Protest and Violence with One White Comparison

	Percent	
	Black	*White*
Protests have helped [1]	90	
Civil rights demonstrations have helped [2]	56	
Would like to see more demonstrations [2]	48	
Violence will never help the Negroes get equal rights [2]	62	
Riots like the ones in Watts help the Negro cause as much as they hurt it [3]	50	
The federal government would do very little about civil rights if it were not for demonstrating [3]	77	
Sometimes I think Negroes should not have supported some of the civil rights demonstrations I have read about [3]	45	
Disturbances are mainly a protest against unfair conditions [4]	56	
Disturbances have helped causes of Negroes [4]	34	
Disturbances have helped and hurt equally [4]	11	
Blacks should be ready to use violence to gain rights [4]	15	
Would join in disturbance [4]	8	
Blacks should be ready to use violence (respondents, age 16–19) [4]	22	
Would join in disturbances (age 16–19) [4]	13	12

[1] NORC, 1963. [2] Marx, 1964. [3] NORC, 1966. [4] Michigan, 1968.

slight decline since 1966 (a decline that may simply be the result of a different wording of the questions).[9]

[9] The measure of decline may be seen by adding the 11 percent who thought disturbances have helped and hurt equally with the 34 percent who thought the disturbances helped the cause of

Forty-five percent of the American blacks in 1966 had reservations about some of the civil rights demonstrations, yet more than half of them in 1968 thought that the urban disturbances were mainly a protest against unfair conditions. In other words, throughout the decade of the sixties, there was general black sympathy for protests (with some reservations about certain kinds of protests and stronger reservations about violence). There was a majority view that urban riots were a protest against unfair conditions, and even more felt they forced the nation to take action on racial problems.

However, in 1968, only 15 percent of the American blacks thought that blacks ought to be ready to use violence to gain rights, and only 8 percent said they would join in an urban disturbance if one was going on in their community. The young were more prepared to support violence in theory (22 percent) or to say they would join it in practice (13 percent); however, the Michigan team discovered that white Americans between sixteen and nineteen were almost as likely to advocate counter-rioting against blacks as young blacks were to say they would join in urban riots (12 percent). The Michigan researchers note that the inclination occasionally to indulge in violence as the means to one's end is not necessarily by any means a black monopoly in American society.

American blacks, then, tend to be integrationists, cultural pluralists, and cautious militants. The overwhelming majority, including the young, reject violence, though at times they are not ready to con-

blacks. That 45 percent from the 1968 Michigan study may be contrasted with the 50 percent who thought riots like the one in Watts helped the black cause as much as hurt it, from the NORC study of 1966.

demn those who engage in violent behavior, partly because they think that the urban riots were a protest over legitimate grievances and partly because it seems to them that the protests may occasionally be necessary to remind the rest of society of black problems.

This strain toward rather cautious militancy is confirmed in the attitudes of blacks toward their leaders, as depicted in Table 12.17. In 1968, the leadership of Martin Luther King, Roy Wilkins, and the NAACP received strong approval from black respondents, whereas only a limited number approved of Stokely Carmichael and H. Rap Brown. In 1968, when the CBS survey asked black respondents to chose one or two black leaders whose positions they thought accurately reflected their own, Abernathy, Wilkins, Stokes, Brooke, and Young were mentioned by 106 percent * of the respondents, whereas Carmichael, Muhammad, Brown, and McKissick were mentioned by only 17 percent. American blacks clearly endorse the moderate middle leadership; they did so when Martin Luther King was alive, and they continue to do so. One may truly marvel that men like Stokely Carmichael and H. Rap Brown received the immense media coverage they did with such little black support.

American blacks are ambivalent about their relationship to their white fellow citizens (Table 12.18). Two-thirds of them regard some white people as friends, but only a little less than two-fifths are convinced that white people would really like to see blacks have their rights.

In the Michigan study of 1968 45 percent said that they felt that many white people dislike Negroes, 12

* Respondents could mention more than one person.

TABLE 12.17
Black Attitudes Toward Leaders from CBS and Michigan Surveys, 1968

	Michigan	
	Percent Approve	Percent Partly Approve and Partly Disapprove
Stokely Carmichael	14	21
Martin Luther King	72	19
Roy Wilkins	50	12
H. Rap Brown	14	13
NAACP	75	11

	CBS	
	Percent Have Heard of	Percent Feel the Same Way **
Ralph Abernathy	83	53
Stokely Carmichael	76	6
H. Rap Brown	72	5
Roy Wilkins	67	25
Elijah Muhammad	57	2
Carl Stokes	48	12
Whitney Young	46	10
Edward Brooke	35	6
Floyd McKissick	34	4
Bayard Rustin	11	1
Ron Karenga	4	1

** "Which one or two on this list seem to feel the way that you yourself feel about these things?"

percent said that almost all white people dislike Negroes, and only 29 percent of the blacks thought that most whites wanted to see them get a better break. In the CBS study of the same year, 28 percent thought that most whites were sympathetic to

TABLE 12.18
Black Relationships with Whites with Two White Comparisons

	Percent	
	Black	*White*
NORC, 1966:		
Regard some white people as friends	67	
Most white people would really like for Negroes to have their rights	38	
When I am around a white person I am afraid he might say something which will show that he is prejudiced	39	
I am afraid that I might tell a white person what I think about white people	37	
The trouble with most white people is they think they're better than other people	83	
If a Negro is wise he will think twice before he trusts a white man as much as he would another Negro	48	
Sometimes I would like to get even with white people for all they have done to the Negro	31	
Remember being insulted by a white adult as a child	45	
MICHIGAN, 1968:		
Many white people dislike Negroes	45	
Almost all white people dislike Negroes	12	
Most white people want to see Negroes get a better break	29	
Most white people want to keep Negroes down	27	
CBS, 1968:		
Most whites are sympathetic to the problems of blacks	28	51
Most whites want complete equality between the races	19	34

the problems of blacks, and only 19 percent thought that most whites want complete equality between the races (only 34 percent of whites thought that most whites wanted complete equality). In other words, many American blacks feel suspicion of and anger toward whites, a tendency fundamentally to distrust white people, and skepticism toward any white commitment to full racial equality. Given the history of American blacks, this suspicion is not surprising; it would be a naïve politician who thought that black commitment to integration and aversion to violence indicates that there is not tension, skepticism, anger, and fear in black attitudes toward whites.

However, despite this anger and suspicion, there is still a fundamental trust in the American system, which leads most blacks to believe that it is possible through individual effort for the American black to overcome all barriers. As the Michigan researchers note, "Faith in the system then is very strong, being held even by many who perceive a great deal of discrimination." [10]

Despite their distrust and anger, American blacks seem to be extremely optimistic about the future as Table 12.19 indicates. In 1963, 69 percent of them thought that a solution would be worked out to America's racial problem. In 1964, 80 percent thought that things were getting better for American blacks, and in the same year, 72 percent thought the day would come when blacks would be fully accepted by whites. In 1966, 66 percent of American blacks expected either complete equality or great improvement in the next decade. In the same year, 59 per-

[10] Michigan survey, 1968, p. 27.

TABLE 12.19
Black Expectations for the Future with Two White Comparisons
(In Percent)

	NORC	Marx	CBS	Gallup	
	Black	*Black*	*Black*	*Black*	*White*
A solution will eventually be worked out (1963)	69				
Things are getting better for Negroes (1964)		80			
The day will come when Negroes will be fully accepted by whites (1964)		72			
Expect complete equality or a great deal of improvement by 1976 (1966)	66				
Position on a ladder between the best possible life and the worst (1966)—percent above 6 on a scale, 0–10:					
today	59				
five years ago	41				
five years hence	90				
See complete equality in less than twenty years			40		
See complete equality never			21		
Feel the world a better place for self in ten years (1969)				51	37
Feel the world a not so good place for self in ten years (1969)				27	29

cent thought that they were closer to the best possible life than the worst possible life, while 90 percent thought that in five year's time they would be closer to the best possible life than the worst.

Two years later, in the CBS 1968 survey, 40 percent of American blacks thought that there would be complete equality in less than twenty years, while 21 percent thought that there would never be complete equality. In the next year, 1969, 51 percent of American blacks thought that the world would be a better place for them in the next ten years, while only 27 percent thought it would not be so good (contrasted with only 37 percent of American whites who thought the world would be a better place in the next ten years). Similarly, in 1969, 76 percent of American blacks said they were satisfied with their work (as opposed to 54 percent in 1963), 44 percent said they were satisfied with their income (as opposed to 38 percent in 1963), and 50 percent said they were satisfied with their housing (as opposed to 43 percent in 1963).

American blacks, then, are inclined to think that their condition has changed for the better during the 1960s, and they project continued and perhaps accelerated change in the years ahead. There is no evidence in the data in Table 12.19 to think that American blacks have increasingly despaired of the "system."

On the contrary, the data collected by the Michigan survey of 1968 shows blacks are perhaps incredibly convinced that the system can work for them *despite* discrimination.

Very large majorities of blacks of whatever age and whatever educational level think that hard work enables the young black to get ahead in spite of prejudice and discrimination (Table 12.20).

The Michigan researchers note:

> *The age and education trends taken together suggest that for males a belief in the value of individual initiative and in the possibility of individual*

TABLE 12.20

"If a young Negro works hard enough, do you think he or she can usually get ahead in this country in spite of prejudice and discrimination, or that he doesn't have much chance no matter how hard he works?" (In Percent)

	Age 16–19 *	8th Grade or Less	9th 11th Grade	12th Grade	Some College	College Grad.
Negro Men	*Age 16–19 **	*Age 20–39*				
Can get ahead	72	68	75	82	81	93
Doesn't have much chance	26	27	24	15	16	7
Don't know	2	5	1	3	3	0
	*Age 16–19 **	*Age 40–60*				
Can get ahead	72	79	83	81	85	91
Doesn't have much chance	26	19	16	14	15	6
Don't know	2	2	1	5	0	3
Negro Women	*Age 16–19 **	*Age 20–39*				
Can get ahead	76	72	72	79	76	72
Doesn't have much chance	18	22	25	18	18	13
Don't know	6	6	3	3	6	15
	*Age 16–19 **	*Age 40–60*				
Can get ahead	76	74	80	80	93	89
Doesn't have much chance	18	20	18	18	4	4
Don't know	6	6	2	2	3	7

* This group combines all educational categories.

achievement continues to reinforce the person who manages to go through school. The more he gets ahead, the more he thinks he should be able to get ahead. But what is often called the school drop-out lacks the possibility of achievement, and apparently in a growing proportion of cases he believes that it is society that is at fault, not he himself.[11]

Protest, anger, even riot, as the Michigan team observed, are calls for reform within the system rather than an attempt to destroy it. The political leader who wants to get black votes should keep in mind two facts (in addition to remembering that 40 percent of American blacks voted for Dwight Eisenhower): (1) American blacks have not abandoned the political and economic system of the country. On the contrary, they endorse it with what must be said under the circumstances to be incredible vigor. (2) They want a legitimate chance for themselves and their children within the system.

In 1966, the principal goals of American blacks were better jobs and better education (Table 12.21). Eighty percent of the respondents in the NORC survey of that year endorsed such goals. Two years later, when the CBS survey was taken (Table 12.22), the emphasis was still on jobs, education, housing, better police protection, and more government effort to help blacks solve their problems. Interestingly enough, most American whites do not object to the items that are high on the black agenda. Only 16 percent of the whites are opposed to job training programs, which 89 percent of blacks want, and only 16 percent are opposed to better police protection for black neighborhoods. Also, only 18 percent of

[11] Michigan survey, 1968, p. 28.

TABLE 12.21
Most Important Goals for Civil Rights Leaders *

	Percent
Better jobs	35
Better schools	15
More school integration	2
More elective offices	10
Bigger poverty program	3
Elimination of discrimination in public places	2
Stopping housing segregation	3
Keeping Negro high school students in school and getting them to go to college	30

* NORC, 1966.

the blacks want preference over whites for jobs and 77 percent of the whites are opposed to it. The principal contrast between a black majority and a white near majority is on more efforts toward providing a minimum guaranteed family income, with 77 percent of blacks in favor of it and 50 percent of the whites against it. The busing issue is also a critical one, since 62 percent of the blacks support it and 40 percent of the whites oppose it. About half the black population is in favor of housing for blacks in present all-white neighborhoods, and about half the white population is against it, indicating that this issue will be an extremely delicate one for political leadership.

Busing, forced integration of white neighborhoods, and a guaranteed family income are three practical political problems on which consensus does not exist between whites and blacks in the United States. However, it is important to note that as far as housing for black families in all-white

TABLE 12.22
Important Black Goals with White Opposition
(CBS, 1968)

	Percent in Favor of *	Percent Object to **
	Black	*White*
More government job training programs for Negroes	89	16
Improving schools and teaching in Negro areas	79	4
More low-cost housing for Negroes	79	25
More effort by Negroes to help themselves	78	–
Better police protection for Negro neighborhoods	78	16
More effort by Negroes to participate in government	77	12
A guaranteed minimum family income	77	50
More attention by local government to solve Negro problems	74	10
Stronger enforcement of present anti-discrimination laws	65	19
Busing Negro students to better schools	62	40
Birth control clinics for Negroes	51	10
Housing for Negro families in present all-white neighborhoods	49	48
Black control of black communities	22	26
Give Negroes preference over whites in jobs	18	77
Whole new communities built just for Negroes	17	42
No choice made	2	4
No answer	1	1

* "Which of the things on this list would you be in favor of? Choose as many as you wish and just read me the numbers."

** "Which of the items on this list, if any, are not such good ideas? Choose as many as you wish. Just read me the numbers."

neighborhoods, a black consensus does not exist either. It would be naïve to suppose that in a society as complicated as the American one, groups with such a long and tragic history of conflict as blacks and whites would agree on all practical political issues. The thrust of the present chapter is not to deny the disagreement but to say that there is still considerable room for coalition and consensus, and to stress, as does Table 12.22, that on some matters of policy there is widespread agreement.

One of the more surprising findings of the Michigan survey in 1968 was that black dwellers in American Northern cities were quite similar to their white counterparts in their judgments on public services (Table 12.23). There are only relatively small differences in the proportions of those satisfied with the quality of public schools and their recreation centers for teenagers. Blacks are less likely to be satisfied with the parks and playgrounds for children, with garbage collection, and with police protection. However, similar proportions of the two groups asserted that they thought they could get city officials to do something about serious complaints, and similar proportions had actually complained about poor service.

Whites were more likely than blacks to think that the mayor and the state government were trying hard to solve urban problems, though blacks were more likely to think that the federal government was trying hard. Nevertheless, substantial majorities of the blacks were likely to give favorable response to government at all three levels as trying fairly hard to solve city problems. The state government got less favorable mention than either the federal or local governments.

TABLE 12.23
Satisfactions and Dissatisfactions
Black and White

	Black	*White*
Percent "Generally Satisfied":		
Quality of public schools	43	48
Parks and playgrounds for children	30	50
Recreation centers for teenagers	24	33
Police protection	46	67
Garbage collection	67	80
Think they can get city officials to do something about serious complaints	48	46
Have complained about poor service	27	29
Percent "Trying Hard" to Solve City Problems:		
Mayor	47	19
State government	33	22
Federal government	39	25
Percent "Trying Fairly Hard" to Solve City Problems:		
Mayor	65	16
State government	41	23
Federal government	17	38
Percent With Complaints about Police:		
Don't come quickly	51	27
Don't show respect	38	16
Search without good reason	36	11
Rough up unnecessarily	35	10

The most serious differences between blacks and whites have to do with the police, though a majority of blacks are critical of the police only on the matter of their not coming too quickly. However, 38 percent say that the police do not show respect, 36 percent say they search people without good reason, and 35 percent say they "rough up" citizens unnecessarily.

Obviously, the political candidate interested in building a coalition will have to give considerable attention to the thorny problem of the relationships between the police and the black community.

Finally, in Table 12.24 we see that large numbers of American blacks are still persuaded that there is considerable discrimination against them in employment, housing, and other areas of urban life, although only a relatively small number report that they themselves have been refused a job because of racial discrimination, or refused promotion because of racial discrimination. It is interesting to note that the situation of American blacks is such that far more of them believe in the possibility of discrimination than have actually experienced it. There is a suggestion here that they misperceive the amount of discrimination that goes on in the job market, that far fewer of them have actually been discriminated against than think that discrimination occurs. Given the past history of discrimination, of course, one can scarcely blame them for being skeptical.

It would be a mistake, then, to think that because American blacks think there has been progress in the last decade and are hopeful for more progress to come, and because they think the federal government at least is trying fairly hard to solve urban problems that they are therefore persuaded that there is no longer any discrimination against them in American society. One may conclude from the data that blacks are moderately satisfied with the progress that has been made, hopeful of more progress in the future, yet under no illusions about the problems that remain.

To summarize the data presented in the second half of this chapter:

1. There is no such thing as an American black

TABLE 12.24
Percentage of Negroes Perceiving Discrimination in Housing and Other Areas *

Believe "many" or "some" Negroes (as against "few") in this city miss out on good housing because of racial discrimination	76
Believe there are "many" places (as against "some" or "none") in this city where they could not rent or buy a house because of discrimination	43
Believe that racial discrimination in housing is increasing or not changing	54
Believe judges in this city are harder on Negroes than on whites	22
Believe "city officials" pay less attention to a request from a Negro than a white person	60

* Michigan survey, 1968.

TABLE 12.25
Percentage of Negroes Perceiving Discrimination in Employment *

Report having been refused a job because of racial discrimination	30
Report having been refused promotion on a job because of racial discrimination	14
Believe many or some Negroes miss out on jobs today because of discrimination	71
Believe many or some Negroes miss out on promotions today because of race	68
Believe there is discrimination in hiring by the federal government	40
Believe there is discrimination in hiring by their city government	50
Believe there is discrimination in hiring in teaching	34
Believe big companies hire a few Negroes only for show purposes, to appear to be nondiscriminatory	77
Believe discrimination in hiring and promotions is increasing or not changing	42

* Michigan survey, 1968.

position. American blacks take stands that run from the very moderate to the very radical. Any attempt to universalize about the black "position" is stereotyping. Unless generalizations are understood as averages or majorities, they are extremely deceptive politically.

2. The overwhelming majority of American blacks are not separatists.

3. The emphasis on black pride and black culture is seen by most blacks as coexisting with the desire for integration. Cultural pluralism does not mean racial separatism in the minds of most blacks.

4. The majority of blacks are sympathetic toward protests and demonstrations, ambiguous about the urban riots, and opposed to violence either as general strategy or personal activity. Blacks are no more likely to say they would engage in riots than are young whites to say they would engage in anti-black riots.

5. Moderate black political leadership still has the overwhelming support of the American black population.

6. Even though there is suppressed anger toward whites among many blacks and widespread suspicion and skepticism of white intentions, American blacks still think that considerable progress has been made in the past and optimistically expect more progress in the years to come.

7. Housing, jobs, education are the principal concerns of American blacks, and while there is potential conflict on such subjects as the guaranteed wage, busing, and forced integration of all-white neighborhoods, there is still considerable areas of agreement between blacks and whites in matters of racial policy.

8. While there are many similarities between

blacks and whites in satisfactions and dissatisfactions with urban problems, and a black willingness to say that the government is at least trying hard to solve those problems, blacks are far more likely than whites to object to police behavior.

9. Even though only minorities of blacks report that they have actually experienced discrimination in employment and promotion, the majority of blacks still think that discriminatory practices are followed in occupational and housing markets.

There is nothing in the above assertions to justify optimism, yet neither is there anything that should prescribe despair. There is a rhetoric of political persuasion that has been extremely popular in the last decade in the United States. It argues that social reform must occur or blacks will give up on American society or, alternately, tear it apart. It seems to me that that rhetoric is of dubious merit. First of all, at the present time it is not true that American blacks have despaired. On the contrary, they are hopeful about the future. Secondly, it is dubious whether the political rhetoric or threat can be productive unless it is used in very moderate amounts. Third, it is very unlikely that any social reform that could possibly occur in the years immediately ahead would satisfy the most militant and extreme black spokesmen. Political reform that is based on the argument that it is necessary to quiet the violent and the radical loses its appeal when it becomes obvious that it will not quiet the violent and the radical.

A far more effective form of argumentation would combine an appeal to the common needs and problems of black and white with an appeal to the American commitment to justice and equality, an appeal, as we noted in the previous chapter, that would correspond to the expressed values of the large majority of white Americans.

The point of this chapter is not that everything is rosy for American blacks. On the contrary, there are no grounds for complacency. But it is not too late, and only those who believe that the rhetoric of apocalypse is absolutely essential to maintain urgency will use it as a justification for complacency.

Political leadership will have to accept the fact that black militancy is a part of the American political scene and will remain so for at least the next decade. Blacks want better jobs, better homes, better education, and more respect from American society. Any political candidate who seems unresponsive to these demands is not going to get black support in elections, and he will not have a black consensus behind him when he attempts to govern. The ways black goals can be implemented may be a subject for debate. Our data would indicate that there are differences of opinion even among American blacks on the question of methods. But a political leader who wishes to govern American society in any kind of peace and harmony will have to convince blacks that he is determined to right the wrongs of the past in his response to their demands for equality in American society. More than that, he will have to show results. Good intentions and fine words are not enough. He will also have to live with the reality that blacks have every reason not to trust white political leadership. And at the present stage of American society, the white politicians are faced with the difficult task of earning black trust, which, if secured, will not be easy to keep. White politicians must also learn to accept an increasingly skillful, vigorous, and militant black political leadership, a leadership that will be all the more effective because it appeals to broad black support, not just to the more militant elements in the black community.

Only the most naïve would conclude from the data presented in this chapter that black militancy is going to go away, or that it will be easy for white leadership or, indeed, the rest of white society to deal with American blacks. It will not be easy at all. But what data we do have indicate that it is still possible. How much time we have left is problematic, but surely there is not enough time to generate complacency. The problems are pressing and demand our urgent attention.

If I have any fear about the liberal response to racial problems in America during the next three years, it is that blacks will go out of fashion again. I have the impression that many liberals are tired of black militancy and disappointed that somehow or other blacks (like the young, of whom they are even more tired) did not prove the kind of strong and enthusiastic and activist supporters of Senator McGovern that the liberals thought they would be. There is, I think, reason to fear that because of sheer exhaustion and discouragement, if nothing else, blacks may be indeed in for a time of "benign neglect" by liberals. And it will not be the sort of "benign neglect" envisioned by Mr. Moynihan, that of ignoring the inflammatory rhetoric; it will be rather a neglect of people and of problems. One presumes that "quotas" (now politely called "affirmative action") will still be pushed and that there will still be some agitation for busing, though I suspect that over the years both these issues will lose much of their energy and force. From a noisy despair about America's racial situation we may turn to an indifference. But hysteria breeds indifference. If problems are insoluble, then why try to solve them? If blacks are about to secede from American society, why worry about trying to integrate them?

Those who are concerned about rebuilding the Democratic coalition can hardly afford that kind of faddism. The blacks are an absolutely indispensable part of the liberal Democratic coalition. I have deliberately piled up statistical tables in this chapter to make as powerful a case as I can for my conviction that a skilled political leader can bring blacks and whites together in a viable political coalition. Moralizing and exhortation to guilt may have to be abandoned. Quick and easy solutions may have to be abandoned. Passion for elegance and balance may have to be abandoned. But coalition is still possible. Indeed, it may be easier than ever before, because racism (here used in the narrow sense of racial bigotry) is a diminishing force in American society. The moralists who wrote the Kerner Commission Report did none of us any favors by using the same word to describe bigotry and the residual structural and cultural effects of past bigotry. There is overwhelming evidence that bigotry is diminishing in American society. There are still bigots around, of course, and there is a bit of bigot in each of us whether we be black or white, Jew or Gentile, Irish or Polish, Northerner or Southerner. But the leaders of the liberal coalition ought to take, as an exploratory model at least, the notion that if one could eliminate crime and violence in the city and find a way to free the white working and lower-middle class from paying disproportionate costs of racial integration, then bigotry might be perceived as a relatively unimportant political and social force. That many urban whites are frightened is unquestionable. That they have nothing to be frightened about is absurd. If the grounds for their fear could be minimized or eliminated, their "bigotry" might not be much of a problem. This is, I would suggest, at least a testable hypothesis, and one that no rebuilder of the liberal Democratic coalition can afford to ignore.

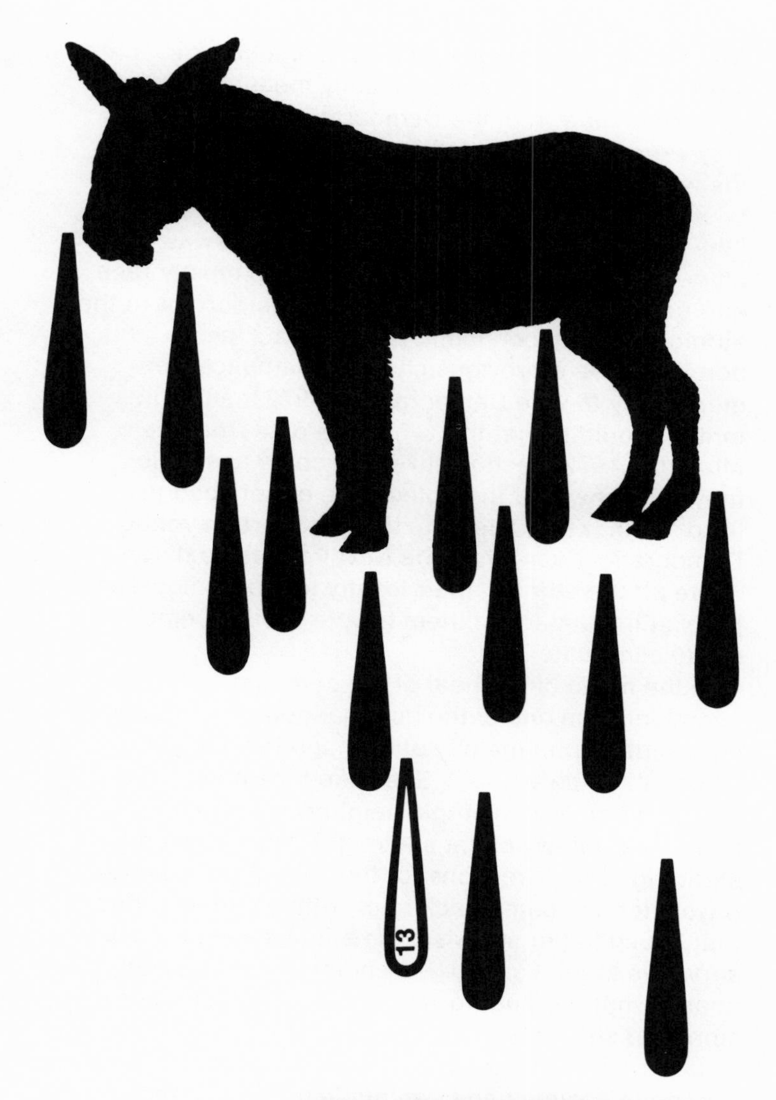

IN DEFENSE OF ETHNICS

One of the great myths of the 1972 election was that the "white ethnics" (which usually meant Catholic) were defecting from the Democratic party because they were "conservative" on racial issues and on the war. It was hoped that Senator McGovern would be able to win some of them back with his stand on "the economic issue." After the election it was concluded that "the social issue" (meaning mostly race and permissiveness) had been more important to the ethnics than the economic issue. In fact, as we pointed out in a previous chapter, Catholics were more likely to vote Democratic in 1972 than Protestants. I would wager that when the data from the Michigan 1972 election survey become available they will show that the Poles were either second or third to blacks and Jews in their proportion voting Democratic. Even when the New Politics coalition wrote off the ethnics, their loyalty to the Democratic party still led many of them to vote for the Democratic candidate.

In the midst of the heat of the campaign a correspondent from one of the national news magazines descended upon the city of Chicago to "study the white ethnic defectors." She asked me about where she could go to find ethnic neighborhoods and ethnics to interview so that she might gain some understanding of their reasons for this defection. Several days later she came back to my office and admitted that, much to her surprise, the ethnics were not conservative at all. I asked her whether there was any chance that her finding would appear in her magazine, and she admitted that it probably would not. And it did not. The minds of those who comment on American society had been made up: the ethnics were "conservative defectors." While intermittent efforts were made during the McGovern campaign to communicate with the ethnic members of the old coalition, such efforts were desultory and futile. (My guess is that many ethnics felt they were thrown out of the party by the convention, and that there was no way of winning them back.)

In the early stages of campaign enthusiasm, the young McGovern enthusiasts were expected to compensate by sheer force of numbers for the defecting ethnics. As time wore on and the campaign became more threatened and shrill with its appeals to morality and more evangelical, all serious efforts to reclaim the ethnics were abandoned.

But the mistakes of 1972 are less important than the possibilities for 1974 and 1976. There is no component of the liberal elitist "picture" of American society that is more stubbornly and wrongheadedly erroneous than the image the liberal elite have of the Catholic ethnic groups. In this chapter, as in the last one, I shall make heavy use of survey data. I fear that the demons of false imagery can only be exorcised by empirical evidence—though there is no special reason that even such powerful formulas of exorcism will have any impact.

The most obvious thing that can be said about the ethnics is that they are Democrats (Table 13.1). The Poles were 21 percentage points more likely to vote Democratic in congressional elections during the last twenty years than were typical Americans, while the Irish Catholics were 15 percentage points more likely and the Italians 7 percentage points more likely to vote Democratic. In the 1968 presidential election (a particularly turbulent year for the Democrats—indeed, for the country), the Irish were 21 percentage points ahead of the national average in voting for Hubert Humphrey, the Italians 15 percentage points ahead, and the Poles (despite all the

TABLE 13.1
Ethnic Democratic Voting Patterns for Congressional and Presidential Elections
(Percent)

	Congress		*President*		
	1952–70 (average percent)	1970	1952–68 (average percent)	1968	1972 *
Catholic					
Irish	70	73	65	65	61
German	57	45	55	55	57
Italian	62	62	60	59	63
Polish	76	73	76	80	72
All Americans	55	54	48	44	55

* Democrat or Democrat leaning.

talk about their support for George Wallace) were 36 percentage points ahead of the national average. Finally, in the spring of 1972, the Irish, Italians, and Poles were more than 5 percentage points more likely than average Americans to describe themselves as Democrats or Democratic leaning independents.

Catholics comprise about one-third of the Democrats in the country and probably close to two-fifths of the Democrats outside the South. It would be very difficult indeed for a Democrat to win a national election without Catholic support.

Furthermore, the issues that the Catholic ethnics are most likely to think are "very serious" problems of the country were precisely those issues that ought to have been the Democratic party's long suit in a national election—war and inflation (Table 13.2). If one compares the Italian and Polish ethnics with the

Anglo-Saxon Protestants, one notes that the order of importance of the first five issues is precisely the same: war, marijuana, inflation, crime, and pollution. However, the Italians and Poles are more likely to see each of these as "very serious" than are Anglo-Saxon Protestants. More than half of both groups think that pollution, inflation, and the war are very serious problems. A campaign geared to respond to these issues might have been especially effective for the Democrats among the Italians and the Poles.

Nor is the fact that half of these two groups (as well as half the Irish) think that crime in the streets is a very serious problem necessarily an indication that these groups are to be written off as conservative, for 65 percent of the blacks in the country also think it is a very serious problem.

However, there is one surprising point in Table 13.2. As of the spring of 1971, three-fifths of the Italians and three-fifths of the Poles thought that marijuana was a very serious problem in the country, placing it in second place in their list of problems. Presumably, liberal political candidates will not be able to understand or effectively respond to this concern about marijuana (which is probably symbolic of the deeper and broader concern about the whole drug problem) until they realize just how intense the concern about it is. (And why are the Irish so much less concerned than anyone else about the marijuana issue?) A liberal political candidate, wishing to appeal to the ethnics, can count on their support for his stand on war, inflation, and pollution, but he will have to find a response to the crime problem that is more reassuring to the ethnics and still in keeping with his liberal conscience. He will also have to take into account their very serious concerns about drugs. However, as the figures in the

TABLE 13.2
Rank Order of
Top Six "Very Serious"
Problems for Ethnics *
(Percent)

Anglo-Saxon Protestant		*Irish Catholic*		*German Catholic*		*Italian Catholic*		*Polish Catholic*	
War	68	War	69	War	62	War	73	War	71
Marijuana	51	Inflation	55	Inflation	49	Marijuana	60	Marijuana	60
Inflation	48	Crime	52	Pollution	46	Inflation	57	Inflation	57
Crime	44	Welfare	42	Marijuana	42	Crime	55	Crime	55
Pollution	42	Unemployment	38	Crime	39	Pollution	54	Pollution	55
Unemployment	30	Marijuana	38	Unemployment	30	Welfare	53	Urban Unrest	35
		Pollution	38						

* NORC 1971 Research Fellows' Study #4119.

column representing the Anglo-Saxon Protestants indicate, all Americans are concerned about both drugs and crime.

Table 13.3 shows the proportions of respondents in each group who express like or dislike for various groups in the society. The overwhelming majority of all ethnic groups are sympathetically disposed to college students, indicating that the younger generation is by no means despised by most Americans. The Irish, Italians, and Poles are somewhat less likely, however, to like college students than are Anglo-Saxon Protestants. Similarly, while the majority of all the groups like college professors, the Irish and the Italians are somewhat less inclined to like them than are the Anglo-Saxon Protestants, and only a minority of the Poles are willing to admit that they like them. However, only a tiny fraction of every group dislikes college professors. But while students and professors get good marks from the ethnics, radical students get very poor marks, with more than four-fifths of each group (and more than four-fifths of the Anglo-Saxon Protestants also) not liking radical students.

There is less admiration for big business among the Catholic ethnics than among Anglo-Saxon Protestants, although only the Italians are notably more inclined to like labor unions. Liberals enjoy a better image with the Irish than they do with the other five groups, though only the Italians are less sympathetic to the liberals than are the Anglo-Saxon Protestants. Similarly, the German, Italian, and Polish Catholics are somewhat less likely to have a favorable image of conservatives than are Anglo-Saxon Protestants.

There is little difference between the Anglo-Saxons and the Germans, Italians, and Poles in their image of blacks. The Irish are notably more inclined

TABLE 13.3
Ethnic Likes and Dislikes of Social Groups
(Percent)

	Anglo-Saxon Protestant		*Irish Catholic*		*German Catholic*		*Italian Catholic*		*Polish Catholic*	
	Like	Dislike	Like	Dislike	Like	Dislike	Like	Dislike	Like	Dislike
College Students	80	3	67	0	80	2	70	0	72	6
Big Business	76	14	42	21	31	26	57	10	33	21
Liberals	27	27	39	28	31	26	15	25	28	21
Blacks	50	12	79	0	49	7	50	2	46	13
Conservatives	46	12	46	18	30	13	38	8	31	13
Hippies	7	77	14	58	3	70	3	66	2	79
Radical Students	4	86	7	86	2	81	14	82	0	88
Welfare Recipients	30	21	28	17	33	28	28	18	10	35
College Professors	63	7	57	10	67	3	57	7	40	2
Police	87	3	86	0	91	5	90	0	78	4
Unions	43	33	43	21	46	30	50	19	45	20
Black Militants *	2	83	0	96	2	83	5	78	4	86

* The black response to this question is Like, 35, Dislike, 37.

to have a favorable image of blacks. However, all groups have a very unfavorable image of black militants—and indeed blacks themselves are slightly more inclined to be unfavorable to the militants than favorable. The Irish, German, and Italians have about the same image of welfare recipients as do Anglo-Saxon Protestants. The Polish image of welfare recipients is distinctly unfavorable. Finally, all five groups are very favorably disposed to the police.

To sum up Table 13.3, a political candidate running as a liberal Democrat need not fear that the ethnics resent either college professors or college students. Nor, apparently, need he fear that they will be antagonized by bad relations with labor unions, though he will find them much less sympathetic to big business than are Anglo-Saxon Protestants. However, they are more inclined, by and large, to like conservatives than they are to like liberals, and they have a distinct dislike for hippies, radicals, and militants. They like the police very much. The candidate, then, who is predisposed to ideological liberalism, is bound to be ill at ease with the ethnics if he is too closely identified with radicals, hippies, and militants and shares their distaste for the police. The candidate might console himself with a mutual dislike of big business and labor, but he should take warning that when advertising himself as "liberal" he may alienate the approximately one-quarter of the ethnics who are suspicious of anyone to whom the term liberal is attached.

So the ethnics are not "pure" liberals; indeed, a substantial proportion seem to dislike them. Would a Democratic candidate therefore be justified in arriving at the conclusion that the Catholic ethnics are not liberal at all? Table 13.4 suggests that ethnic lib-

TABLE 13.4
Ethnic Solutions to Issues
(Percent)

	Vietnam		*Pollution*		*Riots*		*Racial Progress*		*Family Assistance*	
	Withdraw	Victory	Fines and Jail	Nothing	Solve Problems	Force	Speed up	Slow down	Government support	Support self
Anglo-Saxon										
Protestants	40	36	71	19	47	38	40	32	37	40
Catholics										
Irish	64	32	77	23	35	51	57	19	42	24
German	46	28	85	4	58	28	32	27	42	25
Italian	53	32	83	4	40	52	43	40	55	30
Polish	41	30	79	11	59	29	22	35	30	65

TABLE 13.4
Ethnic Solutions to Issues (continued)
(Percent)

	Marijuana		*Rights of Criminals*		*Forced Neighborhood Integration*		*Student Rioters*		*Government Eliminate Poverty*	
	Allowed	Not allowed	More careful	Too far	Government should	Government should not	Should not punish	Punish severely	All resources	Has done too much
Anglo-Saxon										
Protestant	8	87	27	58	22	67	11	74	43	37
Catholic										
Irish	30	52	13	73	34	49	20	67	66	17
German	21	69	19	64	27	55	8	74	45	31
Italian	12	88	33	59	28	55	23	59	62	31
Polish	13	79	17	68	22	23	10	75	74	11

eralism is complicated and rather diffuse, but that there is a strong reserve of potential support among the ethnics for a liberal Democratic candidate. The majority of the Irish, for example, favored withdrawal from Vietnam, stiff punishment for pollution, a speeding up of racial progress, government support for family assistance, and a maximum use of resources to eliminate poverty. On each of these issues, the Irish are more "liberal" than Anglo-Saxon Protestants. A surprisingly large minority of the Irish (30 percent) are also willing to support the legalization of marijuana (perhaps because the Irish romance with John Barleycorn makes them reluctant to deny any kind of narcotics to others). The Irish are also considerably more likely than the Anglo-Saxon Protestants to support government pressure for neighborhood integration and to oppose punishment for student rioters, though in both cases, only a minority of the Irish respondents take such positions. On the other hand, 51 percent of the Irish respondents favored the use of force to end urban unrest. And, finally, the Irish are the most likely of any of the groups under consideration to think that the courts have gone too far in protecting the rights of criminals.

A majority of German Catholics take the "liberal" side on stiff penalties for pollution, though Germans are more likely to be on the "liberal" side than Anglo-Saxon Protestants on the war, on solving the underlying problems that cause riots, on family assistance, marijuana, and on neighborhood integration.

Italian Catholics provide majority support for the "liberal" response on the war, pollution, family assistance, and government efforts to eliminate poverty. They are also more concerned than any of the other groups with the protection of the rights of criminals and the nonpunishment of student rioters.

Finally, even though the Poles are the least likely of the ethnic groups to espouse a "liberal" position, 79 percent of them favor strong punishment for pollution, and 74 percent (highest among all five groups) would favor all possible government resources used to eliminate poverty.

In other words, in 1972, a liberal candidate would have found support among all the Catholic ethnic groups for his stand on the war and pollution, and majority support among the Irish, Italians, and Poles for the elimination of poverty. On most of the other issues, the Irish, the Germans, and the Italians are more inclined to support his positions than are the Anglo-Saxon Protestants. If poverty and pollution are the major issues in American life today, then the ethnics are surely on the liberal side; and if the speeding up of racial progress is a liberal goal, then the Irish are on that side. If government support for family assistance is an imperative reform for the liberals, then the Italians would concur. Similarly, the Irish and the Italians are more likely than Anglo-Saxon Protestants to support liberal views on the subject of forced neighborhood integration. On crimes, drugs, and riots the ethnics are not likely to take a liberal position, but then neither are a large majority of other Americans.

In Table 13.5, we turn to data gathered in the spring of 1972 on certain other critical issues before the American public. The majority of the ethnics are for gun control. Indeed, they are considerably more likely to be in sympathy with such control than are Anglo-Saxon Protestants. On the other hand, the majority of them (in the case of the Poles, three-

TABLE 13.5
Attitudes of Ethnics on Issues *
(Percent)

Issue	Anglo-Saxon Protestant	Irish	Catholic: German	Italian	Polish
For gun control	65	85	72	81	74
For capital punishment	64	60	63	67	75
Would object to black of same class living on the same block	19	8	13	12	20
For school integration (would send children to half black school)	80	80	83	73	77
For busing **	7	10	11	6	9
Allow Communist to speak	63	69	65	54	38
Allow antireligious person to speak	74	79	82	82	64
Would vote for black president	65	85	78	79	66
For abortion if danger to mother's health	83	68	78	88	89
For abortion if mother wants no more children	38	22	31	34	34

* NORC Study #4139, 1972.
** Fifty-three percent of blacks support busing.

quarters) are also for capital punishment. Only a tiny fraction of the ethnic groups would object to a black of the same social class living on the block with them, and the overwhelming majority (between three-quarters and four-fifths) are willing to send their children to schools where half the students would be black. Like all other Americans, however, the overwhelming majority of the ethnics are against busing.

Like most other Americans, a large majority of the

ethnics support the right of an antireligious person to speak, although barely more than half the Italians and a little under two-fifths of the Poles would concede the same right to a Communist (the captive-nation theme is still important to American Poles). Of the Irish, 85 percent, 78 percent of the Germans, 79 percent of the Italians, and 66 percent of the Poles would vote for a qualified black for president (as opposed to 65 percent of the Anglo-Saxon Protestants).

Even though Irish Catholics are less likely to approve abortion than Anglo-Saxon Protestants, there are no differences between the other ethnic groups and Protestants on the subject of abortion. A large majority of Americans are apparently willing to approve it if there is a danger to the mother's health. Only a minority support abortion if the mother simply wants no more children.

Nor do the ethnics (with the exception of the Slavs) do badly on NORC's racial integration scale.[1] (Table 13.6). Jews are still the American religious group most favorably disposed to racial integration. They have changed little in their attitudes between 1963 and 1972. Both Protestants and Catholics, however, have changed substantially. Among the major American ethnic groups outside the South the greatest change in the last two years has been among Italian and Irish Catholics. Anglo-Saxons and Slavic Catholics have also increased their sympathy for racial integration more than the average Northern increase. Scandinavian Protestants and German Catholics have increased less than the Northern average, while German Protestants and Jews have declined somewhat in their sympathy for integration during

[1] For an explanation of the NORC prointegration scale and a description of the Guttman scale, see pp. 300–317.

TABLE 13.6
Prointegration Scale by Ethnicity
(Non-South Only)

	1970		1972		Change 1970–1972
All Northerners	2.88		3.16		.28
Anglo-Saxons	2.80	(220)	3.18	(148)	.38
German Protestants	2.81	(137)	2.70	(142)	−.11
Scandinavian Protestants	2.82	(29)	2.98	(65)	.16
Irish Catholics	3.06	(48)	3.46	(63)	.40
German Catholics	2.97	(41)	3.18	(44)	.21
Italian Catholics	2.65	(38)	3.14	(63)	.49
Slavic Catholics	2.45	(53)	2.76	(49)	.31
Jews	3.79	(24)	3.67	(52)	−.12

the past two years. Jews remain, however, the most sympathetic of all ethnic groups, and the relatively small number of Jews in the sample makes any speculation on the apparent slight decline in sympathy for integration inappropriate.

Do the ethnics, then, belong in the liberal coalition? How would they do on an ideological test of purity? On pollution, poverty, gun control, neighborhood and school integration, and civil liberties they are certainly liberal. On crime, riots, radicalism, busing, capital punishment, and legalization of marijuana they are not liberal, but apparently neither are most other Americans. Surprisingly enough, with the exception of the Irish, abortion does not seem to be nearly as serious an issue for the Catholic ethnic as had been thought. Finally, a liberal candidate is more likely to find support for his welfare measures among the ethnics than he is among Anglo-Saxon Protestants.

Whether the ethnics are to be allowed into a reconstructed coalition depends on how firmly the boundaries of that coalition are to be drawn. If absolute purity is required, the ethnics won't make it (and neither will most other Americans), and no liberal can afford to exclude the ethnics unless he has a compensating presence (like the young) he can count on for more total support.

And if the liberal decides he must attract a substantial number of ethnics to win a majority of votes, what must he do to obtain their support?

He must obviously push very strongly on issues of crime, pollution, elimination of poverty, and the control of inflation. On the other hand, he must reassure the ethnics (and most other Americans, too) that he is not soft on crime, riots, radicalism, drugs, and busing. He must face the fact that however benighted it may be of them, the majority of the Irish, Italians, and Poles think crime in the streets is a very serious problem. A majority of the Italians and Poles also think that marijuana is a very serious problem. Furthermore, while 88 percent of the Italians and 79 percent of the Poles are against the legalization of marijuana, so, too, are 76 percent of the blacks. It would be my guess that in 1976, a liberal candidate who can reassure the ethnics on the question of crime and drugs (and quite likely also on the issue of radicalism) will be able to count on their support in an election. But then it is very unlikely that any candidate who cannot reassure the American public on these three issues stands much of a chance of election—at least in the absence of very notable blunders on the part of his opponent.

Why the myth of the white ethnic hawk and racist hawk was so strong in 1972 is an interesting and important question. Obviously, the myth has been reinforced by the mass media treatment of the "hard-hat" phenomenon and by the articles of writers in elite journals. Middle Americans in general and white ethnics in particular were often presented as primitives, sometimes charming and sometimes frightening, but always uneducated and bigoted. The data I present in this chapter suggest that that image is something the media brought with them to middle America rather than finding it there. The work of Dr. Robert Coles shows that a sensitive observer from the elite world who arrives in middle America without preconceptions discovers something very different and very much more complicated than do other observers of the middle American scene.

From where do the presuppositions that gave rise to the myth of the white hard-hat racist hawk ethnic come? Michael Lerner has suggested that there is a tendency for the intellectual elite, as part of the upper middle class, to feel snobbish toward the lower middle class and working class while it is sympathetic toward the "poor"—a phenomenon characteristic of many societies in which one group is at odds with those immediately below and above it but maintains good relationships with other groups at one remove. It is also true that in certain parts of the country gains for blacks have to be purchased at the price of losses for other groups. Thus in the city of Newark, for example, if black teacher supervisors are to be promoted independently of their performance in exams, the ones who will suffer will be the only other group in the teaching profession in Newark, white Italians. The Italians, who feel, not without reason, that they have yet to get a fair shake for themselves from American society, are likely to protest. The intellectual and social elites of the country need some justification for ignoring this protest and forcing the Italians to pay the required price. To be able to write this group off as benighted and bigoted is one way in which the elite can soothe its conscience. In a somewhat more general way, of course, it is always helpful to have someone to blame for all the wrongs of society. The Catholic ethnics, particularly the Irish, Polish, and Italians, have always been a convenient scapegoat for explaining America's social problems. Why did the war last so long? Why isn't more being done for blacks? An answer that would suggest that we have yet to find the political leadership to mobilize a coalition to cope with urban problems is too complicated even for many well-educated Americans. One needs villains for war and for racism, villains who can only redeem themselves by acknowledging their own guilt. The white ethnic has been such a villain, one who is not likely to be renounced even when overwhelming data demands it.

As a young Polish historian puts it:

> *. . . the American view of the immigrant and his progeny has changed considerably. The brutish, anti-democratic ignoramus; the strike-breaking*

supplanter of honest American labor; the advance guard of anarchism and Bolshevism; the mindless tool of the Papal conspiracy was transformed by the 1940's into the kindly, gentle, slightly comic fellow who, waving his citizenship papers proudly, burbled heartwarming patriotic cliches in his broken, night-school English. Now, he is again transformed into the racist hard hat. These stereotypes, many of them conflicting, reveal much more about the projected hopes and hidden fears of American society than they do about the immigrant.[2]

Clearly, Professor Radzialowski is a pushy Polack. How dare he suggest that the ethnic is an inkblot onto which the liberal elitist projects himself? How dare he imply that the bigotry that the elitist claims to see in the ethnic may really be unconscious bigotry repressed in the depths of his own personality?

But there are probably more important explanations for such complex and perhaps tendentious psychoanalyzing of the American intelligentsia. The simple truth is that most well-educated Americans, particularly those who teach in the major universities, shape the mass media, staff the upper levels of the bureaucracy, and advise important legislative and administrative officials in local and national government simply do not know anything about the Poles and the Italians of the United States, and while they think they know something about the Irish, they really don't know much about them either. Indeed, it can be said that many of those Americans

[2] Thaddeus Radzialowski, "The View from the Polish Ghetto: Some Observations on the First Hundred Years in Detroit," unpublished paper (Marshall, Minn.: Southwestern Minnesota State College, 1972).

who read the *Washington Post* and the *New York Times* every day know more about Nigeria than they do about the northwest side of Chicago, the Italian section of Queens, or the descendants of Studs Lonigan. The Irish, the Italians, and the Poles have not entered into the same world of the upper intelligentsia as have WASPS and Jews. They are not writing doctoral dissertations about their own communities, and the Irish have apparently even stopped writing novels about them. The recent shallow and superficial rediscovery of ethnic Americans indicates not merely how much ignorance there is of the children and grandchildren of the gentile immigrant groups, but how likely this ignorance is to persist.

The tragedy is not that anything particular is being done to most American ethnics (though situations like the Newark teachers are obviously intolerable). The real problem is that fantasies about white ethnics can be very harmful for the possibility of social change when they become the basis for serious political decision-making.

We may dismiss the white ethnics' loyalty to the country as quaint and old fashioned, as super-patriotism, but that does not make it any the less powerful. Most of these people are the children or grandchildren of peasant immigrants who had left centuries of landlessness and oppression behind in Europe. Through hard work (as they see it) they have obtained land, home, financial stability of a sort, and personal freedom. From their point of view, a nation that makes possible both financial security and personal freedom for so many of its citizens *deserves* vigorous defense. To those who point out that we still have our poor and oppressed, the white ethnics respond that they, too, were once poor and oppressed, but that they managed to struggle their way up the economic and social ladder.

The white ethnic, then, simply cannot understand why the children of the well-to-do are so eager to "knock" American society. Hasn't that society permitted them a college education? Granting that there are social wrongs, even granting that the war might have been a mistake, the white ethnic was appalled at the hatred for the United States that he saw displayed on the television screen by the young radicals and some of their faculty patrons. Burning the American flag and waving the Vietcong flag may have been exciting and exhilarating for the son of a well-to-do family, but it was an astonishing and disgusting spectacle to a white ethnic. I don't know the exact cost to the peace movement of such acts of desecration and insult, but my impression is that they were incidents of extraordinary symbolic importance.

Anticommunism is unfashionable now among the American intellectual elites (and this is not to say that it might not become fashionable again). The revisionist historians would persuade us that the cold war was mostly of American doing. Others, not willing to go quite so far, point out the disunity in the international Communist movement and observe that given the schism between China and Russia and the many lesser schisms throughout the Communist world, it is no longer meaningful to speak of an "international Communist conspiracy." These arguments are far too subtle to gain much credence among the white ethnics. In their perspective, it was the international Communist conspiracy that blighted the bright hopes of peace after World War II, that dragged us into the Korean "police action," and that was responsible for the conflict in Vietnam. The white ethnics read the newspapers and learned about Hungary and Czechoslovakia. They were also painfully aware that many of their old homelands are under Communist control and will be until the "captive nations" are freed. It comes as a surprise to many liberal intellectuals to be told that Poles, Lithuanians, Czechs, Slovaks, Hungarians, Estonians, Latvians, and Ukranians accept the Moscow-controlled regimes in these countries about as cheerfully as American Jews would accept Sadat's armies of occupation in Tel Aviv.

Such attitudes may be unrealistic and unappreciative of the complexities of international diplomacy or of the economic progress made in some of the "iron curtain" countries in the last quarter-century. It is nevertheless an extremely important reality for American ethnics.

The "establishment," too, is seen quite differently by the white ethnics. From the perspective of the Polish television watcher on Milwaukee Avenue on the northwest side of Chicago, the long-haired militants were every bit as much a part of the establishment as are the presidents of corporations, Wall Street investment banks, and other Anglo-Saxon and Jewish members of the power elite. In their frame of reference, Richard Nixon, to some extent, and Spiro Agnew, to a very considerable extent, are *anti*establishment figures. Someone like David Dellinger, with his Yale degree, and George McGovern, with his Ph.D., are establishment personages. They saw protesters and militants as sons and daughters of the well-to-do, who attended elite colleges and were supported financially by their parents throughout their radical activity. A Harvard graduate is, after all, a Harvard graduate, whether in a picket line or in a board room of a large corporation. The peace movement was seen as an establishment movement, working against the values, the stability, and the patriotism of the American masses—which masses, incidentally, were seen as footing the bill for establishment games and amusements.

American ethnics are deeply troubled at what they consider to be "changing the rules," a phrase I have heard over and over again. *They* had to work to achieve the social positions they presently occupy, but other groups in American society are demanding these positions as a matter of right. *Their* children had to pass entrance exams to get into college; other men's children (they think) do not. *Their* fathers had to work long hours to support their families; other men's fathers seemingly did not. *They* fought bravely to defend America in World War II and in the Korean war, and now it is being alleged that those who fight and die in wars are immoral or foolish. *They* lived according to the American ethic of sobriety and respectability, and now they see on television the spectacle of the drug-smoking hippies at a rock festival. In other words, the white ethnic feels that he is being told that the rules no longer apply, that others are to achieve what he has achieved (frequently, it seems to him, while he picks up the tab) by doing exactly the opposite of what the rules prescribed for him.

There is obviously something incomplete, perhaps even paranoic, about this "change of rules" analysis, but any liberal who wishes to make converts to his cause among those who think the rules are changing has to cut through layers of resentment and feelings of injustice before he can begin to appeal to reason.

But this chapter is not intended as a plea that ethnics not be called "pigs." It is rather a plea for recognition of the fact that the ethnic component of the old coalition is still available for the pursuit of the coalition's goals. I am not saying that the ethnic component of the Democratic coalition is eager to have black neighbors, but I will say that the image of the ethnic as being an incurable and simplistic racist and hawk is not confirmed by the available research data. There are, of course, racists in the ethnic communities, as there are racists everywhere. There is also a bit of the bigot in every ethnic, as there is in all of us. But the point is that the majority of the ethnics are not simple and uncomplicated bigots; they are, like everyone else, mixtures of bigotry and enlightenment, fear and generosity, liberalism and conservatism. It is great fun, one supposes, to denounce them as bigots, but that is no way to win their support for social change. It is not that the ethnics are opposed to social change but that their coalition partners, not having bothered to try to understand what the world looks like from the ethnics' point of view, have neglected to develop a rhetoric with which to communicate with them. And of course it could be that the ethnics should try to understand things from the point of view of the liberal intellectual. But as the better-educated, more sophisticated, and presumably more tolerant partner of the coalition, the liberal ought to be the one to take the first step.

The ethnics want nothing more than to be a secure and accepted part of American society. Any but the most naïve reformer must realize that the immigrant experience still has a heavy impact on the urban ethnic communities, and that among the older generation the memories of the Great Depression still remain. If one has any sense at all, one does not deal with people who are insecure and frightened by shouting at them, by demanding that they acknowledge their guilt, by behaving in such a way that it looks to them like some of the relatively little they have is going to be taken away from them. If one is persuaded, as many of the intellectual component of the Democratic party seem to be persuaded, that the ethnics are stupid bigots, then there may be no way to deal with them. But the evidence presented in the tables in this chapter scarcely justifies such an assumption. It suggests that the real stupid bigot is the man who does not recognize a potential ally when he sees one.

One may have serious reservations about the immediate likelihood of some sort of black/ethnic coalition in the large Northern cities. And one may be even more skeptical of attempts to organize "militant ethnics" so that they might deal with their militant black counterparts. Such an attempt to transfer the strategy of black militancy to white ethnic neighborhoods is naïve and not likely to be very successful, because the ethnics are already quite well-organized and they do not need a zealous community organizer to create political, social, religious, fraternal, and economic organizations for them. But if black/ethnic coalitions are not likely, it is still true that they have many common goals—better health care, housing, control of inflation, peace, better education, and adequate police protection. They have these goals in common not so much because they are black or ethnic but because they are Americans, whose sophisticated political leadership ought to be able to emphasize this commonality of goals. In fact, it is astonishing that even in a romantic era when all the emphasis is on polarization and not on commonality, more political leaders have not perceived how much commonality there really is.

THE GREAT BEAST

During the month of January 1973, two very distinguished American scholars addressed themselves to the question of legalization of marijuana. In his column in *Human Behavior,* Amatai Etzione, professor of sociology at Columbia, argued vigorously in favor of such legalization. And in his syndicated column, John Roche, professor of politics at Brandeis, argued with equal vigor against legalization. Since I count both professors as friends, I find myself in the awkward predicament of the Irish alderman whose ward was split right down the middle on some critical issue: "Half of my friends say one thing, half of them say the other thing. Me? I'm with my friends."

Both Etzione and Roche have liberal credentials, the latter having once been chairman of the Americans for Democratic Action. Among the devotees of the currently fashionable liberal chic, Roche is somewhat under a cloud, because he worked for Lyndon Johnson and did not oppose the Vietnam war with all the vigor that was *de rigueur* among the liberal academics of the late sixties and early seventies. Yet John Roche is no conservative and Amatai Etzione is no radical. Both are extraordinarily intelligent students of American society. How can it be possible for two such intelligent and warm men to disagree so systematically? What is more puzzling, how can it be possible for Etzione to advance scientific evidence that he asserts proves conclusively that there is no danger in smoking marijuana and for Roche to cite other expert scientific opinion that suggests by no means have all the data on the effects of marijuana smoking been analyzed? Which set of experts, which distinguished social scientist is one to believe?

My own personal inclination prompts me to come down on Etzione's side. I feel there are far more important things for the police forces of the country to worry about than enforcing marijuana laws. The evidence I have seen on the effect of marijuana smoking, while not absolutely conclusive, certainly seems to be persuasive. Surely there is no need to make the possession of marijuana a felony. Yet I must concede some validity to the point made by my fellow Celt: the experimental designs of most of the marijuana research are, to say the least, not all that one would wish for. Roche's argument that caution and prudence should be used before a potentially harmful drug be legalized makes a good deal of sense. What, after all, is the big hurry? People may like marijuana and may continue to use it even if it is against the law, but no one is suffering an undue hardship if they are prevented from smoking it legally.

Perhaps more striking, however, than the disagreement between Etzione and Roche is the one fact upon which they do agree: there are profound and powerful resistances in American society to changing the marijuana legislation. These resistances constitute a strong barrier to what might be considered a dramatic social change. On the whole, Roche seems to think that the fact that we can change only relatively slowly is a good thing. And, on the whole, Etzione thinks it is a bad thing. Roche argues, at least implicitly, that the need to obtain majority coalition support for social change is an extraordinarily important asset to protect the society from foolish change. And Etzione argues that the United States' incapacity to respond quickly to new social situations is a grave defect in a modern urban industrial society. When the difference between the two is stated in that fashion, it becomes obvious, I think, on which side the Madisonian tradition is. Implicit in Etzione's argument is the notion that the social changes that the nation's intellectual and cultural elites deem proper ought to take place quickly without the need for the elite to win the support of a majority coalition. Indeed, Etzione argues in his column that massive public education campaigns should take place to overcome the ignorance of the public on crucial questions like the legalization of marijuana. In other words, the elite members of the society, having determined what is good for the country, will brainwash the rest of the population into accepting the decisions made for them by their intellectual and cultural betters. The capacity of the majority to resist rapid change on certain matters about which it has grave doubts—a capacity that political scientist John Roche so warmly endorses —Etzione seems to believe ought to be eliminated.

I do not want to be unduly harsh on Professor Etzione, but he surely ought to know from the research literature on so-called "educational campaigns" that their impact is feeble when the population has already made up its mind. Unquestionably, the governmental processes in the United States ought to be made more efficient, but the question of whether the United States ought to acquire the capacity for dealing with certain extremely critical social issues with more speed than has been manifested in the past is open for debate. To sacrifice Madisonian democracy in order that marijuana might be more expeditiously decriminalized seems to me to be throwing out the baby with the bath water. One would be hard put to believe that pot is a matter of such critical importance for American society.

Let us suppose that you are an American citizen who has been duly "socialized" into looking to your intellectual betters for cues on how you should respond to important social issues. Under such circumstances professors at Columbia and Brandeis become men of immense importance and prestige.

What happens when you discover that they disagree? Whom do you believe then? Perhaps you fall back on the what may be apocryphal dictum attributed to the mayor of Chicago, "Those experts! They don't know anything."

I would suggest an alternative procedure than the abolition of Madisonian democracy for those who believe that canabis ought to be made legal: Find out why the public is against it, and then see if you can make an adequate response to its fears. Professor Etzione suggested in his column that part of the problem of popular opposition to legalization of marijuana is the fact that it is identified with the counterculture, which is perceived as a major threat by the vast majority of middle Americans. If the legalization of marijuana is correlated with fear of something that is perceived as a clear and present danger by the majority of the population, then that majority of the population will not be won over by all the educational campaigns of the world. Two questions become appropriate: (1) Is the general public really all that threatened by the counterculture? (2) Can a case be made for the legalization of marijuana that detaches such modification of law from identification with the counterculture?

My own impression, based on research of many of my graduate students, is that the salience of the counterculture as a problem to many middle Americans is greatly overrated. Middle Americans do not like hippies, but it does not follow that that dislike is a very important motivation for their behavior. In other words, if you raise the issue of the counterculture, you will find opposition in middle America (what else would you expect to find?); but the counterculture, unless I am completely mistaken, is not something that is anywhere near the top of middle America's agenda of worries.

What middle America is really afraid of is the more dangerous drugs and especially the crime that is believed to result from addiction to such drugs. The fact that blacks, as reported in a previous chapter, are as much concerned about marijuana and as much opposed to its legalization as are whites is perfectly understandable. For it is the sons and daughters of black Americans who are most liable to be swept up in the heroin epidemic. The evidence is overwhelming, of course, that marijuana does not necessarily lead to hard drugs, but it would be foolish to expect ordinary Americans to be persuaded by such evidence until they are assured that effective means had been found to cope with the hard drug problem and its resultant (to them) crime wave.

To put the matter differently. If I were a political leader and convinced of the need to decriminalize marijuana, I would first of all listen very carefully to what middle America is saying, not on *a priori* grounds write off their objections because they are nothing but ignorant bigots. Then I would try to devise a broad program that would persuade my constituency that the legalization of marijuana would be part of a much broader effort that would lead to progress toward a solution of both the hard drug and crime problems. In short, I would build a coalition, including middle America, in which they would get something and my pot supporters would also get something. This may take more time, effort, and patience than one of Mr. Etzione's educational campaigns; it would also, I think, be far more effective.

But here, I suspect, is the rub. Why should it be necessary for those of superior intelligence and virtue to listen to and accommodate their strategies to the fears and worries of those who are their intellectual and moral inferiors? Educate them? Yes. Bargain with them? Make coalitions with them? Hardly.

The American public is the Great Beast, the enemy on which everything can be blamed, the cause of all our problems, the obstacle to all change, the collectivity, which Anthony Lewis has told us is bound for eternal damnation (how splendidly Protestant!). The American public is guilty of war, crimes of racism and genocide, of preparing for environmental cataclysm—indeed, of just about every crime in the book. Father Philip Berrigan assures us that it is impossible to be an American as well as a Christian too. It is necessary for the American public to change, to be educated, to return to virtue, to "come home again," to stop being beastly. And the elite leadership finds that it only needs to harangue the public much like a Puritan New England parson would exhort his congregation.

Frank E. Armbruster in his book, *The Forgotten Americans,* cites an immense amount of survey evidence for overwhelming public support for the dissemination of information about and the means to fight venereal disease (between four-fifths and seven-eights of the population in all surveys supported those programs). Nevertheless, the *New York Times Magazine* quoted in 1971 the following comments:

> *One of the reasons for the continued existence of gonorrhea and syphilis is the widespread belief that decent people don't acquire the disease, decent people don't talk about the disease, and decent people shouldn't do anything about those who do become infected.*[1]

One could multiply examples of such statements —and Armbruster does. The interesting question is

[1] From a "recent publication" of the Los Angeles Health Department, quoted in Cokie and Stephen V. Roberts, "The Venereal Disease Pandemic," *New York Times Magazine* (November 7, 1971), p. 67.

why would someone write something like the above? Why would someone with full access to the survey literature still feel the necessity of blaming the public (or as it is called here, "decent people") for the existence of the problem. The public is perfectly willing to do something about it.

But the most spectacular manifestation of misunderstanding the public was the Vietnamese war. It is a matter of absolute faith among those who think the public is the Beast that it was the young, the college educated, and the "nonethnic" who were most likely to be opposed to the war. However, Professor James Wright at the University of Wisconsin, in an exhaustive and systematic study of attitudes from the beginning of the war almost to its conclusion, discovered almost exactly the opposite phenomenon.[2] It was the working class (those much abused hard-hats), the ethnic, and the older segment of the population who were most likely to oppose the war. The young, the better educated, and the nonethnic were most likely to support it. A study done in New York City, I am told, also discovered that the white occupational class most likely to be opposed to the war was quite literally the hard-hats, that is to say, the construction workers.

Wright concludes his paper with the blunt statement that resistance to the war was strongly among the "non-affluent, the uneducated, and the non-young." But the objection comes immediately from those who find it impossible to convert Professor Wright's evidence. The old and the uneducated and the ethnic and the nonaffluent were against the war for the wrong reasons. They were against it because Americans were being killed and because the war

[2] James Wright, "Popular Misconceptions, Public Opinion, and the War in Vietnam," unpublished paper presented at The Society for the Study of Social Problems, August 1972.

was not being won. The right reason for opposition was that it was a war of unjust aggression.

Professor Howard Schuman, in an article in the *American Journal of Sociology,* investigates two sources of antiwar sentiment. He finds that the difference between "college-based" protest and "general population" protest is that the former was essentially "moral" and the latter essentially "pragmatic." Schuman hastens to add that the moral-pragmatic distinction is by no means perfect. There was pragmatic opposition to the war among college respondents and moral opposition within the general population. Nor does he think that "moral" opposition to the war necessarily makes college respondents superior human beings. In his words:

> *Nor is it necessary or wise to assume that the distinction represents characterological differences between the campus and the city. We are dealing here with ideology, not with personality. While it is probably true that some of the leaders and participants in the college-based protest movement are motivated by deeply held ethical principles, it would obviously be a mistake to infer individual character directly from verbal reasons for opposition to the war. College students provide moral criticisms primarily because they are exposed to, and learn such criticisms on campus. In addition, they are intellectually equipped to elaborate their sense of dissatisfaction with the war, and to turn personal concern about participating in it into a critical examination of its goals . . .*[3]

Thus what may seem to be a difference in reasons for opposing the war may very well be only a difference in style and vocabulary and educational level.

[3] Howard Schuman, "Two Sources of Antiwar Sentiment," *American Journal of Sociology* 78, no. 3 (November 1972): 534.

At least the members of the educational elite should display enough humility to consider the possibility that the rest of the population might articulate its opposition to the war in less precise and sophisticated categories than those available to the elites. Schuman's penultimate paragraph may well be the best epitaph on the peace movement, including its more highly publicized clerical leaders, the brothers Berrigan:

> *From a policy standpoint, the main overall implication of our argument is that the president has never had much to fear directly from the college antiwar movement, because the latter does not speak the same language as the general public. Public disillusionment with the war has grown despite the campus demonstrations, not because of them. The president's primary enemy is and always has been the Viet Cong and the North Vietnamese, for it is their resilience and success that undermine larger public support for the war. The antiwar movement is not wholly ineffective: it influences commentators and columnists, who in turn (but in different words) influence the public. And it provides energy and money in political campaigns. But attempts by moral spokesmen against the war to proselytize the general public directly are likely to fail or even prove counterproductive unless carried out with more skill and less righteousness.*[4]

Unless you can understand and sympathize with those whose support you are trying to win, you may very well become counterproductive. Just because your potential supporters use very different rhetoric from yours and apparently have a different perspec-

[4] Howard Schuman, "Two Sources of Antiwar Sentiment," *American Journal of Sociology* 78, no. 3 (November 1972): 534–35.

tive from yours, there is no reason to write them off as being part of the Great Beast bound for eternal damnation. For the Puritan minister, ranting at his congregation, it was necessary to do the right thing for the right reasons—that is to say, his reasons. But the founder of a political coalition should only find it necessary that his adherents support the right things—for whatever reasons.

Armbruster suggests that what is ultimately at issue are two different views of where American society is at the present time. If you take the first view, then the public is beastly and must be educated, charismatized, or forced into virtuous behavior. Armbruster characterizes one view in four points:

> *1) The period in which we live is one of great, almost inevitable change in all areas, and in the past few years, in a direction that is basically good and to which we must accommodate ourselves.*
> *2) This trend must, in many cases, not only be tolerated but encouraged.*
> *3) Values must be re-examined in the light of these new ideas with a readiness to jettison parts of our traditional system.*
> *4) Opposition to change (often, if not usually, represented by the majority) is traditional and can generally be looked on as simply another part of the problem to be overcome, seldom as part of the solution.*[5]

The position stated above seems a fair enough description of much of the rhetoric one can read in the elite national journals and heard in the McGov-

[5] Frank E. Armbruster with contributions by Doris Yokelson, *The Forgotten Americans: A Survey of the Values, Beliefs and Concerns of the Majority* (New Rochelle, N.Y.: Arlington House, 1972), p. 342.

ern campaign. However, Armbruster (himself, hardly conservative) says there is also another viewpoint:

> *On the other hand, a sympathetic, but seldom articulated characterization of another point of view (which perhaps would be subscribed to by a majority of all employment and income categories of the population), holds that since ours is a sensitive societal structure, stemming from, among other things, a basic value system, changing this value system can have many grave effects on our society. Hasty, perhaps ill-considered changes have often proved to be counterproductive, sometimes in the very areas they were meant to improve, oftentimes in other vital areas that were not taken into account, but nevertheless were highly sensitive to the change. Those who are sympathetic to this viewpoint are likely to ask for the credentials of those who encourage any program, which goes against their own judgment, particularly a domestic program; they are quite likely to risk not achieving the benefits of programs pushed by those whom they consider to be unreliable (and they may occasionally miss substantial benefits this way), rather than risk the losses which implementation of the program might entail.*[6]

If you subscribe to this second view of what is happening in American society and how American society works, then the public is not so stupid and ignorant. It may be inarticulate and confused, it may be uninformed and at times wrong; but it has a certain grim, instinctive wisdom that is a very useful

[6] Frank E. Armbruster with contributions by Doris Yokelson, *The Forgotten Americans: A Survey of the Values, Beliefs and Concerns of the Majority* (New Rochelle, N.Y.: Arlington House, 1972), p. 343.

brake on the oftentimes shallow and faddist enthusiasms of the elite.

The prior perspective may masquerade as one based on superior knowledge and intelligence and sensitivity to the fundamental forces at work in society, but I doubt that any sober social scientist, looking carefully at his data or projecting carefully from his theories would say that the first-mentioned vision of things has been validated. On the contrary, the second viewpoint described by Armbruster is, I think, much closer to the perspective of sane social science.

Whichever perspective one takes, however, an effective coalition can never include people who are defined as part of the problem. Armbruster says, ". . . this great cross-section of America makes up 'the bone and sinew' of that nation; if its members falter, the republic could be in trouble." [7] It is precisely this "great cross-section," this "bone and sinew" that many of the New Politics liberals saw as a beast before the election of 1972. After the election they became even more convinced of it, though Senator McGovern said he was more sorry for it than he was for himself.

Frank Armbruster suggests that much of the anger directed at the Great Beast results from the failure of the reform efforts of the 1960s:

> *Efforts in the 1960s to solve some of our outstanding problems did not bear fruit quickly enough for some, so that by the late 1960s a significant amount of the effort was spent blaming people for the problems. This is perhaps normal when would-be reformers experience the frustrations of trying actually to implement changes in any society. The failure of the Left to effect an immediate shutdown of military operations in Viet-*

[7] Ibid., p. 406.

nam, of course, probably helped to magnify our "defects" for them.[8]

The liberal left was quite properly affronted by both the war and racism. But with an intolerance that showed neither sensitivity nor political skills, it expected that once it had decided that the war and racism were wrong, both must end. Unfortunately for the human condition, things never work that quickly and easily. The war did end eventually, and progress against racism, while it is steady, is still too slow. As Armbruster notes:

> *More civil rights and social legislation was passed in the mid- and late 1960s than in the first few years of the decade, and . . . attitudes toward integration and equal opportunity for Negroes became more and more favorable. In fact, some government actions . . . and much non-government action, initiated in the rush to "stamp out injustice" and help the underprivileged, seem to have been somewhat ill-advised, both from the point of view of the amount of benefit that could be expected to accrue to the main objective, and the bad side effects. Yet even these programs were initiated.*[9]

But the left-wing enthusiast, seeing that despite his enthusiasm, his efforts, his intelligence, his superior morality, peace could not be achieved and racism could not be ended immediately, had to find someone to "blame." The imperfections and the difficulties of the human condition were not an adequate explanation. The slowness of social change was unsatisfactory as an explanation. His own failure to win allies was an intolerable explanation.

[8] Frank E. Armbruster with contributions by Doris Yokelson, *The Forgotten Americans: A Survey of the Values, Beliefs and Concerns of the Majority* (New Rochelle, N.Y.: Arlington House, 1972), p. 405.
[9] Ibid.

Hence, the only one left to blame was the American public, who the intellectual left never liked much anyway.

Never mind that the American public is more sympathetic toward racial integration than the public of any large multiracial nation of the world. Never mind that the United States is the first superpower ever to be forced out of a war because the public turned against it. It is not enough that the public came down finally, if imperfectly, in its own rhetoric on the side of virtue. It must instantly, completely, and in the rhetoric of its elite endorse that virtue that the elite presently deems appropriate.

The critics of the American public would argue that the public is paranoid, because it sees everywhere threats to its values and its most cherished beliefs. In fact, the research evidence indicates that some people see some beliefs threatened and other people see other beliefs threatened, but broad, sweeping generalizations about threats the middle majority perceives are not grounded in solid and durable data. However, if the American majority thinks that a certain small but articulate and influential segment of the American intellectual elite is indeed engaged in an assault on the fundamental political and social values of the country, they are quite correct in such an analysis. This is exactly what is happening. This assault is on the fundamental values of Madisonian democracy. Many New Politics liberals no longer believe in the necessity of coalition politics. When Ken Bode enthused at the 1972 Democratic convention that it was the most representative in the history, he really meant that it was most representative of those whose intellectual and moral superiority gave them the right to govern, that is to say, liberal elitist New Politicians like himself. Because it could not quickly get out of the Vietnam quagmire and immediately end racism (by which of course is meant the residual effects of the racism of several centuries), both American democracy and the American people were judged by this liberal elite and found wanting. The issue between them and the rest of us, then, is whether the United States ought to continue with the kind of political society it is, or whether it ought to be replaced by some modernized form of Plato's republic with Ken Bode or some other New Politician reigning as philosopher king.

The debate may be an interesting one. It is to be supposed that those who wish to abolish Madisonian coalition democracy can make a convincing argument for their case, convincing, that is, in theory. Those who push this argument reject the necessity for winning majority support of their opinions (save for appeals to morality or by the trickery of charisma) but, in order to achieve power, then, short of force (which seems extremely unlikely), the New Politicians must either abandon their efforts for social reform or accept, however reluctantly, the strategies of Madisonian democracy. They must, in other words, give themselves over to coalition building.

In practice, the argument over whether the American public is the Great Beast or not is irrelevant. If you are going to play the politics game in the United States, you will have to enter into coalition with at least some of the Beast, and you better learn to listen to, sympathize with, and even respect your fellow citizens, who may not be as well-educated and may not express their morality in precise and elegant terms as you.[10]

[10] An appalling possibility which must be faced is that given the speed with which the pendulum of intellectual faddism swings, we might move from despising the American public to worshipping it. The American elite seems to have a very difficult time maintaining a stable middle ground.

He who aspires to rebuild the Democratic coalition must not permit himself to despair over American society and the American public. For if he despairs, he will surely lose, and the purpose of an election is to win. More than that, he should rid himself of advisors and speechwriters and strategists and experts who believe in the Beast theory of the American public. It may well be that those apocalyptic prophets who envision the eternal damnation of the American public will be proven right by history, but if so, there is nothing the rest of us can do. In any event, they will plague and blight and perhaps ultimately destroy any attempt to rebuild the coalition if they get too close to those who are directing the reconstruction.

The most impressive young people I have ever met are those who went out canvassing for liberal, peace-oriented candidates in 1968, 1970, and 1972. Most of them had the integrity and the sense to listen as well as talk. They did not abandon their principles or ideals but returned from their canvassing with a good deal more sensitivity to ordinary people. They discovered that there is no such thing as the American public; rather, there are many millions of individuals with hopes and fears, problems and potential, nobility and selfishness all wrapped up in a complicated mixture that is the human person. Politics is about gaining the support of enough of those people to, first, win an election and then to begin to implement the social policies you have promised. There is, of course, the risk inherent to Madisonian democracy that if you do not do a good job in delivering on promises, you will not be reelected. Newspaper columnists, television commentators, and full professors do not have to stand for reelection.

CONCLUSION

The argument of this book can be summed up in the following propositions:

1. Given the size, geographical distribution, and diversity of American society, the American political system works remarkably well. Close to seven-eighths of the American public seems to be basically satisfied with it.

2. While there is unquestionably both evil and immorality in American society, their elimination would bring only marginal improvements in most of our social problems. Those problems are complex and could not be solved by easy, simple moralistic answers.

3. There is not a power elite or an establishment that controls American society. Quite the contrary, one of the principal obstacles to social reform is the wide distribution and diffusion of power.

4. There exists in American society wide support for basic social reforms, though this support does not extend to those "issues" deemed important by the "politics of style" practiced by the New Politicians.

5. Racial prejudice is declining, the lot of American blacks is improving, and, while blacks are not as satisfied with American society as whites, they are still relatively satisfied.

6. Most young people are not part of the radical counterculture. On the contrary, George Wallace's support was strongest among the young. Even among college youth, counterculturists are among the minority.

7. What American politics needs is not more enthusiastic, self-righteous amateurs but more skilled politicians who understand the complexities of social reality.

8. Contrary to the mass media, American society is not polarized. For example, in the 1968 election only 13 percent of the electorate supported George Wallace and only 3 percent were doves in sympathy with the Vietnam protesters of the Chicago convention.

9. Given the nature of American society and the traditional style of American politics, the only way to accomplish meaningful social change is through reform coalitions.

10. The white ethnic component of the old Democratic coalition is not made up of bigoted hard-hatted white racists. On the contrary, it is sympathetic to reform. Without its support reform will not occur.

11. At the present time most "style-oriented" social protests are counterproductive in that they drive away support for the causes they promote.

12. While peace and prosperity are still the fundamental issues in American politics, a new issue that emphasizes control of and respect from the great corporate bureaucracies is beginning to emerge in American society.

13. The key to the future of American politics is to rehabilitate and reactivate the reformist Democratic coalition inaugurated by Franklin Roosevelt. For all its troubles this coalition is still the majority of the American electorate and is still favorably disposed to social change. It ought to be relatively easy for a political candidate to communicate with this coalition if he can avoid the polarization rhetoric of the "politics of style" that some of his intellectual advisors might like to force upon him.

14. The American public is apparently quite ready for its political leadership to speak of the complexities of problems that cannot be solved immediately,

of difficult choices to make, and the need to experiment. Simple answers, scapegoating, demagoguery of the Left or the Right are distinctly unpopular in the republic at the present time.

15. Scammon and Wattenberg are correct when they argue that American politics is necessarily a politics of the center—despite the ideologues of both the liberal and conservative "attentive audience." However, the center is not so rigidly fixed that an astute political leader cannot move it in his own direction. The leadership of the real coalition is faced with the challenge of finding the rhetoric to integrate the common interests of both the white ethnic and black components of his coalition.

If the radical fringe of American liberalism denies the existence or the importance of the old coalition, it is simply wrong. There is overwhelming evidence that the majority of Americans are in support of liberal social change, peace, racial justice and harmony, honesty about complexity, and protection of the environment. And while there is not absolute evidence for it, it still seems to be a safe hunch that the new issue of organizational control and responsibility will become an extremely important one.

Furthermore, the radical fringe of American liberalism is simply wrong when it thinks that it can put together a winning coalition that excludes the white ethnic working class. It is also wrong when it thinks that the old coalition has collapsed, for despite the efforts of the New Politicians to drive the white ethnic working class out of the coalition, it has not been successful (except in New York). The old coalition is still there, waiting to be energized by a political leader who can break out of the rhetoric of the liberal audience and its emphasis on hate, fear, polarization, and destruction.

Politics is a coalition-forming, alliance-building, conflict-managing affair. In a society like ours, politics has been assumed to be oriented toward the achievement of the national goals of freedom and equality. The precise specifications of these goals have changed with time and they have frequently been honored more in theory than in practice. Politicians have often been content with building coalitions to stay in power instead of using the power of coalition to achieve more adequately the goals of the society. There are "good" coalitions and "bad" coalitions only in the sense that some have facilitated the development of equality and freedom and others have not. "Good" coalitions cannot do a perfect job; indeed, they may be barely adequate, but at least they move society closer to equality and freedom.

By and large, the old coalition, which was put together by Franklin Roosevelt some four decades ago, has been a good coalition. It has provided the political muscle that enabled national leadership to enact most of the agenda of the liberal elites of the past. Some of these programs worked brilliantly, others were less than successful, and still others failed. But the old coalition can hardly be blamed for the failure of a welfare system, for example, that its liberal element of the 1930s strongly endorsed; nor can it be blamed for a foolish and corrosive war that its liberal element of the 1960s was instrumental in involving us in.

But whatever its successes or failures, the old coalition is still the only one presently available that offers much hope of responding to the nation's critical problems.

Politics is not a game unto itself. It must be goal-oriented. The coalition must exist to do something, to achieve some ends, to implement some values. Save for intermittent periods, the old coalition has been deficient in goals for the last two decades, but it is still there and still waiting for the political leadership that can articulate goals and values to restore its momentum. This leadership must be able to understand the problems and speak the language of the various components of the coalition, but it need not be imprisoned by what is commonly held to be the limitations of its rank and file membership. They may be complex and inconsistent, but they can be stirred out of their limitations by imaginative and vigorous leadership. Besides, as we have observed in the last three chapters, many of the presumed limitations of the rank and file members of the coalition do not in fact exist. It has been axiomatic in most political and journalistic circles for the last several years, for example, that the Catholic ethnics were hawkish on the war in Vietnam. Thus it was felt that coalition leadership had to reckon with this Catholic superpatriotism or risk offending an important component of its support. However, the data show that Irish, German, and Italian Catholics were substantially more likely to be at the "dove" end of the continuum than were typical Americans.

There are still two signs of hope in the data presented in the last three chapters: (1) The majority of black members of the real coalition have not yet despaired of American society; and (2) the majority of the white ethnic members of the coalition are far more enlightened on questions of race than anyone has been willing to admit.

To say that these two phenomena are grounds for hope is not to say they are grounds for complacency. Hope can no more be equated with complacency than panic can with a sense of urgency. The argument of this book is that hope and urgency can be combined; indeed, they are corollaries of one another. Panic and complacency prevent effective action, panic because it asserts that there is no time left, complacency because it asserts that there is plenty of time left. The argument of this book is simply that there is time left—certainly enough time if political leadership realizes that there is a potential, indeed, a desperate yearning in the American people for social movement and progress.

The emphasis in this book has been on coalition rather than goals, because in the eschatological and apocalyptic climate of the day it frequently seems that the absolute necessity for coalition formation is forgotten. A politician can easily be so fascinated by the mechanics of the coalition-politics game that he forgets it has a purpose beyond itself. On the other hand, an enthusiastic social critic can be so dazzled by the enthusiasm of his own vision that he forgets it can only be implemented through skill and persistent practice of the mechanics. Both the skillful coalition builder and the enthusiastic social critic are necessary if society is to move ahead. In some instances—all too few—they can be found in the same person, but when they occupy different bodies it is incumbent that the politician and the critic listen to each other and try to cooperate. Neither can be really effective without the other. The tragedy for the old coalition during the late 1960s and the early 1970s is that the critics and the coalition builders stopped listening to each other, occasionally shouting foul words in the other's direction.

A contemporary mythology depicts the American people as uncertain, afraid, defensive, polarized, repressive, losing faith in political democracy, involved in a massive "backlash" or "swing to the

Right." There was little evidence to support this mythology in the 1972 election returns, and almost no evidence for it in the data presented in this book. On the contrary, it is astonishing that in spite of the turbulence of the 1960s, the coalition still exists, shaken somewhat, but still very much alive.

Why, then, are so many people convinced of the mythology? Politicians tend to overreact to slight shifts in public opinion, because such shifts can be enough to eject them from office. Journalists—even those very wise ones, the national columnists—deal in the sensational and the dramatic. In their hands, slight shifts are transformed into massive, long-range trends, and even "revolutions." The politicians believe what they read in the newspapers, and the newspapers report in turn what the politicians believe. The collapse of the working-class or middle-American support for the liberal coalition has been cheerfully predicted on all sides for more than two decades. One remembers, for example, the time when Joseph McCarthy was expected to be the Pied Piper who would lead the Catholic ethnics out of the Democratic party. Joseph McCarthy is gone, another McCarthy came and went, and the Catholic ethnics still vote Democratic (at least most of the time) and still support liberal political positions.

No one who has eyes to watch television will deny that there has been a notable increase in tension and conflict in the United States in the last decade. Yet Adlai Stevenson III, son of the famous liberal Democrat and an egghead in his own right, with his attitudes on war and race unmistakably liberal, nonetheless swept into office with large majorities in precisely those white ethnic working-class wards where a backlash or a swing to the Right was supposed to be occurring. He did so against a candidate who was running with the vigorous support and the personal presence of the vice-president, who was supposedly the symbol of the middle-American backlash.

Might there be a cataclysm in American society? Possibly. Might there be a radical political realignment? Perhaps. Might there emerge a totally new form of politics that has nothing in common with the politics of the past? Probably not, but it could happen. Before there is a cataclysm or a radical realignment or a totally new kind of politics, American society will have to undergo much more severe traumas than it has experienced in the past decade. There is precious little evidence to indicate that American society is coming apart. It might well come apart, of course; things might continue to go from bad to worse; the clouds on the horizon might become ominous thunderheads. The important point, however, is not that there could be a cataclysm but that there does not need to be one. Disaster is not inevitable.

There is still considerable strength left in the American polity, enough strength to enable us to cope with our most pressing social problems. We will not cope with them automatically indeed, we will do so only with courageous and imaginative political leadership and with a rank and file that is willing to pay the cost of social change. Urgency is essential. We will not be served by defeatism, by apocalyptic rhetoric, or by panic. Only the political leader who can combine a sense of urgency with confidence will be able to lead us out of the morass of hesitancy and uncertainty in which we are presently bogged down. (Of course, in all likelihood, twenty years from now we will find ourselves in still another morass—but that's another book.)

Social change does not come inexpensively, but yet, as the National Urban Coalition's *Counter-Budget* [1] demonstrates, it is possible to make solid beginnings in the next half-decade on the problem or race, housing, health, crime, and resources—human and natural—without a drastic shift in the balance of the American economy. The counter-budget assumes that the war is over, that military spending is substantially reduced (though by no means eliminated), that prosperity (in the sense of the full-employment economy) is achieved, that the users of certain specialized government services pay more for these services (harbors and airports, for example), that there is a reform in the tax structure eliminating many of the present inequities, and that there would be a 10 percent surtax, which would still leave taxes of the United States lower than most other countries in the Western world, indeed, lower than they were here before 1960.

The counter-budget is a realistic and hardheaded proposal, one might almost say conservative in its assumptions. Even a 10 percent tax surcharge ought to be acceptable to a majority of Americans. They accepted a surcharge during the early years of the war, and they indicated in the survey data cited in Chapter 12 that they were willing to pay such a price to achieve racial peace. What is lacking, then, is not the technical feasibility to make considerable progress in the solution of our most serious social problems nor a popular readiness to pick up the tab for such progress. What is lacking is the political leadership with the courage, the imagination, and the rhetorical skills to begin.

[1] Robert S. Spencer and Harold Wolman, eds. *Counter-Budget: A Blueprint for Changing National Priorities* (New York: Prager, 1971).

I am sure that my efforts in this volume will be criticized on the grounds that I emphasize the continuity of American coalition politics rather than change. I talk about James Madison and about the old Roosevelt coalition. Haven't I heard about "future shock," or the "new permissiveness," or the "new women," or the "new militants," or the "new young" in our society? I have indeed heard of all these groups and movements that have been baptized by the adjective "new." But on the basis of the available evidence, I simply do not believe that such groups are particularly representative of the majority of American society. They are not unimportant, but it does not at all follow that they are the waves of the future. There is, of course, change in human affairs; there is also continuity. I am profoundly skeptical of scholars, preachers, and prophets who think that they have so clearly understood the wave of history that they are able to climb aboard and ride with it. Frederick Dutton, perhaps more than any other recent American political writer, thought he had diagnosed the wave of history in the changing demographic and educational patterns of the American public. How wrong Dutton was became clear in the shambles of the 1972 campaign. That demographic and educational changes are occurring in the society and that they do have considerable cultural import cannot be denied, and if Dutton had been content with such modest but not unimportant points, both he and Senator McGovern would not look nearly so bad. That the population is younger (until zero population growth catches up with us) and much better educated is a new and important factor in American politics, but it does not change the whole political game. Some human events move very rapidly, others at a moderate

TABLE 15.1 *

"As far as the people running these institutions are concerned, would you say you have a great deal of confidence, only some confidence, or hardly any confidence at all in them?"

	Great Deal	Only Some	Hardly Any	Not Sure
Major Companies				
1971	27%	50%	15%	8%
1966	55	35	5	5
Organized Religion				
1971	27	40	25	8
1966	41	32	17	10
Education				
1971	37	46	15	2
1966	61	32	5	2
Executive Branch of Federal Government				
1971	23	50	18	9
1966	41	42	11	6
Organized Labor				
1971	14	42	35	9
1966	22	42	28	8
The Press				
1971	18	51	26	5
1966	29	50	17	4
Medicine				
1971	61	29	6	4
1966	72	22	2	4
Banks and Financial Institutions				
1971	36	46	13	5
1966	67	26	3	4

TABLE 15.1 * (continued)
"As far as the people running these institutions are concerned, would you say you have a great deal of confidence, only some confidence, or hardly any confidence at all in them?"

	Great Deal	Only Some	Hardly Any	Not Sure
Television				
1971	22	48	25	5
1966	25	44	26	5
Mental Health and Psychiatry				
1971	35	40	15	10
1966	51	32	6	11
The U.S. Supreme Court				
1971	23	41	27	9
1966	51	29	12	8
The Scientific Community				
1971	32	47	10	11
1966	56	25	4	15
Congress				
1971	19	54	19	8
1966	42	46	7	5
Advertising				
1971	13	42	40	5
1966	21	43	30	6
The Military				
1971	27	47	20	6
1966	62	28	5	5
Local Retail Stores				
1971	24	56	15	5
1966	48	42	7	3

* Harris survey, the *New York Post,* October 25, 1971.

pace, and others with glacial slowness. Only the naïve analyst confuses a rapid change in one dimension of human behavior (marijuana smoking, for example) with long-range change in fundamental human patterns (the importance of the family or coalition politics, for example). If it is the mistake of the conservative to underestimate potential for change in society, it is equally the mistake of the liberal to overestimate the fact of change. If this volume emphasized continuity rather than change, it is not because the author is unaware of, much less opposed to, change. In the present crisis of the liberal coalition it is necessary to insist on continuity, since so many members of the liberal wing of the Democratic party seem temporarily to have forgotten about it. One can easily lose an election by thinking that nothing has changed; it is equally easy to lose an election by thinking everything has changed.

But there are, of course, important changes going on in the American society. As Verba and Nie and I will demonstrate in our forthcoming analysis of "national election and attitudinal data since 1950," the Catholic population has moved Left dramatically. The "New Issue" of participation with respect, which I described in a previous chapter, is an extraordinarily important change and one that can easily be documented. The problems of crime, equitable distribution of the cost of integration, social problems that win broad support because there "is something in them for everyone," and reform of corporate bureaucracies so that they become responsible and responsive are not exactly new problems, but it is evident at the present time that we need new solutions to them. It is also abundantly clear, I think, that some (though by no means all) of our enthusiastic ventures designed to eliminate poverty have not been particularly successful. This, of course, does not mean that we should abandon the attempt to eliminate poverty, but it does mean that we need new and creative techniques (the costs of which, let it be emphasized should be equitably distributed) to fight against demoralizing and dehumanizing effects of poverty and injustice. We probably also need much more modest expectations about the proportions of social programs that will be effective. We should foster the capacity to eliminate programs that turn out to be ineffective.

Surely, then, in terms of problems and challenges, many things have changed in the American society since the creation of the New Deal coalition. There will be no lack of exciting and difficult challenges for those who choose or are chosen to lead the reconstructed coalition. But if many things have changed, one thing has not: One still needs a plurality of votes to win an election.

The accompanying table based on Harris survey data of October 25, 1971, ought to be material for daily meditation for every politician who aspires to put the liberal Democratic coalition back together again. The American public has systematically lost confidence in virtually *all* large corporate bodies—companies, religion, schools, the Supreme Court, Congress, the executive branch of the government, the military, the scientific community. The smallest drop of confidence has been in the press, television, and advertising—and the public never had much confidence in these three media industries to begin with. Unquestionably, the war, protests, racial disturbance, and the ill-feeling (generated mostly by the war) had a profound effect on the confidence the American public had in its major institutions. Now that the Vietnam war is receding into the past (and may very well be an unpleasant memory repressed in our collective unconscious, just like the Great Depression,) it may well be that confidence in the major corporate structures will increase once again. A replication of the Harris questions in early 1974 should be extremely interesting.

There are those, of course, who are delighted that the American public is systematically losing confidence in its institutions. For such a loss of confidence, they argue, is the beginning of the collapse of a corrupt middle-class society. Presumably, a political leader interested in reassembling the Democratic coalition is not enthused at the thought of American society's collapse. He would therefore be greatly concerned about the loss of confidence documented in Table 15.1. It is reasonable to expect that with the war over, confidence will begin to rise; however, it does not seem likely that the present administration has the capacity to restore strong faith of Americans in their social structure.

On the other hand, the Nixon years, particularly the second half, may provide a breathing space for the liberal coalition in which it can rethink its priorities, strategies, its policies, and its tactics. To charge into the 1976 election with the same set of mindless clichés that guided the 1972 election would be to commit political suicide—and this time there may well be no ashes from which to rise again. It is time to focus on how American coalition politics works (and this book is an effort to do that). It is also time to rethink what being liberal means in American society. Surely it must mean something more than ever increasing power to the government and more strident demands for virtue.

And what about the most obvious leader of the reconstructed coalition? The problem of Camelot was not that it got us into a war, but that it was destroyed by a madman's bullet. If a reconstructed liberal Democratic coalition does not produce something rather like Camelot, it had better resign itself to Spiro Agnew or John Connally in the White House. Senator Kennedy may or may not be the man to rebuild the Democratic coalition; but if he is not the one, it had better be someone who stands for the same combination of liberal values and political skills for which his brothers stood.

Senator Kennedy has assets and liabilities as a presidential candidate that are so obvious they need not be listed in this book. Among the assets, however, charisma should not be included; it is not a liability either. But unless I completely misunderstand the temper of the American people, charisma without honesty, intelligence, compassion, and, above all, political shrewdness is completely irrelevant. The quintessence of political shrewdness at the present time in American history is the ability to listen once again to what nonelite America is saying. If Senator Kennedy wants to be president, he will have to learn how to listen sympathetically, though not uncritically, to what nonelite America is really saying. If he can do this effectively and respond to the hopes and fears, the anxieties and the generosity of those who were both turned off and turned out by the 1972 New Politics, then there is not much doubt that Senator Kennedy can be president. Whether he can, in fact, exercise such political coalition skills should he make up his mind to be president is a question that I am not qualified to answer. Those who know him, and whose judgments I respect, say that he can. I hope so.

One gets a peculiar sensation while writing a book like this. It is like wading through an endless swamp—I keep slogging on, getting nowhere. My argument in this book is against profound and massive assumptions about American politics and the American people that are strongly held, if not by "everyone that matters," at least by a substantial proportion of them. To contend against "images" and "pictures" that represent these assumptions is like a religious argument—you never win but you keep on arguing.

The radical says that everything about America is bad; the conservative says that practically everything is good. My middle position is that everything is complicated but many things are possible. The radical sees eternal damnation for America; the conservative says "love it or leave it," and Philip Berrigan says you can't love it without leaving it. I say, "Damn it all, let's win the next election, and win it big."

And I won't apologize for saying that.

INDEX

ABOUT THE AUTHOR

Fr. Andrew M. Greeley was born in Oak Park, Illinois. He received his Ph.D. in sociology from the University of Chicago, where he also lectured. An authority on ethnic groups in America, he is now the director of the Center for the Study of American Pluralism, National Opinion Research Center in Chicago.

He has written over fifteen books including *Unsecular Man, That Most Distressful Nation: The Taming of the American Irish,* and *Why Can't They Be Like Us?* a pioneering study of American ethnic groups.

Building Coalitions: American Politics in the 1970s is an important and timely analysis of the political scene today. Fr. Greeley deals with political reality and how effective leadership is necessary for a party to win elections through coalition building.